Sea

Sukarnopura

New
Guinea

West Irian

NEW GUINEA

Papua

Port
Moresby

Arafura Sea

Darwin

Coral Sea

Cairns

Northern

Territory

Queensland

South

Brisbane

Australia

New South

Wales

Sydney

©Canberra

Adelaide

Victoria

Tasman

Sea

Melbourne

Tasmania

Hobart

PARLIAMENT OF A THOUSAND TRIBES

PARLIAMENT
OF A
THOUSAND TRIBES

A Study of New Guinea

———

OSMAR WHITE

THE BOBBS-MERRILL COMPANY, INC.
A Subsidiary of HOWARD W. SAMS & CO., INC.
PUBLISHERS/INDIANAPOLIS • NEW YORK • KANSAS CITY

ORIGINALLY PUBLISHED IN GREAT BRITAIN BY WILLIAM HEINEMANN LTD.
LIBRARY OF CONGRESS CATALOG CARD NUMBER 66-28338

FIRST AMERICAN EDITION

PRINTED IN AUSTRALIA BY HALSTEAD PRESS, SYDNEY

To Mollie and Sally

Acknowledgements

AMONG the many people who helped in the preparation of this book, I would like particularly to thank Professor W. Macmahon Ball, of the Department of Political Science, Melbourne University, who was kind enough to read and comment upon the text; my wife and two daughters for useful discussions and their perceptive secretarial work; and Mr R. D. Ewins, B.A., Dip.Ed., for his crucial assistance to my wife in the important but deadly task of indexing.

In research I had considerable help, notably from the late Mr J. A. Feely, State Librarian of Victoria, and Mr Roy Weston of the Herald and Weekly Times Ltd., Melbourne. I am also grateful for the courteous co-operation of the Australian News and Information Bureau which supplied the illustrations.

The inspiration to attempt an interpretative study of this kind derived from an old and valued friendship with the distinguished American anthropologist, Dr Margaret Mead.

O.E.W.

Foreword

In essence, this book is a simplified outline of what has happened in eighty years of conflict between men of the modern world and men of the Stone Age in the jungles, swamps, mountains and grasslands of New Guinea.

It is a story about cannibals, head-hunters, sorcerers and pygmies; of treasure hidden in lost valleys; of simpletons and saints and statesmen; of heroes and boozy freebooters looking to make their fortunes out of black slaves, gold, sandalwood, pearls and bird-of-paradise plumes.

Yet the reader should be warned that in these pages he will not come close to people as personalities, for the book is concerned more with vicissitudes of communities than of individuals. Those who wish to meet the remarkable characters of New Guinea's history and share vicariously the perils they encountered and the wonder of the strange things they saw will fare better elsewhere in the copious literature of the South Seas—in the memoirs of Luigi Maria d'Albertis the naturalist, Hubert Murray the administrator, or J. G. Hides the explorer; in the anthropological works of Malinowski and Mead and Worsley; in the modern travel tales of Colin Simpson and Ion Idriess or the not-so-modern novels of Beatrice Grimshaw.

These and many others have written about New Guinea with the intense subjectivity of participants in a play set on a preposterously exotic stage, for the great dark island has qualities which fire the human spirit and imagination. On its forbidding shores evangelists who coveted the martyr's crown found many wide-open gateways to heaven—and the wicked who once fled there from pursuit found just as many wide-open gateways to hell.

In such a country the blaze of deeds done by the adventurous too often dims the outline of their effects, so I have deliberately muted the colour of personalities and the excitement of their exploits in order to emphasize the distinction between what is historically significant and what is merely amazing.

In selecting from a vast store of available material what facts to quote, in arranging them as a coherent narrative, and in attributing to them relative emphasis, I have been motivated by the desire to avoid any distortion of the whole truth. Judgement is, of course, a subjective function, and such judgements as I have expressed or implied in this book are based not only on a close study of documentary evidence but also on long experience in New Guinea and neighbouring countries as a reporter and commentator for Australian newspapers.

This personal experience of the region I have acquired intermittently, on tours lasting from a few days to many months, over a period of more than thirty years. It has included three crossings of the eastern end of the island on foot during the Pacific war and many journeys with peacetime patrols in both controlled and uncontrolled sectors of Dutch and Australian territory. It has involved personal friendship and free interchange of information and opinions with the most—and least—distinguished members of the European community and with many highly intelligent and admirable New Guineans.

Some of these people will agree with my version of the New Guinea story and the conclusions I draw from it. Others will feel that I have made sinful omissions or failed to achieve accurate perspective; others still may hold that my generalizations are so broad as to be offensive to the conscience of the expert. I can only plead that I am not like the Apostle Paul, 'made all things to all men'. This book is one man's version of the truth in New Guinea.

It has been a difficult task attempting to describe briefly, simply, yet accurately, the impact of Western civilization on more than 1,000 tribes speaking 750 different languages. In such a situation no generalization can possibly be wholly valid for every particular instance. I have often been forced to pass over the fascinating exception in giving due emphasis to the crucial rule.

Information of what has happened, what is happening, and what may happen in New Guinea is, I believe, much more important to the modern world than is commonly realized. Events there will increasingly affect the political status of Australia and its Pacific allies. Events there may even re-delineate the oceanic frontiers of Asia.

The way in which the authority of the United Nations influences Australian policy and administration in the eastern half of the New Guinea archipelago may put to conclusive test the competence of that great organization to regulate beneficially the dealings of advanced nations with retarded societies.

Is it possible, in the man-shrunken world of the twentieth century, for ethnic groups which are grossly inferior to others in social organization and technical achievement to be accorded, and to enjoy and preserve, genuine political independence?

Can programmes of education and aid, conducted by the advanced nations for the benefit of the backward, eliminate the disturbing effect of the inequalities imposed by nature upon different societies of men?

In New Guinea, the last great wilderness left on earth, at least part of the answer to these vital questions could be found. It is a laboratory in which an ambitious experiment —an attempt to accelerate social evolution by various processes of prohibition and education—is now drawing to its close.

In this laboratory the unflinching observer may still study the crude essence of human inequality. He may judge for himself whether or not social science can discover a reagent to neutralize the bitterness which the pain of realized inequality has injected into race relationships since the beginning of time.

Contents

List of Illustrations

1

Dragon Island

NOBODY can hope to understand the people of New Guinea and their unusual relationship to the rest of the world without first acquiring at least some elementary knowledge of the physical nature of the country they live in. The New Guinea tribes have for centuries remained cut off from the mainstreams of humanity, denied by an accident of geography the stimulations which make for evolutionary change. The situation, topographical character and climate of the country into which their migrant forbears were forced, probably by pressure of competition in the lands of their origin, offered them a refuge so secure that even today there are tens of thousands of square miles in the western half of the island which have had no contact with the civilizations of the twentieth century.

After Greenland, New Guinea is the largest island in the world. It is shaped like a dragon. It lies with its head facing west just under the equator and with its body and tail lying to the north of the eastern half of the Australian continent. The mainland is nearly 1,500 miles long and about 500 miles wide at its thickest. North and east of the tail, a crescent of large and small islands comprising the Bismarck Archipelago sweeps up towards the equator again, while to the south-east the Solomon Islands chain runs downward roughly parallel to the Queensland coast.

The area ceded to Indonesia by the Dutch in 1963 totals 151,700 square miles, and the area under Australian administration is 183,500 square miles. The mainland rises above the sea from the northern edge of the Australian continental shelf and was joined to Australia by a land bridge during the

Pleistocene period about half a million years ago, when the greater part of Europe and North America was covered by ice.

Although Australia and its great offshore island stand on the same foundations, they are totally unalike. Australia in the geological sense is an old, flat, worn-down country with vast plains and deserts and few mountains. New Guinea is a young country born in comparatively recent times as a result of a gigantic wrinkling of the earth's crust which buckled and smashed the bed rocks of ancient, vanished oceans and piled them on top of each other in a series of central ranges, of which the highest peaks rise more than 16,000 feet above sea level. These mountains were formed in much the same way as the Himalayas and the Andes. The ranges are not continuous. They are closely spaced, parallel cordilleras running mainly from north-west to south-east and together they form the backbone of the 'dragon' all the way from its thin neck in West Irian to its stumpy tail in Australian New Guinea.

The remarkable thing about New Guinea mountains is the steepness with which they rise and the narrowness of the valleys between the main ridges. It is not uncommon to find 10,000- or 11,000-feet peaks within 30 miles of the sea, or a large river flowing through a canyon with a depth of 3,000 or 4,000 feet and the lips only a mile or so apart.

Perhaps one third of New Guinea's total area is made up of mountains of this kind—ridge after ridge of razorbacks separated by deep valleys through which swift rivers leap down to the lowlands or the sea.

Extensive swamps are also a feature of New Guinea. They are only a few feet above sea level and are laced with innumerable muddy, sluggish waterways. They lie mainly on the breast and belly of the dragon from the Mimika Coast to the Gulf of Papua, although there are also vast marshlands north of the mountains in the Lakesplain of West Irian and the middle reaches of the Sepik River.

The remainder of the island comprises the alluvial plains of big rivers like the Fly, Sepik, Ramu and Markham in the east, and the Digoel and Idenburg-Mamberamo in the west; the Great Papuan Plateau north-west of the Gulf of Papua; a few large highland valleys and tablelands, and even fewer areas of coastal plain where the land is not violently contorted.

So much for the naked body of the dragon, with its thick, bristling spine of mountains, its soft underbelly of swamps and its sparse, blotchy flesh of easily habitable land. Half an hour spent studying a relief map will serve to fix in the reader's mind the essential anatomy of the country—how its parts are put together. But what an ordinary relief map will not show, or even suggest, is the violence of the terrain, the dizzy heights of its peaks, the depths of its ravines, the expanse of its swamps, the volume of water discharged by its numberless rivers into the shallow, reef-studded seas.

Few if any equivalent areas on earth are subject to such physical fragmentation or to such contrasts. This fragmentation and these contrasts must be understood, and indeed *felt*, by anybody who wants to understand the nature and the habits of the primitive men who made New Guinea their home.

The next factor of importance is climate. The top of the dragon's head is almost on the equator, and its tail at the tip droops just a little south of the 10th parallel. This means that at sea level its climate is hot at all seasons and the temperature varies little between day and night. However, the equatorial heat is tempered with heavy rainfall and high humidity borne by the prevailing winds from the south-east or the north-west which carry moisture-laden air from both the China Sea and the South-West Pacific.

In coastal New Guinea the thermometer seldom rises above 90 degrees or drops below 70 degrees, and the humidity hovers around 70 per cent at sea level. The average annual rainfall is from 100 inches to 780 inches—except in the relatively dry 'rain shadow' areas about Merauke and Port Moresby. When the north-west monsoon blows, normally between May and October, the warm, moist winds from the China Sea strike the mountains and precipitate in rain on the northerly slopes. In the season of the south-east monsoon or trade wind, between December and March, the cool, moist air from the Pacific brings rain to the southerly slopes.

However, the distribution and intensity of rainfall in any one district of coastal New Guinea vary according to the height, shape and lie of the nearby mountains. In the highlands it rains almost all the year round, no matter what monsoon is blowing. Precise records have yet to be kept, but some observers believe that the average annual rainfall of certain mountain districts in West Irian may be as high as 1,180 inches.*

Average temperature of course falls as altitude rises, and because altitudes in New Guinea can vary so abruptly it is possible for the people of a coastal settlement to be sweltering in turkish-bath heat while mountain villagers only thirty or forty miles away are shivering in bitter cold. The climate is as fragmented as the land itself. Its only really consistent factor is the high humidity.

How then does nature clothe the dragon island? Soil and climate are of equal importance in producing a flora. New Guinea's climate varies widely—and so do its soils.

Most of the high mountain chains are formed of sedimentary rock—limestones, sandstones and laterites originally laid down in the beds of ancient lakes and seas and forced up to great heights by titanic convulsion. But even as these mountains were being thrust up, rain and frost and wind started to tear them down again and streams and rivers carry them back to the sea whence they came.

Soils derived from such sedimentary rock are not fertile until they have been changed and enriched by weathering and by the addition of decayed vegetable and animal matter. They lack the minerals and organic chemicals on which plants thrive.

Since the country is geologically young, the soils formed from the breaking down of its sedimentary mountains are naturally poor and shallow on the mountain slopes and in the high valleys. The rate at which they could develop fertility is slowed down by heavy rains leaching or washing out humus and useful chemicals almost as soon as they are deposited.

The weathering of New Guinea mountains is rapid because of their steepness and the rainfall. The rivers score out valleys and carry off vast quantities of silt. Where the mountains drop sharply to the sea, this silt is discharged and most

* *Handbook on Netherlands New Guinea,* The New Guinea Institute of Rotterdam, 1958, p. 11.

of it is quickly taken away by tides and currents; but where the rivers discharge on to a coastal shelf the silt accumulates in alluvial flats, or is trapped and builds up swamps according to the lie of the land and the natural drainage.

Most of New Guinea's rocky skeleton is covered by soils of these kinds—shallow and poor on the mountainsides and sour and swampy in the broad river valleys or along the coast.

There are, however, a few districts where the land is fertile because of old and new volcanic activity. The long chain of volcanoes which runs down the western extremity of the Pacific Ocean, all the way from the Kurile Islands through Japan and Indonesia to New Zealand and Antarctica, touches the north-eastern coast of New Guinea and runs on through New Britain, the Solomon Islands and the New Hebrides. On the New Guinea mainland small areas enriched by volcanic dowry lie at the south-eastern end near Mount Lamington and Mount Victory and in some valleys in the central highlands near old peaks like Mount Hagen and Mount Ialibu.

Yet New Guinea looks a fertile land to the casual eye. The whole island, except for the highest mountaintops and the broad valleys, is densely clothed with trees of one sort or another. They flourish in the warmth and wet, sending their roots far and deep into soil which would not grow good pastures and crops. Enthusiastic explorers used once to declare that the island was a second Java—a natural treasure house awaiting exploitation. But the modern soil chemist, geologist and agronomist have exploded that myth. The prolific forests of New Guinea are deceptive. They do not denote agricultural potential.

What is the appearance of this contradictory land? The seafarer from the south may sight the New Guinea coast where it is either swampy or mountainous.

If the coast is swampy it appears as a low bank of dull green foliage where mangrove trees grow densely on the tidal mud-flats. The whole outlook is depressing and monotonous. Clouds veil the distant mountains and the sea is discoloured by muddy water from innumerable rivers and creeks. It is hard to imagine a less inviting landfall than the south coast from, let us say, Kokonao in West Irian to the eastern limits of the Gulf of Papua.

Closer examination does nothing to improve the first impression. Behind the belt of mangroves, in places many miles wide, the freshwater swamps begin. They are enormous expanses of mud and rotting vegetation alternately flooded and drained by a lacy maze of waterways and covered by dense reeds, wild sugar canes and trees in which the nipa palms and sago palms with their long vicious spikes predominate. This is an eternally hot, wet, stinking region which winds rarely penetrate. One can fly over it for hundreds of miles and see only the metallic glint of ground-water through the feathery canopy of palm tops thirty or forty feet high. Here and there islands of more solid land—anything from a few square yards to a few hundred acres—are being gradually formed by the accumulation of silt and humus.

Behind the coastal swamps, which may extend more than 100 miles inland at the outlet of larger rivers, is usually a belt of lowland jungle not easily distinguishable by the layman from the jungles of tropical Asia, Africa or America. Fingers of swamp thrust into it along the course of the streams, but the ground underfoot is comparatively firm. There is a dense undergrowth and many of the trees are giants reaching a height of more than 200 feet. Mostly they are festooned with flowering creepers and bear a bewildering mass of parasitic and saprophytic plants—orchids, staghorn ferns, and 'mistletoes' of strange hue and shape. The sun's light rarely penetrates to the floor of the jungle where hundreds of species of trees and thousands of species of smaller plants riot in disorderly variety all together.

Should the voyager to New Guinea steer clear of the swamps and make landfall where the coast is mountainous he would probably navigate along the north side of the island— the top of the dragon's head, its neck, shoulders, back, and its tail on both the upper and lower surfaces. Here the high, blue-black, jagged mountains stand above a bank of rain-clouds and the approach to the coast is often complicated by coral reefs and islets on which coconut palms are growing. The estuaries carry the inevitable growth of mangrove, but long stretches of shore are fringed by narrow beaches with palms or small jungle trees overhanging the water. In the 'rain shadow' areas about Port Moresby and Merauke, which get only about forty inches of rain annually, the coastal strip is backed by savannah—rolling grassland timbered sparsely with eucalypts, casuarinas and paperbarks—which create a resemblance to parts of northern Australia. In the wet districts, however, the lowland jungle reaches close to the shore and ends in a fringe of coconut palms, which flourish in sand moistened by brackish subsoil water.

In the New Guinea hinterland, as the ground rises steeply from plains or valleys into foothills the nature of the forest begins subtly to change. Soil is shallower and rainfall higher. The mixed undergrowth of the lowlands thins out. Many varieties of trees develop enormous buttressed roots to help them keep foothold on the sharp slopes and in eternally sodden soil. The struggle for survival in this rain forest is fierce. Growth, decay and death are all rapid so that the parasites and saprophytes luxuriate in the thickening canopy of creepers bearing strange flowers and fruits. In the lower levels of the hill forest grow wild nutmeg trees, taun, kwila, erima (valued building timbers) rosewoods, mahoganies and New Guinea walnut. Higher there are red cedars, beeches, oaks, and isolated stands of *klinkii* and hoop pines reaching heights of more than 250 feet. Many of the trees are deciduous.

Above 5,000 feet, however, the size and solidity of the trees start to diminish. The slopes are even steeper and the soils poorer, but because rainfall and humidity are higher the cycle of germination, growth, decay and death is faster. The forest lives on the product of its own wet rottenness. Mosses, ferns, lichens and fungi are everywhere. The moss forests are eerie place at these altitudes. It rains continually and when it is not raining the hills are mostly blanketed in chill mists. Large areas are infected by luminous fungi so that at night every trunk, branch, twig and leaf is outlined in pale green and blue fire. It is possible for a man to topple down a sizeable tree with a single axe blow because the fungus has so weakened its trunk, and one falling tree may bring another dozen or so crashing with it.

Above 7,000 or 8,000 feet the forest becomes scanty and stunted. Alpine shrubs abound. At about 11,000 feet the dwarf forest gives way to moorland plants, snow grasses and mosses. Here sleet and snow often fall, but permanent snowfields and glaciers do not form at altitudes lower than about 15,000 feet. The only New Guinea mountains which are capped by eternal snow are the Juliana, Wilhelmina and Carstenz tops in West Irian. The highest peak in the Australian half of the island, Mount Wilhelm (15,600 feet) is frequently clear of ice and snow.

There remain only three other important categories of regional vegetation in New Guinea—that of the flood plains of rivers like the Ramu and Markham in Australian New Guinea; that of the valleys, and plateaux of the eastern, western and southern highlands, and of the Bailem River in West Irian; and that of the swamp plains in the middle reaches of the Sepik and Idenburg Rivers.

The flood plains are covered by reeds, canes and tall, coarse grasses. The plateaux are lightly timbered, with reeds in the depressions and drainage channels; and the inland swamps are not unlike those of the coast.

Some areas of inland New Guinea, particularly at moderate altitudes in the Australian half of the island, are clothed by a coarse spear grass common in South-East Asia, called *kunai*. Agronomists believe that these *kunai* patches, which cover many thousands of acres, established themselves after primitive agriculture destroyed the forest. When trees are felled and undergrowth cleared, the rank *kunai* moves in so quickly that seedling trees cannot compete with it.

Even the most generalized description of New Guinea is not complete without reference to its animals, birds, fishes, reptiles and insects, for they are there in variety as profuse as the plants and trees.

The warm, reef-studded seas teem with life. There are coral fish of every imaginable kind, many brilliantly coloured and some poisonous, schools of pilchards, sardines, tuna, mackerel and snapper. There are sharks, eels, rays, squids and octopuses; turtles; shellfish in abundance from giant clams, pearl oysters, and bailer-fish eighteen inches across to minute univalves smaller than a pin's head; crabs, sponges, jellyfish, pearly nautilus and sea slugs, marine worms and big sea snakes banded in glossy black and yellow. That oddly ugly marine mammal, the dugong, frequents New Guinea waters, particularly in the west. But the ugliest and most dangerous customers of the whole lot are the estuarine or salt-water crocodiles which often swim many miles out to sea on hunting forays.

Ashore, life is hardly less prolific. There are few large land animals native to New Guinea, but its marsupial population includes many smallish wallabies, opossums, kangaroo rats and tiny pouched mice. The elephants, tigers, lions, buffaloes, deer and monkeys of Asia did not migrate so far to the southeast. Even the native pigs and dogs which the white man found in the country were almost certainly domesticated animals brought in the first place by human migrants.

Far more noticeable in the New Guinea scene than marsupials, however, are the reptiles, birds and insects. There are more than fifty species of snakes, ranging from pythons twenty feet long down to minute nocturnal serpents of only a few inches. One third of the snakes are venomous, but the venomous breeds—with the exception of the sluggish death adder and the deadly taipan which grows to a length of twelve feet—are usually too small to be dangerous. Numerous reptiles of the lizard family in New Guinea vary in size from big monitors to tiny skinks and geckoes. Amphibious animals have also found the environment favourable, and many kinds of frogs and toads set up a deafening chorus in the lowlands at night.

Bird life on the island includes a prodigious variety of species—parrots, kingfishers, egrets, hornbills, crested pigeons, megapod fowl which hatch their eggs in great heaps of decaying vegetable matter, bower birds which make brightly decorated playpens in the forest, the flightless cassowary with a horny 'hat' on its head for cracking open tough jungle fruit, and no fewer than eighty varieties of birds-of-paradise. On the mainland alone, naturalists have listed more than 1,500 species and sub-species of birds, many of them unique.

But it is in the evolution and sustenance of insect life that New Guinea is extraordinary. Few regions on earth support such a huge and spectacular insect population—spiders, beetles, crickets, ants, ticks, mites, bees, butterflies, grasshoppers, wasps, flies and, above all, mosquitoes. Only the Arctic tundras in summer are comparable with the swamp plains of New Guinea as breeding grounds for mosquitoes. They—and the mountains—are the gross factors of the New Guinea environment affecting the life and development of the men who came through the ages and made the dragon island their fortress and their home.

Mystery clouds the human story of New Guinea and the origins of the vast majority of the people who now inhabit it. No one can say for certain whence or when they came, but the probabilities are that the big island and its smaller neighbours were colonized by successive waves of migrants from lands to the north and west.

The first men in New Guinea may well have been ethnic cousins of the aborigines of Australia, the Dravidians of India, and the Sakai people of the highlands of Malaya. They arrived when there were still land links between New Guinea and part of Asia. They were eventually displaced or absorbed by newcomers who also crossed before the land bridge disappeared. Just when the migrations began and over what period they extended is at present an exciting guessing game for ethnologists. In time, scientists may collect enough information to change speculation into accurate deduction, but probably the pioneers were a woolly-haired Negrito or pygmy type believed to have originated in Malaysia or Indonesia.

The next waves of immigrants are thought to have been tall, dark-skinned, curly-haired negroid people with prominent noses who were classed thirty years ago as 'true Papuans'.

In the third migratory wave were the Melanesians—a vigorous, seafaring people who, in their wanderings over the Indian and Pacific Oceans by outrigger canoe, had picked up by intermarriage a confusion of physical traits including wide range of skin tints and some resemblance to both the mongoloid races of South-East Asia and the negroes of West Africa. They almost certainly arrived after the bridge with Asia had been cut.*

The three basic racial types did not, however, remain separate. They intermarried to some degree and thus acquired

* An excellent introduction to the study of Western Pacific migrations is Malinowski's *Argonauts of the Western Pacific*, Routledge, London, 1958.

such an extraordinary mixture of race characteristics that it is difficult today to say any one New Guinea tribe is predominantly Melanesian, Papuan or Negrito. The ethnological picture has been further confused by the discovery in recent years of tall, light-skinned, mountain people who don't seem to fit at all into any combination of Melanesian, Papuan and Negrito.

The peoples of New Guinea are not, therefore, of any fixed, definable type. They are an almost incredible agglomeration of racial types which have remained only imperfectly mingled because of the extreme difficulty of moving about freely in the New Guinea terrain. Thus a New Guinea native's skin can be any colour from pale biscuit brown to blue black. His hair can be almost straight, woolly, frizzy, curly or wavy. His natural stature can range from a strapping six-foot to a freakish four foot three inches. The shape of his nose can be flat, semitic, straight or aquiline. And he can be round-headed, broad-headed or long-headed. At the extremes of difference one New Guinea tribesman can be as unlike another as an Eskimo is unlike a Hottentot, or a Laplander unlike a Sicilian.

The almost limitless variety of physical dissimilarities is paralleled by language differences. In the Australian half of the island, more than 500 mutually unintelligible languages have been officially listed among a population of about 2,000,000—and the list is growing as the last areas unknown to Europeans are being explored. Before the Dutch handed over West New Guinea to Indonesia in 1963, they had listed in their territory more than 200 languages among about 500,000 people of a total population estimated at 700,000.

In coastal regions it is rare for tribal groups speaking a common language to number more than 5,000 people—although the Tolai language of the Gazelle Peninsula of New Britain is now spoken by about 40,000. In the more densely populated highland valleys, however, there are several language groups numbering more than 30,000—but in the most rugged and inhospitable regions tribes of a few hundred have a distinct language of their own and no knowledge of any other.

In the field of language, the old-fashioned arbitrary classi-
fications of 'Melanesian' or 'Papuan' are more useful and
accurate than they are in describing the physical or cultural
characteristics of a New Guinea tribe. Generally the Melanesian languages are spoken round the coasts of Australian
New Guinea and along parts of the northern and western
coasts of Indonesian New Guinea. They have a relatively
simple grammar and many of the words are obviously derived
from common roots, as in the Germanic languages. They
do not penetrate far inland.

The Papuan languages are spoken in the hinterland and
predominate along the south coast of the island west of the
Fly River. Their grammar is fantastically complicated and
root relationships are very difficult to detect. Both classes of
language are, by comparison with European and the more
advanced Asian tongues, poor in vocabulary and unsuitable
vehicles for the expression of abstract thought.

It will serve to emphasize the remarkable fragmentation
and confusion of human groupings in New Guinea to note
that tribes with a preponderance of Melanesian physical characteristics may very well speak a language of Papuan type, or
vice versa.

One might go on endlessly listing the dissimilarities of New
Guinea tribes, but it is probably more useful to seek the rare
but important similarities which occur in all or many of the
diverse inhabitants of New Guinea and its adjacent archipelago.

The most significant similarity is to be found in basic
technical achievement. Practically all the tribes had learned
how to make and polish tools and weapons of stone, but none
had learned how to work metals. The stone-working skill of
the most advanced New Guinea artisans was roughly equivalent to that achieved in Western Europe about 6,000 or
7,000 years ago, at the end of the Mesolithic or the beginning
of the Neolithic era.* They could shape, grind and mount
stone axes, adzes and smaller tools much more accurately and

* Comparison between the Stone Age cultures of New Guinea and those of
Western Europe, the Mediterranean basin and Asia Minor may conveniently
be made by reference to *Prehistory and the Beginnings of Civilization* by
Jacquetta Hawkes and Sir Leonard Woolley, Allen and Unwin, London, 1963.

efficiently than Paleolithic people of the old Stone Age, and with these implements they were able to work wood with comparative precision, build permanent dwellings and fence plots for cultivation. Those who lived on the coast or by large lakes or rivers fashioned good dugout canoes from hollowed tree trunks.

It seems probable that the Papuan and Melanesian migrants brought this stone-working skill with them from the lands of their origin—and other skills as well. The Neolithic and Mesolithic peoples of Africa, Asia and Europe had learnt how to cultivate crops. They had domesticated animals and were no longer wholly dependent for sustenance on hunting or gathering food. They could afford to settle down in one district and build permanent hamlets and villages. They were not forced to lead nomadic or semi-nomadic lives and find shelter from the elements in caves or temporary huts.

So it was with the later waves of migrants which populated New Guinea. They brought with them early Neolithic techniques and adapted them to the new environment, but lacking the stimulus of necessity in an abundant equatorial land they did not develop those techniques rapidly or establish civilization—a condition of human evolution which implies town dwelling, specialization and the inter-dependence of the specialized elements with a complex social structure.

In harsher climates Neolithic man learnt fairly quickly to till the land and improve grain crops, to herd animals, to build in a variety of materials, and to extend the political dominion of the most vigorous and adaptable groups.

In New Guinea and the tropical islands of the Pacific generally, it sufficed to be a gardener and a hunter rather than a farmer and a herdsman, and the terrain militated against expansion of the more vigorous strains. There is some historical and anthropological evidence to suggest that the Papuan and Melanesian peoples were degenerating rather than evolving racially and socially when European influence began to assert itself towards the end of the nineteenth century. Populations were static or declining as a result of incessant inter-tribal warfare, destructive magico-religious practices, and diet deficiencies following the gradual extinction of more easily hunted game. A shortage of animal protein in the native diet remains to this day one of New Guinea's most perplexing medico-economic problems.

When the white man appeared in their world, most New Guinea tribes were gaining the bulk of their subsistence from a primitive but fairly efficient horticulture. They cut down saplings with stone axes, cleared and fenced garden plots, cultivated the soil with fire-hardened digging sticks, planted cuttings of yam, taro, sweet potatoes, manioc, bananas and sugar cane. Usually they moved on to new sites in the forest when the fertility of cultivated soil was exhausted, leaving the old gardens to be taken over by *kunai* or rehabilitated by secondary forest growth. On the steep hillsides of the interior where severe erosion often followed cultivation, a few highland tribes learned the value of efficient terracing, composting, and irrigation with ditches or bamboo water-pipes. But shifting horticulture was the rule.

The starchy food produced by cropping was supplemented everywhere by birds, small animals, fish, reptiles and insects, and on the coast by coconuts and wild fruits and vegetables as well. In the mountainous districts, the dietary was naturally more restricted, and in the true swamps the staple was sago starch washed from the pith of wild palms felled and split with stone axes. Garden produce raised on the limited areas of dry ground provided a little variety, and in places far from large waterways or the sea, protein supplement was obtained from gathering grubs which thrived in the decaying shells of felled palms, and by netting small fry which were often incorporated in the sago starch when it was heat-dried and smoked for storage.

Food growing and gathering of this sort naturally called for a division of labour between the sexes. Apart from their function as warriors, the men did the heavy work of tree felling, splitting and fencing. The women dug, planted, weeded and harvested. Men were the hunters and fishermen, women the gatherers of forest foods. The only domesticated animals contributing to pre-European dietary were pigs, and dogs* of sadly inbred strain, which were eaten only on ceremonial

---

* Pigs were introduced to the South-West Pacific by early European navigators. Dogs probably accompanied the migrants on their long canoe journeys.

occasions and which performed important functions as village scavengers of waste and ordure.

Food was mostly cooked by roasting over open fires or in ash pits, although a number of tribes made moulded or coiled clay pots, fired them and traded a surplus with any neighbours with whom they were not feuding at the time. Clay cooking-pots were thus fairly widely distributed among tribes living on the coast or along waterways navigable by canoe.

New Guinea hunters used rough wooden bows strung with slivers of bamboo or cane bark, firing unfeathered arrows with reed stems and elaborately carved tips of wood or cane. (Stone arrow heads were rare.) They also employed stabbing and throwing spears, stone-headed clubs, and in some districts sling-shots.

Fishing methods were not very advanced. Most fishing was done with spears in shallow reef waters, although some tribes twisted vegetable fibres to make lines and carved shell to make hooks. Others used small hand nets, but it is noteworthy that the coastal peoples never achieved a skill in net-making comparable with that of their Polynesian and Indonesian neighbours.

An equable climate, and an abundance of timber and thatching material in the forest, provided little stimulus for the development of building techniques. Generally tribesmen were content with thatched huts of grass or palm, framed and raftered with sapling poles lashed together by split canes or creepers—a type of construction common to every kind of shelter, from the extremely primitive dwellings of the high mountain tribes to the huge, elaborate 'man houses' of the Fly River and Gulf districts and the towering 'tamboran (spirit) houses', sometimes seventy feet from floor to ridge-pole, of the Torricelli Mountains near the mouth of the Sepik. Coastal or swamp people often built their houses on piles and made a decking of poles and woven canes, but mostly the primitive New Guinean lived on the ground under his thatch, cooking his food and warming himself at night at a crude stone hearth. Frequently he shared his single-roomed habitation with his pigs and dogs.

The lay-out of villages varied considerably between district and district, as did the shape of the buildings and the degree of craftsmanship used in their construction. The mountain peoples were as a rule more primitive in their methods than the coast and plain dwellers. For defence they usually sited their villages on narrow ridge tops, often far above the nearest running water. In some areas the villages were surrounded by elaborate moats* and palisades of sharpened stakes; in others the dwellings were small and dispersed in deliberately preserved undergrowth to make surprise attack on the whole group more difficult. A few swamp tribes built tree-houses far above ground level. Rarely did any village or complex of hamlets have a population exceeding two or three hundred people. Usually the number was much less.

Domestic furniture and utensils were simple and sparse. Among more advanced communities the list might include clay cooking- or water-pots, sleeping-mats woven of palm fronds, gourds and carved wooden bowls; and among the less advanced perhaps only gourds for water, net bags to contain dry food, native tobacco and betel nut, and small tools made of stone, shell, bone or bamboo.

In most areas the techniques of spinning vegetable fibres manually and of knitting, plaiting and weaving were fairly well established. The string bag for carrying food and personal belongings is ubiquitous in New Guinea to this day. Some tribes, mainly in the eastern islands, were skilled in basketry and weaving mats. Others made girdles, bracelets and head-bands woven in geometrical designs with dyed fibres. Small cowrie shells were often skilfully incorporated in these personal ornaments. All the same, it cannot be said that the New Guinean before he came under European influence had made more than a beginning in the art of textile manufacture. He wore clothing for ceremonial or decorative reasons rather than for protection against the elements. At one end of the scale some tribes (on the Sepik) went entirely naked; at the other, the women customarily wore elaborate grass skirts and the men loincloths of beaten bark. Most people, however, were satisfied with pubic coverings of net, bark, grass, fronds, shells or gourds according to local custom. Even in the high mountains, they did not protect themselves

---

* In the Tari district of the southern highlands of Papua a maze of fighting ditches up to thirty-five feet deep extends over the countryside.

against the cold with anything more imaginative than a liberal coating of pig fat or coarse cloaks of bark or leaf.

It was in personal and non-functional adornment that the primitive New Guinean employed the greatest creative ingenuity. Many coastal and plain peoples were practised in the fabrication of shell and bone necklaces, bracelets, and ear and nose ornaments. They made spectacular ceremonial cloaks, and carved and painted masks of wood or bark. In the highlands, the craft of making fantastically complicated headdresses of feathers and fur was well developed. Here, among a large group of people, huge wigs of human hair (that of the owner and of his family, friends and enemies) were major status symbols. Tattooing, both by dye injection into the skin and by keloid scarring, was a precise and delicate art in some districts.

Beyond fabrication of personal ornaments, New Guineans had few artistic accomplishments. The tribes of the Mimika Coast in West Irian and of the Sepik district of the Australian Trust Territory carved detailed human and animal figurines from wood. In the Torricellis the 'tamboran houses' were furnished and decorated with traditional grotesques representing natural and supernatural beings. Canoes, prows, drums, wooden bowls and even clay pottery sometimes bore carved, modelled or painted designs of a conventional kind. But on the whole the artistic achievement of New Guineans could not be compared favourably with that of their contemporaries in Oceania or equatorial Africa. Some anthropologists believe that their art was deteriorating when the white man arrived.

New Guinea music was even more primitive. The only instruments were wooden drums with heads made of dried reptile skins and, in a few areas, conch shells and pan-pipes and flutes of reed or bamboo. Drum rhythms were simple, repetitive and monotonous, as were the themes of flute music and songs. Much the same may be said of the dance forms which, though often performed in splendid panoply, were not graceful and demanded little physical discipline except stamina.

The similarity of New Guinea cultures is discovered in the upper limits of their material attainment. They were alike only because none had progressed beyond certain critical levels in human mastery of environment.

This similarity of limitation extends inevitably into the field of social organization. The village was the most advanced political and social unit evolved indigenously. A number of villages might be allied by language and blood, but with few exceptions there was no centralized tribal government with authority over all the allied villages. Each village had its chief or chiefs and managed its own inter-communal relationships within the pattern of kinship taboos.

Occasionally one village or tribe might conquer a neighbouring village or tribe, perhaps exterminate or enslave an enemy population—but the conquest never had political implications. New Guinea produced powerful, feared tribes and formidable war chieftains, but they never attempted to build little empires or assert permanent political authority beyond their own communities. Probably the difficulty of travel and communication in such broken and rugged country made such enterprises physically impossible. Only in the Trobriand Islands did a system of hereditary chieftainship evolve and a paramount chief exercise authority over lesser chiefs.

In such circumstances one might expect that the tribesmen would have lived together more or less peaceably, but this was far from the case. Before the coming of Europeans, each tribe was in a state of almost uninterrupted low-grade warfare with its neighbours. Why, since ambition for permanent conquest was either absent or never realized, did this condition of continual conflict exist?

There may have been causes which might broadly be described as economic—disputes about the ownership of land, trespass, theft, raids to obtain women or slaves, the need for increasing tribes to extend their gardens or their hunting grounds. But I am inclined to think that the real causes of the endless hostility were to be found in mental attitudes rather than in direct physical needs. Primitive man is completely exposed to, and intensely aware of, the favourable and unfavourable elements in his environment. To him Nature is a paradox, giving and taking away without rhyme or reason. The paradox of Nature, apparent in any part of the world, must have seemed especially puzzling to the races which inhabited New Guinea. It was a country which in many ways sustained life easily. There was plenty of food to be had from the sea and from the lowland and foothill forests. Men never went hungry for long, although diet was unbalanced. The crocodile, shark and snake were almost the sole visible, comprehensible enemies of man in the animal kingdom.

On the other hand, diseases—invisible and incomprehensible enemies—took heavy toll. Mortality among babies and young children was high. Adults too were apt to sicken and die from no apparent cause. Trivial wounds and injuries infected quickly and sometimes resulted in prolonged suffering and death. It has always been in the nature of man to ascribe supernatural explanations to circumstances or events which he does not understand. The migrants to New Guinea doubtless brought with them their own primitive religion and code of beliefs to explain what they could not understand about life; but their new country was to present such a violently contrasted complex of elements so unpredictably favourable or unfavourable that the religions themselves had soon to be greatly complicated and intensified to provide satisfactory answers.

As far as we can make out, the primitive religions of all the diverse New Guinea tribes are fundamentally similar. They believe that the affairs of this world and the lives of the people in it are very largely managed by the inhabitants of a spirit world. The inhabitants of the spirit world are various —sometimes of superhuman extra-terrestrial origin, sometimes superhuman but terrestrial, but more often simply the ghosts of the dead. All the tribes seem to ascribe to the individual soul a persistence, either permanent or impermanent, after physical death. Furthermore, all the tribes seem to believe that communication between the material and spirit world is possible in a number of ways, and that the behaviour of the spirits can be influenced by the behaviour of living people. There is also a practically universal belief that some spirits are good and friendly, others are bad and unfriendly, and *all* spirits can be placated, propitiated or circumvented by ritual actions.

Close resemblance between tribal or regional religions does

not go much deeper than this; but a great majority of the people believed, and indeed still believe, that accident, illness, death, defeat in combat, and such disasters as freakish floods or crop failures, are caused by the intervention in human affairs of hostile supernatural forces. Since the actions of living people affect the actions of the spirits, a man's enemies are primarily responsible through the agency of sorcerers or magic rituals for the ills that befall him. The primitive New Guinean believed absolutely that systems of efficacious sorcery and magic (and of counter-sorcery and counter-magic) were necessary for survival. Without that belief, the paradoxes of his environment would have confounded him utterly.

Perhaps all humanity has passed through this stage. But in New Guinea progress beyond it was hampered by the nature of the country. In other parts of the world, groups of human beings were able to make contact readily with their neighbours; to expand by conquest; to merge through clearly apparent mutual interest; to trade freely and to exchange ideas. In New Guinea the steepness of the hills, the deepness of the rivers, the impenetrability of the forests and swamps, made mergers virtually impossible. The terrain clogged the normal evolutionary development of human society. Little groups of people lived for centuries isolated from each other in every activity except war, preserving and evolving their own language, customs and magico-religious rituals. To such groups, everybody beyond the valley or the swamp island or the mountainside that provided sustenance was the enemy— the enemy who made the hostile magic that caused death, disease and suffering, and against whom one must in self defence make hostile magic and counter magic.

The same terrain and climate that inhibited contact and checked social development produced food liberally in return for little effort. With the exception of the nomadic tribes which range the infertile high mountain tracks to an altitude of 7,000 or 8,000 feet, New Guineans did not have to spend much time hunting, or growing or gathering food—not at least by comparison with other primitives such as the Australian aborigines or the Eskimos. They occupied a great deal of their life in magico-religious ceremonies and in warfare.

The ingrowing nature of their cultural development resulted in a very complicated and variegated structure of superstitious beliefs and practices, many of which are abhorrent to the sensibilities of Western civilization. Cannibalism, although by no means as universal in New Guinea as people used to think, was practised by tribes both on the coast and in the mountains. In some cases, parts of the human body were ritually eaten in the belief that strength or some other desirable quality was thereby transmitted from the dead person. Many tribes ate parts of dead friends or relatives as a mark of respect or affection. Others ate parts of enemies killed in battle to acquire their courage and cunning. There were also those who ate human flesh because they enjoyed it and saw no moral reason for wasting edible meat.

Head-hunting is another practice objectionable to civilized conscience. Many tribes hunted enemies and preserved their skulls as trophies in the belief that their influence with the spirit world as well as their current social standing was thereby enhanced. Among these peoples the taking of heads was often associated with the magical rites of initiating youths into the status and responsibility of manhood. Some anthropologists hold the opinion that head-hunting is the degraded vestige of an earlier religion which demanded human sacrifice to propitiate the gods. Even among people who do not actually hunt heads the collection and preservation of skulls and bones supposedly possessing magical properties was a widespread custom. In the Sepik district and elsewhere widows were confined in a hut with the bodies of their husbands until such time as they could emerge with the skulls and bones, from which the decayed flesh had fallen away.*

It is always difficult if not impossible to make a distinction between customs and practices that are purely of religious significance and those which are predominantly related to social organization. In New Guinea the difficulty is especially pronounced. Propitiation by ritual of the all-powerful spirit world and the observance of customs evolved to protect the viability and solidarity of the village-state were matters inextricably woven together. Some tribes had an almost incredibly

---

* This custom prevailed among many tribes of the Lower Sepik until the 1920s.

C

complicated system of sex *tabus*. These probably began as behaviour patterns to safeguard the group against degenerative inbreeding, but they became so elaborate that to the mind of modern man they seem completely illogical and far more destructive of human happiness and community efficiency than preservative of reproductive vigour.

Birth, the attainment of maturity, procreation, death . . . these were the milestones watched jealously by the spirit world. The traditional forms and observances had therefore to be observed. But in less vital matters there was room for human variability and human decision, and we descend from the realms of supernatural or divine law into the realm of ethics.

Ethically, the vast majority of New Guinea tribes believed implicitly in an ancient precept: 'And thine eye shall not pity; but life shall go for life, eye for eye, tooth for tooth, hand for hand, foot for foot.' Fanatical subservience to this ethic perpetuated never-ceasing war and feud. It reinforced the terrain in preventing disparate peoples from mingling and emerging as a homogeneous nation.

If we are to understand the obstacles in preparing New Guinea peoples for partnership in a modern world, we must realize how complete was their belief in the existence of a world inhabited by good and bad spirits with power over human life and happiness; and how complete was their acceptance of the idea that the greatest attainable virtue in living man was the courage to exact an eye for an eye and a tooth for a tooth by any natural or supernatural means. This dual code was in effect religious law; and in New Guinea communities it governed many everyday activities. The breaking of religious law was rare. When the breach occurred, it was either publicly apparent or divined by sorcery. It was mercilessly punished. Crimes such as incest and adultery were usually punishable by death. Accused persons who denied guilt were subjected to trial by divination or ordeal.

Religious law did not, however, cover simple crimes of violence or offences against property. There was no *law* against murder or theft; indeed there was no moral revulsion against murder or theft as such. But by binding custom murder or theft had to be 'paid back' by the relatives of the victim, and there was moral revulsion against those who neglected through lack of courage or strength to pay the debt. Again by binding custom, the reprisal in its turn demanded counter-reprisal—and so on, endlessly. It was, of course, perfectly logical for the people involved in the vicious circle of payback to invoke the aid of sorcery in their immediate enterprise.

The Stone Age men of New Guinea did not evolve for themselves any system of criminal or civil law which is recognizably the prototype of civilized systems of criminal or civil law. They had no form of impartial judiciary, nor any concept of social or individual morality compatible with civilized conscience. Human life was not regarded as sacred, or property as inviolable. There was no inhibition against inflicting intense physical suffering on an enemy or an animal, and there was a marked and quite genuine inability to distinguish between fact and fantasy. Happenings in a dream are just as real to a New Guinea primitive as the events of waking life.

Warfare, except in the case of a few highland tribes, was usually stealthy and total, casualties among women and children often exceeding those among the warriors. Villages were burned, and where prisoners were taken they were brutally killed either for their heads or their flesh. Chivalry and what more advanced peoples regard as martial virtues, such as personal courage in combat or generosity to a defeated enemy (again with the highland exceptions), was notably absent in the pattern of New Guinea tribal war.

Among New Guinea peoples generally there was little social stratification. Leadership was not a matter of birth but of individual qualities, and the power exercised by leaders was strictly limited. Frequently the function and responsibilities of leadership in a village were divided among several persons. One man was the war chief, another led hunting or fishing expeditions, a third organized and directed the clearing and planting of gardens. Another claimed, and was believed to possess, occult powers which might qualify him to become the chief priest or sorcerer. Activities might to some degree be specialized, but specialization did not of itself imply social privilege or superiority. In general, however, the wisdom of age was respected and the elders spoke with powerful voices in community discussions.

In most communities, concepts of social organization, however widely they might differ in detail between groups, incorporated incentives to accumulate wealth. Elaborate systems of gift exchanges were common, probably as a means of insuring group solidarity by inter-dependence or mutual indebtedness. Marriages among New Guinea primitives were invariably accompanied by the payment of a bride-price in the currency of the particular region. This could be dogs' teeth, boars' tusks or live pigs (mainly though not exclusively in the coastal areas) or different sorts of cowrie, pearl or marine snail shells (mainly though not exclusively in the highlands). A man achieved social status, but not necessarily leadership, by the accumulation of wealth which he disbursed by purchasing wives, by contributing ostentatiously to ceremonial feasts, or by making rich gifts to those over whom he wished to obtain social advantage.

Except for some seafaring villagers in the Bismarck Archipelago who turned to professional trading because they had little productive land,* New Guineans were, and remain, untalented in commerce. The sea shells which were the currency in the highlands reached there by long and devious trading routes, bartered for stone implements, food and forest products over many hundreds of miles. Similarly, tribes with such specialized utilitarian skills as making pottery, sago or salt, partly depended on barter with their neighbours who in turn passed on surplus acquisitions. By and large, however, the primitive tribesman showed little or no interest in accumulating profits from his small trading activities—or at any rate, profits in the European sense of the term. The wealth of the rich villager in every group was singularly unnegotiable and peculiarly expendable.

Land was held in general by the tribe and in particular by the clan, and systems of tenure and utilization varying from group to group seemed incredibly complicated to Europeans. Inheritance and familial authority were mainly matrilineal

* Notably the Manus islanders studied in detail by Dr Margaret Mead, the authoritative American anthropologist.

among peoples speaking Melanesian languages, and patri-
lineal elsewhere.

Among the Melanesians of the Bismarck Archipelago, however, certain crude forms of class distinction were evolving at
the time the first traders and missionaries arrived. Secret
societies, unlikely to have had religious origin, existed among
the men. Such associations as the Duk-Duk and the Iniet on
New Britain, where members went masked on ceremonial
occasions, made extortionate demands on the uninitiated and
had established a brutal reign of terror over large populations. Left to their own devices, perhaps these societies may in
time have taken political colour and radically changed the
old order.

There remains only one significant aspect of primitive New
Guinea life to summarize before passing to the firmer ground
of recorded history. That aspect is the dissimilarity in temperament between New Guinea's Stone Age peoples and the
white men who infiltrated their country and established
domination over them from the late nineteenth century
onwards.

To the white man, the New Guinean of any tribe appeared
emotionally unstable, highly excitable and totally unpredictable. The earliest administrators and missionaries remarked
in horrified wonder at the natives' apparent lack of inhibition
in personal relationships. They were amazed by a man who
would burn down his hut or shoot arrows indiscriminately in
any direction simply because he felt frustrated or depressed,
by a woman who would commit suicide to shame a husband
who had spoken unkindly to her, by whole tribes whose
people would mark grief, humiliation or mere ill-temper by
lopping off a joint of their own fingers or toes with a stone
axe.*

These people appeared to have no belief whatsoever in the
sanctity of human life or any regard for physical suffering.
They killed one another or themselves on what seems, to us,
the most trivial provocation. To them the waking world and
the dream world were equally real—and the ghosts of the

* Self-mutilation of this kind is practised extensively among many highland
tribes in both Australian New Guinea and West Irian. It is not so common
among lowlanders.

mind as indisputably a part of existence as the bodies of friends or enemies, the horizons of sea and earth, or the shape of clouds.

Practically no feature of the social structures they had evolved or of their individual behaviour was compatible with the institutions or standards of Western civilization.

2

Partition in the Wilderness

EXCEPT for the Amazonia province of Brazil, New Guinea resisted European penetration longer than any other habitable region of its size on earth. The maze of offshore reefs and shoals made its approaches perilous for all but the most skilled seafarers in the smallest of sailing craft, its terrain blocked efforts to explore the hinterland, and the reputation of its savage tribesmen was so forbidding that even the treasure-hunters of the sixteenth, seventeenth and eighteenth centuries gave it a wide berth.

Historians believe that two Portuguese navigators, Antonio d'Abreu and Francisco Serrano, were the first Europeans to sight the mainland in 1512 on a voyage of exploration from the East Indies. In 1526-7 another Portuguese, Jorge de Meneses, looking for a route from the Malay Peninsula to the Spice Islands, landed on the shores of western New Guinea and called it 'Ilhas dos Papuas'—the land of frizzy-haired people. Ten years later the crew of a Spanish ship out of Peru mutinied and murdered their captain, Hernando de Grijalva, shortly before the ship was wrecked somewhere on the north coast. They were taken prisoner by the natives and those who survived were liberated after years by Portuguese traders from the Celebes. In 1545 Ynigo Ortiz de Retez, a Spaniard from Tidore, landed in the extreme west and claimed possession for his country of the territory which was later to become Dutch New Guinea. He named the place New Guinea because he thought it resembled the Guinea Coast in West Africa. But Spain made no attempt to consolidate Retez's claim.

During the next three hundred years practically every great

27

maritime explorer of the Indian and Pacific Oceans touched New Guinea and mapped parts of its coast. Torres discovered the Louisiade group and charted Milne Bay and parts of the north-east coast in 1605. Jansz, Le Maire and Willem Schouten made voyages along the north coast. In 1642 Abel Tasman reported that he believed the island had agricultural and trading possibilities. William Dampier named New Britain in 1700. Cartaret, Bougainville, Cook, Hunter and McCluer all sighted and examined sections of the New Guinea coast and filled in blank spots on the charts of their times, but it was not until 1793 that the British East India Company, acting on a report by McCluer that there were possibilities for the spice trade east of the Moluccas and Ceram, made a half-hearted attempt to establish a settlement on Geelvink Bay. Captain John Hayes, in the warship *Duke of Clarence*, raised the flag at Restoration Bay and built a small fort which he named New Albion, but the annexation was never confirmed and the post soon abandoned. For political reasons the British decided to allow the Dutch a free hand in the area, and in 1814 recognized the ancient claim of the Sultan of Tidore to overlordship of the West New Guinea tribes. As the Sultan himself owed allegiance to the House of Orange, this was tantamount to ceding sovereignty to the Dutch, but it was a surrender of small significance in those days.

Tidore's claim to rule West New Guinea dated back to the thirteenth or fourteenth century, but with little practical substance. A few Indonesian trading prahus* had irregular contact with Papuan coastal communities in the western half of the island, but at no time were those communities brought under powerful or permanent Indonesian influence, and much less were they conquered or governed by the agents of the Sultanate. New Guinea and its people were a combination which for hundreds of years resisted the expansionism of both East Indian princelings and European empire-builders alike. Until the middle of the nineteenth century even the coastal tribes had little contact with the outside world of either East or West, and the inland tribes had virtually no contact at all.

* Malay sailing canoes.

Beyond minor adaptations which enabled them to cope better with their immediate environment, the peoples of New Guinea in all probability changed their ways very little in the millennia which passed between their original occupation of the archipelago and the coming of the white man. It is even possible, as mentioned earlier, that their skills and cultures were declining rather than evolving in the protection of the many-celled fortress where they had found refuge from the pressures of the Neolithic migrations which in prehistoric times swept slowly back and forth across the continents and oceans. The Melanesians encountered by early European explorer-navigators and traders must have appeared repulsive and bestial compared with the far more advanced inhabitants of the East Indies and the gentler peoples of Micronesia and Polynesia.

The first white men to seek prolonged contact with coastal New Guineans were not explorers but maritime traders based on Australia. By the middle of the nineteenth century small sailing vessels, usually out of Sydney or Auckland, were making more or less regular expeditions to the Solomon Islands and New Guinea. It was a time of rapid commercial expansion in Oceania. The colonial empires of the British, Dutch and French were well established in Asia and Australasia, and the Americans were colonizing and developing their own West Coast. The Pacific Islands had become the new frontier—a frontier pioneered, as usual, by individualists who were rugged indeed and who sought fortune and freedom beyond the ordered preserves of the great trading companies.

First came the whalers and sealers. Whale oil was in those days a commodity of much greater economic importance than it is today. Until the development of coal gas and paraffin it was the main domestic and industrial lighting fuel of Europe and America. Whale ships scoured the Pacific from the fog-banks of the Aleutian Islands to the ice packs of Antarctica in one of the most highly organized, ruthless, physically demanding and profitable hunts ever undertaken by man, whose history has shown him to be the most rapacious of all the predatory animals. The rapacity of the whalers was matched only by that of the sealers, whose brutal greed and haste were so insensate that they often skinned their prey alive in the rookeries.

After the sealers and whalers came the tropical traders: men who were equally ruthless and who regarded the savages of the 'cannibal islands' as mere animals to be exploited for whatever profit could be wrung out of them. The traders sought pearls and pearl shell, trochus and tortoise-shell, sandalwood and ebony, guttapercha, wild rubber, coconuts, coconut oil, dried coconut meat, and bêche-de-mer, a marine slug abounding in the coastal lagoons which, when dried and smoked, was a food prized by wealthy Chinese. Natives who supplied these commodities were paid with axes, hatchets, knives, nails, tools, metal utensils, beads, mirrors, calico, rum, and sometimes with firearms and ammunition.

Copra began to assume increasing importance in European commerce as ways were found of making soap from vegetable oil and manufacturing stock food from the residue when the oil had been expressed. Soon the demand for Pacific copra outran a supply dependent upon trade with natives who gathered nuts haphazardly from wild groves by the seashore. Europeans moved in, acquired land by purchase or seizure, and made plantations, first in Polynesia where climatic conditions were easier and the native population resisted white encroachment less vigorously, and later in the more isolated Melanesian islands. Profitable sugar plantations were also started in Queensland, Hawaii, Samoa and Fiji.

By the 1870s various trading and planting concerns had made considerable capital investment in organized tropical agriculture in the Pacific. Profits and expansion were, however, limited by scarcity not of suitable land but of cheap labour, a factor which planters in the Americas had encountered some two centuries earlier and overcame by importing slaves from Africa. No such solution was available to the planters of the Pacific, unless covertly. The British Parliament had outlawed slavery in 1833 and the Abolitionists were on the winning side in the American Civil War of 1861-5. Nevertheless, emancipation for the agricultural labourer in the tropics was to remain for another half century far more a legalism than a social reality.

As early as 1847, European traders began to recruit Melanesians as labour for the Peruvian mines under an indenture system. Later they recruited for the sugar plantations of Queensland, Fiji, Samoa and elsewhere. In the nineteenth century Pacific the verb 'recruit' was a euphemism for the act of cajoling, tricking or forcing primitive men into a 'contract' to work for specified periods in places far distant from their homes, and in conditions and for material rewards often inferior to those provided by most American slave-owners before emancipation.

The techniques of recruiting varied. Traders who had established friendly relations with groups of natives might perhaps offer inducements of gifts and promises to any young men who would enter into a contract to work for a white master in some fabulous land beyond the sea for a specified term and for specified wages. The young men who accepted this proposition, either for greed or in a spirit of adventure, rarely if ever understood what sort of bargain they were making. They had no conception of the value of money, of the kind of labour they would perform, of the conditions in which they would live, or even of the exact meaning of the specified labour term.

Yet such recruiting was by far the least brutal and dishonest of the methods employed. Other kinds of recruiters obtained labourers by getting them paralytically drunk on board ship and sailing off before they sobered up—or by bribing village leaders to induce or order them to accept indentures. Some recruiters encouraged powerful tribes to raid their traditional enemies for slaves and then hand over the slaves, unprotest-ing, naturally enough, as recruits. Still others treacherously invited young men aboard their ships, enticed them below, then simply clapped the hatches on and sailed before the men realized what had happened. Thirst, starvation and terror soon sapped their will to resist. The callousness of Pacific recruiters in 'blackbirding', as the debased trade was known, was often comparable with the brutality of the West African slave trade during the previous century. It can, however, be said to the credit of European conscience that blackbirding in its crudest form was tolerated for less than fifty years, thanks largely to the growing political influence and activity of the Christian missions who had fought so successfully for the abolition of legal slavery in the Americas.

A proportion of indentured labourers was, of course, repatriated at the end of the term, although worse off materially and socially than they had been before they were recruited. Others died of alien diseases against which they had acquired no natural resistance. The remainder, forever detached from their kin, was absorbed and consumed in the expendable mass of native labour which drifted in dribs and drabs about the Pacific until well into the twentieth century.

It is clear, therefore, that the first prolonged contact between Europeans and the Western Pacific islanders was painful; and that the Europeans treated the islanders with as little understanding and humanity as previous generations of conquerors had treated the American Indian nations which had been almost exterminated during the three centuries following the voyages of Colombus. It should nevertheless be remembered that humanitarian treatment by conquerors of the conquered is a relatively new manifestation in the history of man. It certainly did not exist among the primitives themselves.

The early traders, recruiters, planters and prospectors in Melanesia as well as Polynesia were often misfits in their own society—men who had not found profitable employment or security at home and who sought to make or restore their fortunes in regions free from the inhibitions of civilized law, custom and tradition. Some were criminals, debtors, or political refugees; most were simply social rebels or adventurers irked by ordered conformity. They possessed extraordinary physical vigour and, often, reckless courage. They were as pitiless as the savages they sought to subdue and exploit with their superior weapons, tools and tactics. They had little care for human life and suffering or property rights. Among them and the savages it was the accepted code that the strong and the cunning should take what they wanted from the weak and the ingenuous.

The influence of men of this type upon accessible island communities tended rapidly to destroy the old social order. Metal tools and implements alone wrought cataclysmic changes in the economy and the living pattern of those who acquired them. With a steel axe land could be cleared and fenced, or building materials obtained from the forest, perhaps ten or twenty times as fast as with a stone axe. Steel adzes revolutionized canoe-making. Indestructible iron pots replaced fragile clay ones. Calico was more colourful, versatile and durable than bark cloth. Rum was a more potent euphoric drug than betel nut. A gun killed game—or an enemy—far more efficiently than an arrow or a sling-shot. It is difficult for any European who has not observed the pattern of activity in a Stone Age community to appreciate how completely the introduction of simple steel tools can change living habits and the basic economy of a primitive people, or how rapidly this change can destroy the existing motivation and structure of society.

The upheaval caused by the arrival of white men with axes to trade for pearls or bêche-de-mer or coconuts was not confined to chain reactions from technical innovations. Europeans brought with them diseases against which the islanders had developed no natural immunity: measles, whooping cough, typhoid, syphilis and gonorrhoea, tuberculosis, influenza. These were killers in unsalted communities. Within a few decades of the first trading contacts, a tragic depopulation began in island communities which the newcomers visited.

Yet it must be emphasized that New Guinea, New Britain and the larger islands of the Solomons and New Hebrides groups were less affected by the coming of the whites than the islands of Polynesia where the people were less warlike and the country more easily penetrable. The rugged terrain which had prevented free mingling of the Melanesian tribes before the arrival of Europeans also prevented intruders from infiltrating the hinterland to any great extent. Sporadic trade contacts and later agricultural expansion were restricted to a few of the more accessible coastal districts. Only a minor percentage of the total population felt the European impact during the early years.

The presence of occasional small Australian trading vessels off the south coast of New Guinea was remarked by British naval commanders as early as 1840. In 1846, Lieutenant Charles Yule in *Bramble* made a leisurely examination of the coast and took possession of it in the name of Queen Victoria, but the British Government, which had signified its indifference to the region eighteen years before by acknowledging without argument Dutch claims to sovereignty over the western half of the island, refused to confirm Yule's annexation. It could foresee no profit, commercial, strategic or political, in accepting responsibility for the government of these remote and unattractive 'badlands'.

During the next twenty or thirty years, however, the growth of trade and tropical agriculture in adjacent areas of the Pacific altered the opinion of far-sighted men. The Polynesian islands were becoming an important source of raw materials, and small enterprises which had originally been speculative began to establish themselves as regular and high profit earners. Big companies began to interest themselves in preserves which had hitherto attracted the attention only of wandering freebooters.

The Germans were in the field early. In 1857 the powerful Hamburg firm of Godeffroy and Sons acquired freehold land in Samoa with the support of the Hanoverian Government, and during the next fifteen years this company established a formidable network of trading agencies throughout the Central and South-West Pacific.

It was also an era of keen public interest in scientific exploration. The reports of F. P. Blackwood, Owen Stanley and John Moresby, who examined and mapped long sections of the New Guinea coast, were widely studied by patrons of natural philosophy.

By the early 1870s, Godeffroy agents were operating as far afield as New Britain, New Ireland and neighbouring groups. Blackbirding was at its peak and missionaries were for the first time setting up permanent stations in the New Guinea area. Their reports, and the reports of brother missionaries elsewhere in the South Seas, began to rouse public concern about the excesses of the traders and recruiters. As early as 1864 representations were made to the British Government that annexation was the only means by which a rule of law could be established. Ten years later further approaches were made and Captain Moresby took possession of East New Guinea in the name of the Queen. Again Whitehall refused to act.

Meanwhile the successes of Godeffroy were alarming smaller competitors and consolidating the interest of German commerce in the area. An ambitious visionary, Adolf von Hansemann, formed the South Seas Trading Company and after early reverses succeeded in obtaining the approval of the Imperial Chancellor, Prince von Bismarck, who at this stage was unwilling to saddle a newly unified Germany with colonial responsibilities.

British and Australian interests who wanted to attempt organized exploitation of the area were unable to get Government support. The Colonial Office quashed the proposals of a British syndicate in 1876 (and of an Australian syndicate as late as 1898).

Events, however, outstripped official thinking. The influential Anti-Slavery Society and various missionary organizations were putting heavy pressure on the British Government. In 1874 the Colonial Secretary, Lord Carnarvon, invited the opinion of the Australasian colonial governments on annexation. They replied rather lukewarmly in favour of it but were reluctant to undertake financial responsibility for administering new territories. The matter was dropped. But by now political factors, as distinct from commercial and moral considerations, were becoming important. The Australian colonies were frightened of German, Russian and French intentions. They saw their defences as extremely vulnerable if Britain failed to assert naval control of strategic areas. The sections of people who entertained these fears made common cause with the humanitarians who pointed out that race relations were going from bad to worse in Melanesia, where natives were now committing crimes of murder and minor piracy by way of indiscriminate reprisal for the activities of lawless whites.

Speculatively-minded men added their voices to the clamour for annexation. The major gold strikes in California, Victoria and New South Wales had stimulated European colonization and development on both sides of the Pacific, but by the 1870s bonanza days were over and an energetic search for new fields had begun. Minor discoveries in Queensland caused some movement of population northward and the eyes of ever-hopeful, ever-restless prospectors turned to

the great dark island across the Coral sea, the name of which
—for no valid reason—had for centuries been popularly associated with gold.

In 1870 a naturalist, Richard Daintree, submitted to the
Ministry of Public Works in Queensland a paper suggesting
that the gold-bearing structures in North Queensland continued across the Coral Sea and would be encountered again
in south-east New Guinea. Three years later the observations
of Captain Moresby indicated that such a geological continuity did, in fact, exist. In 1877, a discovery of trace gold
near the future site of Port Moresby started a minor rush of
excitable prospectors who were soon to regret their rashness
in challenging a country far more formidably hostile than
north Queensland. None found gold in payable quantities.
Many died of malaria and exposure or were murdered by the
natives.

These were the days of the romantics and the romanticists.
New Guinea was the *Ultima Thule* of people who made a
cult of travelling in, or even just dreaming about, strange,
savage places; it was a paradise for the ambitious naturalist
and a lodestone for the treasure seeker and the religious with
a yearning for martyrdom.

In the west as in the east, the missionaries were early in the
field although, being more concerned with the salvation of
souls than the elucidation of geography, they rarely scored
exploratory 'firsts'. In the 1850s, Dutch Protestants established themselves on Mansinam Island in the far west, almost
at the same time as French and Italian Catholic missionaries
were forced after a siege by disease and cannibals to abandon
their station on Woodlark Island in the extreme east.

The first naturalists on the mainland—men on the whole
better endowed with imagination than scientific detachment
—achieved little but temporary notoriety until Luigi Maria
d'Albertis, an Italian adventurer with some knowledge of
natural history, led a number of remarkable voyages in Dutch
territory and up the Fly River, the first occasions on which
white men had penetrated deep into the heart of the island.

About this time a Russian biologist, Baron Nicolai Mik-
luho Maklay, landed on a beach in Astrolabe Bay in what
was to become German New Guinea. Having established

friendly relations with the tribes there by his instinctive understanding of primitive psychology, Maklay remained for about fifteen months to explore the Rai* Coast and observe its fauna and flora. He later did field work in Dutch territory and twice returned to the scene of his early adventure. His contribution to nineteenth-century knowledge of New Guinea is qualitatively unparalleled.

Unlike the quiet, efficient, intuitive Russian, the Italian d'Albertis conducted his explorations with a kind of exuberant exhibitionism, concerned only to establish crude geographical facts and the merest superficialities in the field of ethnology, and to collect rare specimens.

D'Albertis had no time for the bare-bottomed savages who stood in the way of 'scientific' inquiry. When in doubt he resorted to dynamite or gunpowder.

Nevertheless, after some time spent in collecting specimens and in minor exploration from a base on Yule Island, d'Albertis made the three expeditions up the Fly River which revealed to the world for the first time specific facts about the interior.

The second of these voyages in 1876 was brilliantly successful. In the steam-launch *Neva* d'Albertis travelled 540 miles upstream, almost to the geographical centre of the country. No real opposition from the river tribes was encountered on this occasion, but d'Albertis's collecting methods were so predatory and he was so impatient in his dealings with primitives that on the third voyage a year later, he met serious trouble. He used dynamite bombs, fireworks and flaming petroleum to scare off war parties who tried to drive him out of their lands. For half a century afterwards the river people remembered the swashbuckling Italian with hatred and gave other travellers who followed his route as bad a time as they could contrive.

The writings of Maklay, d'Albertis and other explorer-adventurers in the 1870s aroused interest throughout Europe and stimulated a number of colonization schemes.

By the early 1880s, however, the New Guinea problem was becoming critical for Australians. The South Seas Trading Company had been liquidated because of the pressure of

* Rai is a native corruption of Maklay.

D

British creditors scheming to control its policy, but von Hansemann formed a new syndicate to colonize the northeast coast of New Guinea. Bismarck still officially denied expansionist intentions but Australian traders in the Western Pacific were not convinced. Fears grew apace that political action would soon be taken to protect the commercial gains of private or semi-private German interests.

Nor was Germany the only European power which Australians suspected of casting acquisitive eyes on the Pacific no-man's-land. The French had annexed the mineral-rich island of New Caledonia in 1853 and were probing the New Hebrides. Even the Russians were thought to be looking at New Guinea in a speculative light after the reports of Maklay.

The schemes of cynical and irresponsible speculators added to the general confusion. The most flamboyant was that of the Marquis de Rays, a French nobleman who tried to restore his fallen fortunes by promoting a fantastic plan to colonize New Ireland. He sold £300,000 worth of 'shares' to gullible French, Italian and Belgian shopkeepers and small farmers by promising them land and houses in a mythical colony which he called 'Nouvelle France'. De Rays knew nothing of the Pacific except what he had read in the papers of d'Albertis, but he managed to persuade 600 innocents to subscribe up to £75 a head, in return for which he promised each subscriber 50 hectares of fertile land, a house, six months' free rations, and a 'patent of nobility' in this South Seas Utopia.

In 1880, 300 men, women and children left Barcelona in two old steamships and after three months' voyage were landed at Port Breton on the southern end of the island. No arrangements had been made to receive them. Unprovisioned and unequipped, the wretched dupes had no chance of establishing themselves. Within six months more than fifty had died of malaria and dysentery, and the rest were ill and starving. They persuaded the captain of one of de Rays's chartered immigrant steamers, the *India*, to take them to Sydney. But the *India* broke down and was forced to put in to Noumea in New Caledonia, where the destitute refugees were a grave embarrassment to the French authorities. Eventually most of the survivors reached New South Wales. They were helped and given land grants near Woodburn on the Richmond River by the Premier, Sir Henry Parkes.

The arch-trickster, de Rays, continued to publish fictitious accounts of life in idyllic 'Nouvelle France' for a long time after the Port Breton settlement had ceased to exist, but he was eventually exposed and ended his days in a madhouse. The scandal convinced the last doubters in the Australian colonies that the need to establish law and order in the islands could no longer be ignored.

Queenslanders were particularly alarmed by fresh rumours that the Germans planned a land grab in New Guinea, and early in 1883 the Premier, Sir Thomas McIlwraith, instructed the Resident Magistrate on Thursday Island, Mr H. M. Chester, to annex the eastern half of the mainland in the name of the British Crown. This Chester did on 4 April, 1883, at Port Moresby; but the British Government promptly repudiated the action. It wanted no further expansion of the Empire that might precipitate trouble with Germany, and it was doubtless influenced by the opinion of the pioneer missionaries, Lawes and Brown, that Queensland's interest in annexation largely stemmed from a desire to ensure continuity of recruited labour for the northern sugar and cotton plantations.

There was immediate and excited reaction in the colonies to the British Government's repudiation. In November and December, 1883, an Intercolonial Convention in Sydney unanimously urged the United Kingdom to annex eastern New Guinea and agreed to contribute £15,000 a year to the cost of administration. This time the colonies' clamour was too loud and angry to be pigeon-holed. In August, 1884, the British and German Governments held informal discussions and Britain announced that it would declare a protectorate over the territory lying between the agreed Dutch boundary and the 145th meridian. Germany protested strongly, and the British accordingly agreed to confine their claims to the south coast. On 6 November, Commodore J. E. Erskine declared the British protectorate. Ten days later Germany proclaimed its protectorate, naming the whole of the north coast and the islands of the Bismarck Archipelago. It was Britain's turn to protest, and Germany compromised by setting its boundary at the 148th meridian on the north coast of the island. Island frontiers between the two protectorates were later negotiated and the partition was ratified by treaty in June, 1885.

Australian reaction to these arrangements was again antagonistic. The States were agitated because Germany had now gained a footing in the strategic area, and felt that Britain had been humiliatingly outsmarted—at the cost of Australian security. For the first time the Pacific colonies were solidly unified in disapproval of British policy, and some historians see here the germ of the federation of the Australian States achieved about twenty years later.

At long last the occupation of the Pacific no-man's-land by Europeans was a political and legal reality, but many years were to pass before political and legal reality had much practical effect on the majority of the native inhabitants.

It should be remembered that the complexity of events leading up to the establishment of the British and German protectorates in New Guinea did not in any sense imply that there was already massive contact between native and European as there had been in Oceania. Some thousands of coastal tribesmen had been affected by the activities of a handful of white traders, recruiters and missionaries, but there were hundreds of thousands inhabiting the hinterland who were untouched. This is an important fact to bear in mind when evaluating the early European influence. A large proportion of the mainland population was not to experience white civilization for more than seventy years after the proclamation of the protectorates.

Although the British and German Governments had in theory accepted responsibility for supervision of the New Guinea territories, this did not in itself eliminate the lawless and brutal European elements, pacify the warring tribes, or at first check the rising tide of reprisal murders committed by native groups who had suffered from the depredations of traders and recruiters. From the beginning the British and Germans tackled their colonization problems in entirely different ways and, until the occupation of German New Guinea by Australian troops during the First World War, policies and race relations in the two territories evolved striking dissimilarities once basic authority had been established at the seats of administration.

At official level the British were genuinely indifferent to economic development. They were concerned only with pacification and the protection of British lives and property. Towards the end of 1884, Major-General Sir Peter Scratchley was appointed Special Commissioner of the British New Guinea Protectorate, but delays in London and consultations with the colonial Governments kept him out of the field until August, 1885. Meanwhile two deputies, H. H. Romilly and Anthony Musgrave, made a valiant but futile start with the business of restraining unruly native groups in the vicinity of Port Moresby. In most native attacks on white men reported to the deputy Commissioners, the whites had obviously offered provocation, but even had this not been so, little could have been done to punish the aggressors. Romilly and Musgrave had no physical resources—or for that matter clear legal authority—to enforce the peace and punish misdemeanours by either whites or natives.

When Scratchley arrived to take up his official duties he too laboured under the same handicaps. He was, however, a man of enormous energy and vision, and he immediately undertook a strenuous reconnaissance of his domain. He collated and checked a vast amount of information in a short time, and from it developed views which were to exercise considerable influence on the policy-making of his successors.

Scratchley lasted only three months in New Guinea. He contracted cerebral malaria and died on board his chartered steamer while being taken to Cooktown in Queensland; but his voluminous notes were preserved and carefully studied by the Australian authorities. Scratchley took the view that undesirable traders and recruiters had no just claim on the Government for protection. They had brought their troubles on their own heads. He accepted the need for pacification and suppression of barbarous practices, but at the same time favoured conservation of native lands and those elements in native social structure which were compatible with civilized conscience.

In February, 1886, John Douglas, Resident Magistrate at

Thursday Island, was appointed to succeed Scratchley. He held office until November, 1887, when Dr (later Sir William) Macgregor, Government Medical Officer for Fiji and Deputy Commissioner for the Western Pacific, was appointed Administrator. Macgregor arrived in Port Moresby on 4 September, 1888, the day on which Britain officially announced annexation of the New Guinea Protectorate as a Crown Colony.

The deputy Commissioners, lacking both legal status and the resources to govern, had done little to change the situation in the islands since the declaration of the Protectorate, but during their terms of office a great deal more was learnt about the country and its people, and the knowledge was disseminated in Australia.

Journalist explorers backed by Melbourne newspapers, *The Age* and *The Argus*, made limited explorations of the country in the vicinity of Port Moresby, and quickly learned at first hand how tremendously difficult it would be to subdue the natives and make a going concern of the colony.

George Morrison (later world-famous as 'Chinese' Morrison, the journalist-sinologist and influential political adviser to China's leaders) represented *The Age*, and was gravely wounded by arrows when ambushed after he had shot a thief who had been raiding expedition stores. Morrison survived only by virtue of his courage and amazing constitution. Captain W. E. Armit, a tough Queensland policeman recruited by *The Argus*, was personally more fortunate in a journey which penetrated as far as the lower foothills of the Owen Stanleys, but he lost one of his companions, sixty-year-old Professor W. Denton, from malaria and exhaustion.

Both correspondents wrote lively and colourful accounts of their brief but hair-raising adventures.

The hapless public servants charged with the administration of the new colony soon realized—when they attempted to assert the authority of Her Majesty's Government by punitive naval expeditions against recalcitrant coast villages harbouring the murderers of white traders—that New Guinea would never be pacified by gunboat diplomacy. Bombardment by small warships of the Royal Navy inflicted few casualties and did little damage. Douglas indeed came to the conclusion that such forays harmed rather than enhanced British prestige and the use of naval forces was soon discontinued.

When Macgregor assumed office his resources were hardly greater than those commanded by Scratchley, Douglas and the deputy Commissioners. He had a staff of only four 'career' officers and had to appoint private individuals to honorary magistracies and other public posts. But he was remarkable for his great physical and mental vigour. Like Scratchley he immediately set about familiarizing himself with the country and people at first hand, and in the main he agreed with Scratchley's intuitive conclusions. He had no time for freelance traders and was determined to protect the natives from them. He was quick to appreciate the value of missionaries as agents of tacit conquest, offered them what scant protection he could, and encouraged their then very modest work in the medical and educational fields.

As his knowledge of the country increased, Macgregor began to assemble a tiny but functional machine of government. He appointed a Legislative and Executive Council and framed basic ordinances. Although his funds were still limited to £15,000 a year, he established by 1890 a small native constabulary of Solomon Islanders with Fijian NCOs. When suitable Papuans became available, they supplemented and eventually replaced the foreign islanders. With this force Macgregor gradually brought under control some accessible villages and demonstrated that deliberate flouting of the white man's law incurred unpleasant penalties.

He discovered, as so many New Guinea administrators were to re-discover after him, that the condition of almost perpetual warfare between tribes did not arise so much from the natives' love of fighting as from an ignorance of how to avoid fighting—a dilemma which plagues civilized nations today as sorely as it did New Guinea's savage clans then.

Macgregor and his men found it fairly easy to negotiate peace treaties between traditionally hostile communities, but extremely hard in practice to maintain the peace when the negotiating authority could not enforce sanctions against the parties which breached agreement. However, even with his few police, Macgregor managed to achieve a good deal on the south-east coast. By New Guinea standards the people there were not particularly virile and belligerent. They lived in constant terror of raids by the fierce hill tribes, and since they were unable to get rid of the white men they were willing to accept whatever protection the whites could give them. It is worthy of note also that they degenerated the most rapidly when exposed to undesirable aspects of white influence.

In the hinterland Macgregor's pacification programme did not go so well. The Government could travel reasonably fast in small ships along the coast or up navigable rivers, but to journey by land was a different matter. To trek maybe 100 miles into the interior involved major organization and imposed severe physical strains upon Europeans. The climate was enervating, disease was rife, and the terrain appalling.

Nevertheless, Macgregor himself actively explored the jungle-smothered Owen Stanley Range behind Port Moresby, climbed several of its highest peaks, and gained what was then a unique knowledge of the practical difficulties which stood between an approved policy of pacification and its actual accomplishment.

Macgregor to the modern mind might appear as a self-contradictory and unpredictable character. There is no evidence that he either understood or sympathized with the primitive people whom he governed, or tried to govern, with benevolent intent. Indeed few Europeans of his generation, including the missionaries, really understood or sympathized with them. They seemed cruel, treacherous, intransigent, idle, dirty, bloodthirsty and stupid, possibly a little more than wild animals but certainly something less than men. Missionary and administrator alike regarded them as an onerous component of the white man's burden, a responsibility of civilized conscience to be accepted in expiation of original sin or to be tamed and disciplined as the patriotic duty of the chosen proconsuls of a master race carrying the torch of enlightenment to barbarian lands. Traders and planters were on their part persistently inclined to look on natives as low-grade, raw animal material from which profit could be extracted only if the operator was ruthless enough.

Macgregor appears to have been moved by the conventional sense of duty inculcated by his Colonial Office training. With ludicrously inadequate resources he established a workable skeleton administration. He divided the colony into magisterial districts, framed ordinances imposing a form of licensing control on traders and timber-getters, and prevented the alienation of native lands except by sale to the Crown. Evidently he realized that opening the area to unrestricted European exploitation would seriously harm the natives and probably impede the prime objective: pacification and the imposition of British law.

To deal with rivalry between denominational missionaries Macgregor allocated clearly defined spheres of influence to the London Missionary Society, the Anglicans, the Wesleyans and the Roman Catholics. He worked steadily towards complete abolition of labour recruitment for foreign service and outlawed the sale of liquor and firearms. Towards the end of his term he did what he could to encourage responsible European settlement as a means of developing the country's agricultural potential. In broad outline, his policy can be described as enlightened and highly practical by the standards of his day. He certainly implemented his theories with energy and consistency.

The growth of mission influence, preservation of native land, and the discouragement of lawless traders and recruiters combined to inhibit commercial exploitation of the new colony. New Guinea was no longer a country from which the callous adventurer could extract quick profit for slight effort. Indeed the restrictions proclaimed by the British administration on white commercial enterprise soon disheartened the speculators who had been most vociferous in demanding annexation. New Zealand, Western Australia, Tasmania and South Australia repudiated the agreement under which they were to contribute to the cost of governing the colony, and Queensland, New South Wales and Victoria were left to share the financial commitment. Some Australian newspapers acidly criticized a native protection policy which they claimed prevented sound economic development and foredoomed New Guinea to be a heavy drain on Australian resources. It was certainly true that under Macgregor's regime trade did not greatly prosper and no planting of any account was done by Europeans. Macgregor himself was very well aware that the country required investments, but he was so busy trying to create some order out of chaos that it was not until his term was nearing an end that he began to frame and press for a land tenure system attractive to white investors and at the same time protective of essential native interests.

Commercial gold strikes, first on the offshore islands of Sudest and Woodlark, and later on or near the Yodda Valley on the mainland, generated some of the additional money Macgregor needed to build his administration and yet paradoxically added almost intolerably to his responsibilities. In 1895, more than 200 white prospectors rushed to the alluvial fields of the offshore islands, crossing the Coral Sea from Queensland in all sorts of sailing craft from Chinese junks to square-rigged ships, and Macgregor was deeply concerned by the thought of what would happen when unsuccessful diggers tried to retrieve their luck by prospecting the mainland. Accordingly he concentrated on pacification in the south-east segment and tried to exert some authority in the mountainous hinterland.

Macgregor's methods if practised today would be condemned as ignorant, arrogant and brutal. When hostile natives attacked his patrols and pressed the attack, they were 'taught a lesson'. They were shot down and their villages burned. That many attacks were motivated by perfectly natural fear did not weigh with efficient officers of Her Majesty's Colonial Service. They honestly believed that *force majeure* was the quickest way of getting results and that in any case they were wholly justified on grounds of self-defence. So long as the results were confined to making the white man feared and the brown man subservient, the formula worked.

Macgregor, like most of his contemporaries, was assiduous in establishing white prestige by the lawman's gun and only slightly subtler methods. It is for instance reported of him that when he called on the paramount chief of the relatively advanced people of the Trobriand Islands, the chief received him sitting on a high, decorated throne with the lesser chiefs grouped about and below him. Macgregor seized the man by his frizzy hair and flung him violently from his seat, declaring that no one should sit higher than he, the representative of the British Crown.

Yet, despite many stories of similar theme told about Macgregor, he *did* protect the New Guinea subjects of Queen Victoria from greater indignities and brutalities at the hands of commercial exploiters.

Unhappily he was not successful in his effort to impress the mountain tribes in the Owen Stanleys that white men were dangerous to resist. He lacked the force and the time. As he had feared, raw prospectors did come to the mainland, and eventually discovered and worked alluvial gold deposits in the Yodda Valley. The hardships endured by the miners in the rush of 1896-7 were horrifying. The majority were men without experience of life and travel in a hard equatorial country. Without adequate equipment, food or medical supplies, small parties of them plunged recklessly into the jungle. They died in scores—from malaria, dysentery, typhus and pneumonia, or infected wounds and exposure. They suffered heatstroke, skin diseases and deficiency diseases. They sweated in the lowland swamps, shivered and froze in the high mountain passes, and they went in continual peril of sneak attack by the frightened and angry tribesmen whose gardens they often pillaged for food. How many of these foolhardy men perished in the Yodda goldrush will never be known. Their arrival and departure were uncontrolled and unrecorded, but it is safe to assume that a significant proportion of their casualties was caused by native attack. It is also safe to assume that, because the whites had firearms, the attacking warriors themselves suffered heavily. The Government was able to intervene in only a few cases with exemplary hangings of men unfortunate enough to be identified as raiders of miners' parties.

Miserable coastal natives recruited as carriers were also involved in the sordid and senseless tragedy. It is highly probable that even more casualties occurred among the carrier lines, both from disease and violence, than occurred among either the Europeans or the bands which ambushed and harassed them. The mountain people made no distinction between brown and white invader. They attacked, killed and often ate both with equal enthusiasm.

Macgregor, who was promoted to another Colonial Office posting in 1898, had been able to do very little to remedy the situation caused by the Yodda goldrush. He concluded logically that the country would be able to afford effective government only when it could support soundly based, non-speculative industry. One of his last major administrative acts was to allocate to the British New Guinea Syndicate, a company financed by English capital, an area of 50,000 acres for agricultural and mining development. However, the federation of the Australian States was by now imminent and colonial politicians were reluctant to allow English investors too great a hold on New Guinea. Macgregor's concession was cancelled. Not long afterwards a somewhat similar development scheme backed by Australian capital was also rejected. Public opinion at this time was extremely sensitive to criticism of labour-recruiting methods and allegations of exploitation and maltreatment of Pacific Islanders, voiced mainly by missionaries.

Macgregor had on the whole, in spite of his tactlessness and haste to establish British prestige at gunpoint, lived up to his own dictum that 'one of our first duties lies in dealing justly and righteously with the native inhabitants'. He was succeeded first by Sir Francis Winter, in office for only a brief period, and then by G. R. Le Hunte, a man of very different temperament. Whereas Macgregor had thrown himself with furious energy into field work and delegated much administrative detail to his tiny staff, Le Hunte was determined to tidy up the machinery of government and to build up the public service as well as possible within the limits set by available finance. The service did in fact grow but, because its salary scale was so low and it could offer no security of tenure, it attracted only zealots or incompetents, and the zealots were hopelessly outnumbered.

Very little extension of Government influence was achieved by the Le Hunte administration and except for the exploitation of the Yodda goldfields the colony remained economically stagnant. The missions, however, were very active along the south coast and by the turn of the century had established some sort of contact with most of the large coastal communities from the Dutch border to the south-east tip of the mainland.

One of the most energetic and courageous missionaries in this field was the Rev. James Chalmers who, after experience in Raratonga, had joined Lawes of the London Mission Society at Port Moresby in 1877. Chalmers was undoubtedly one of the great missionaries in an age of heroic mission work. He travelled mainly without European assistants. With only a retinue of mission converts on a small schooner, he made the acquaintance, and sometimes won trust and friendship, of the cannibal villagers between Port Moresby and Daru, a tiny outpost near the Dutch border.

On 4 April, 1901, Chalmers left Daru on a voyage that was intended to fill in one of the few gaps in his knowledge of the south coast. He wanted to make contact with the tribes on Goiarabari Island in the Gulf of Papua. The Goiarabaris were swamp-dwellers, head-hunters, cannibals, and stout, cunning fighters. They had never seen Europeans but had undoubtedly heard alarming stories about them. On this occasion Chalmers, now sixty years old, permitted a young missionary, the Rev. Oliver Tomkins, to accompany him. In addition to his boat crew he also had nine Papuan mission students and the chief of the Kiwai tribe which lived on an island near the mouth of the Fly River.

After an uneventful voyage, the *Niue* anchored off the village of Dipoma. The schooner was soon surrounded by scores of canoes manned by hundreds of hostile warriors who eventually swarmed aboard. Their leaders demanded that Chalmers go ashore but he refused, knowing that it was local custom for war captives to be executed in the *dobus* or men's clubhouses, compartmented grass huts up to 600 feet long which were adorned with the skulls and bones of victims. Chalmers, a man of forceful presence, managed to get rid of his murderous visitors at nightfall by promising them through his interpreter that he would come ashore the following morning.

For some unknown reason, possibly the belief that he could not escape, or in defiant and fatalistic quixotry, Chalmers remained at anchor that night and the following morning kept his promise. He went ashore in the whaleboat with Tomkins, the Kiwai chief and the mission students. Immediately they entered the *dobu* all twelve were clubbed to death, their heads cut off and their bodies dismembered, cooked and eaten. The *Niue* was looted, but its Polynesian skipper and crew were spared and by 27 April news of the massacre reached Port Moresby.

Le Hunte had been preparing to go to Cooktown in the Government steamer, *Merrie England*, but as soon as he heard of the murder of the Chalmers party he cancelled his plans and mounted a punitive expedition. A force of five Europeans and twenty-four native police was recruited in Port Moresby and was reinforced by two Europeans and twelve police from the Government station at Yule Island, and by two officers and ten men of the Royal Australian Artillery from Thursday Island.

The *Merrie England* was challenged by a fleet of war canoes off Dipoma and returned the volleys of the Goiarabari bowmen with the massed fire of fifty-four rifles. After the brief encounter twenty-four bodies were counted floating in the sea or slumped in abandoned canoes, but it is probable that three or four times as many casualties were inflicted. Next day a party from the steamer landed, burned down twelve *dobus* along the foreshore, and took one prisoner whose fate is not recorded. The remainder of the population fled into the swamps where nobody was foolish enough to pursue them.

Le Hunte then returned to Port Moresby satisfied that the white man's 'payback' had been exemplary, but by no means happy on the score of its moral justification. Le Hunte's doubts about holding a whole community responsible for its leaders' acts were reflected soon afterwards in his reaction to a punitive operation authorized by the Government officer at Daru against a Gulf village called Baramura. The Baramurans killed a mission native who had stolen a valued wooden image from their manhouse, and in reprisal a force of police from Daru had burned down the great grass structure which had taken the village more than two years to build. When Le Hunte heard of the incident he sent an expedition to apologize to the villagers and pay them compensation in trade goods.

Ten months after the Goiarabari massacre he himself returned to the island to retrieve the skull of Chalmers, give the villagers peace offerings and assure them the account was closed. He established friendly relations and there would probably have been no further trouble if it had not been for the stupidity of C. S. Robinson, the man who temporarily succeeded Le Hunte as administrator after he retired in May, 1903. Christopher Robinson was a young and inexperienced lawyer who had been chief judicial officer in the colony for a couple of years. He had no understanding whatsoever of New Guineans and was intellectually and temperamentally unfitted for the office to which he succeeded and the almost insoluble problems that went with it. He had always held that the men responsible for the Chalmers murders should be hunted down and punished, and he did not favour Le Hunte's peace treaty at Goiarabari.

Robinson began a tour of the colony soon after Le Hunte's departure. He started his inspection on the north-east coast and attempted to reach the Yodda goldfields by a new route. A severe outbreak of measles among his carriers and repeated harassment by hostile natives turned the expedition into a fiasco. The administrator, by now suffering recurrent bouts of malaria, was forced to retire. He later reached the Yodda Valley by the regular route, tried and hanged a couple of murderers on the way, and promised to do what he could to afford the miners additional Government protection against native raiders.

After return to Moresby, Robinson rested briefly and then set out to show the flag and demonstrate his policy in the west. At Daru he fell under the influence of the Resident Magistrate, a man named Jiear, who strongly urged that the individuals actually responsible for the killings should be arrested and punished and that the villagers should be forced to surrender the skull of Tomkins which they still retained. Robinson agreed and the two men took the Government ship to the Goiarabari coast where they were received as friends. Jiear however claimed that among the natives boarding the ship he recognized two men as members of the group which had enticed the missionaries ashore and murdered them. He ordered their arrest. As soon as the native police forcibly

seized and handcuffed them, their companions in the wel-
coming canoes became agitated and fired a desultory volley of
arrows at the ship. Jiear ordered immediate retaliation and
the police party poured intense rifle fire into the massed
canoes, killing or wounding about fifty men and boys. The
Goiarabaris again took to the swamps and no further arrests
were made. Robinson continued his tour of inspection on
other parts of the coast and eventually returned to Moresby
to face a storm of indignant condemnation from missionaries
and others who had already learnt of the incident and reported it to the authorities. The second massacre caused
almost as much furore as the first. The angry moralists contended with justification that Robinson's repudiation of Le
Hunte's understanding with the Goiarabaris debased Government tactics to the kanaka level. One might have expected
such behaviour from the victims of the reprisal, but not from
the head of an administration charged with the responsibility
of exemplifying civilized standards. Robinson had undoubtedly made a tragic mistake in heeding Jiear's advice on how
to 'handle' savages, and he was quick to realize it.

The Australian Government had been considerably embarrassed by the whole Goiarabari affair and the strong probability that further trouble would occur on the coast unless
the administration of native affairs could be improved.
Humanitarian elements in the electorate were bitterly critical
of Robinson's brutal and unnecessary reprisal. They scented
scandal in the whole Port Moresby set up, and pressed for a
Royal Commission.

On return to the tiny capital after the second Goiarabari
affray, Robinson received orders recalling him to Melbourne
for an inquiry and appointing his Chief Judicial Officer, Captain F. R. Barton, to administer the colony until the inquiry
had recorded its findings. Worn down by malaria, worry and
the physical strain of touring, Robinson shot himself in the
grounds of Government House in June, 1904.

The affairs of the colony were by now in hopeless confusion. Even its precise political status was unknown, for
although the British Government had transferred sovereignty
to the new federation of Australian States in 1901, formal

The peak in New Guinea architecture. A House Tamboran (dwelling for spirits) at Maprik, Sepik District.

The mighty fisherman. A Goroka brave of the eastern highlands is happy with his minute catch from the Government ponds. Any protein in the diet is better than none.

acceptance was still delayed and indeed was not forthcoming from the Australian Parliament until 1906. No one, least of all Barton, knew what courses of action would be approved either in handling native affairs or in regulating commercial or mission activities.

After Robinson's suicide, he carried on for three years the job of trying to hold together the embryonic public service built up by Macgregor and Le Hunte. It was a thankless, hopeless task, for the young Australian Commonwealth was still half a century away from according to the New Guinea colony the attention and the financial and human resources that its proper government needed. Port Moresby was a tiny, poverty-stricken outpost of European rule on the fringe of a vast and savage wilderness. Its inhabitants, Government servants or otherwise—following the tradition of early colonization in the deep tropics—were either refugees from the irksome restraints of their own social order or would-be exploiters of the 'lesser breeds'. The town dwellers were mainly alcoholics, eccentrics, or little men disguising their lack of social and intellectual stature behind a front of starched tropical drill. The jungle travellers differed from them only in their physical courage and the furious vigour with which they sought escape from their own kind, or the means of satisfying their greed for material wealth or the heady drug of danger.

Barton, himself an officer of the West Indian Regiment with an undistinguished career, was no man to stem the demoralizing rot which had set in at Port Moresby after the Colonial Office shed its New Guinea responsibilities. He was a weak, amiable person with a faculty for making useless friends and dangerous enemies, and these in a community which then comprised only sixty-six permanent European residents living in squalid little iron-roofed houses on the stony hillsides about the harbour. The centre of social life in this isolated, malarial place was an appalling tavern near the waterfront where the riff-raff of the Pacific occasionally came ashore from their trading ships to get speechlessly drunk and engage in bloody brawls. Its centre of commercial life was a tumbledown trade store given over mainly to the buying of sandalwood and the selling of cheap grog. Under

E

such conditions, only a leader of great personal magnetism and purpose could have maintained the morale of the low-grade public servants stationed in the settlement—and Barton certainly possessed no dynamic qualities. In the three years he held office, the Government service was cleft into two warring factions, each of which accused the other in extravagant terms of inefficiency, drunkenness, corruption and immorality. All source material preserved from those days is so tainted with self-interest and malice that it is hard now to discern the flavour of the truth; but it would seem that an old Colonial Office faction, left over from the days of Scratchley and Macgregor, allied themselves against Australian newcomers and the disaffected few who sympathized with the newcomers.

Barton had the misfortune to attract the support of a dipsomaniac Scot named David Ballantine who in time came to dominate his chief, while the Australian faction had the luck to find leadership in the veteran Government Secretary, Musgrave, whose need to seek relief from boredom and frustration in alcohol in no way impaired his expertise as a double-dealing bureaucrat. Musgrave was destined to play a large part in the downfall of Barton and his clique, but he was not the architect of that petty but perhaps fortuitous victory.

The man who brought about the changing of the white guard in British New Guinea was of very different calibre: a scholar, athlete and eccentric who was to become in his own lifetime a legendary figure in the history of colonial administration in the Pacific.

He was Hubert John Plunkett Murray, who had been appointed to succeed the unfortunate Robinson as the territory's Chief Judicial Officer after being sent to Port Moresby as Royal Commissioner to inquire into the Goiarabari troubles.

Murray was a man of exceptional intellect, personality and physique. He was the second son of Sir Terence Murray, a distinguished Irishman who served with the 145th Regiment in New South Wales from 1817 until 1824, transferred to India and returned to Australia later to become a pioneer pastoralist in the Canberra district and build a successful career in State politics.

Hubert, no less versatile and even more talented than his father, was brilliantly successful as a student at Sydney Grammar School. At the age of nineteen he entered Magdalen College, Oxford, from which he graduated with a Double First in humanities four years later. In this brief time, he found the surplus energy to row for Oxford against Cambridge, win the amateur light heavyweight boxing championship of Great Britain and become a skilled swordsman. After coming down from Oxford, he read law in London for a year and was called to the Bar, but decided to return to Sydney. There, after admission to the Australian Bar, he practised his profession for some years.

Through an oddity of personal address or manner difficult to define, Murray was not popular as a barrister and few lucrative briefs came his way. He finally accepted a post as Parliamentary Draftsman and Crown Prosecutor—work which on his own admission bored him to distraction, but from which he could see no practical avenue of escape. He found some diversion in amateur soldiering, was prominent in the establishment of the Irish Rifles in 1896 and soon rose to become the regiment's commanding officer with the rank of major. Four years later, in 1900-1, he served with the Australian contingent in the Boer War, attained the rank of major in the British Army and of lieutenant-colonel in the Australian forces. In a less peaceful age he might have turned to professional soldiering, but as things were he was compelled to resume the dreary legal routine.

When he was offered employment in New Guinea, no doubt through the good offices of political friends, he accepted eagerly, first as Royal Commissioner and then as Chief Judicial Officer to fill the vacancy created by Robinson's suicide. There is little evidence to suggest that he had at this time any interest whatsoever in New Guinea or in the subject of colonial administration, but there is a good deal to indicate that he began a new career at the age of forty-five because he found the life of a mediocrity in Sydney's legal life insufferably dull. One more misfit escaped to man an outpost of empire!

But between Murray and the rest of his contemporaries on the island there was a great difference. The Chief Judicial Officer was a man of high education, iron self-discipline, sensitivity and intellectual resource. He had not been long in New Guinea before he saw far beyond the horizons of the miserable, sweltering little capital and responded to the spiritual and physical challenge of the untamed wilderness on whose flank it was set. He decided his destiny lay in governing this place and its people.

For some two years, during which he coped quietly and efficiently with the varied but petty judicial business of the colony, Murray made a detailed and penetrating assessment of the strengths and weaknesses of his fellow public servants. He was well aware that Barton, to whom he accorded a civil deference in spite of the contempt in which he held him, must soon come to grief and that there must be a thorough administrative purge. He allied himself unobtrusively with the Musgrave faction and set about collecting evidence of Barton's ineptitude and the drunken misdemeanours of Ballantine.

By 1906, affairs had become so chaotic that the Federal Government could no longer ignore what was happening and the Prime Minister, Alfred Deakin, asked Murray for a confidential report. At the same time Barton himself, aware that the ship was breaking up under him, requested a Royal Commission and a firm policy directive. Deakin, no doubt influenced by Murray's report which one must assume to have been impeccably factual, appointed three Commissioners. They spent about twelve weeks taking evidence and conducting first-hand investigations in every part of the colony to which white influence extended. Soon afterwards they announced their findings—to the effect that after twenty-two years of Imperial rule the industrial development of the colony was negligible and no measurable progress had been made towards civilizing its people. European settlement had been discouraged by a policy of native protection which did not in fact protect but destroyed tribal entity in the process of pacification by *force majeure*. The public service was riddled with backbiting, intrigue, insubordination and inefficiency.

Much of the evidence on which this damning judgement was founded was given or assembled in convincing form by Murray, whose critics bitterly accused him of treacherously plotting Barton's downfall from the beginning. But whether or not he did plot Barton's downfall from the beginning, the evidence he accumulated was no more nor less than the truth and the Australian Government had to do something about it.

Barton was retired and subsequently received a minor Colonial Office posting at Zanzibar. Ballantine and Musgrave, as ringleaders of the warring factions, were also retired. Murray was appointed acting Administrator with an assurance from the Prime Minister that when legislation was proclaimed officially declaring British New Guinea a dependency of the Australian Commonwealth to be renamed Papua, he would receive the post of Lieutenant-Governor.

Deakin's Government was to fall and the Labor administration of Andrew Fisher was to take office before that promise could be redeemed. But Murray survived despite frantic efforts by his enemies to undermine his position and to promote the claims of a rival nominee, M. Staniforth Smith. He survived for the very good reason that no one else with his qualities was available to do an unenviable job in what was then regarded as an extremely unpleasant part of the world for men of culture and intelligence. His appointment as Lieutenant-Governor was confirmed by Fisher at the end of 1908. The brilliant but unsuccessful barrister had indeed found himself a career—and a new era in colonial administration in the South-West Pacific had begun.

3

The Law Bringers

THE REPORT of the Royal Commissioners on Barton's administration of British New Guinea was the first comprehensive balance sheet produced on European enterprise in this part of the Pacific. It made dismal reading because it indicated very clearly that nobody, white or brown, had derived much profit from attempts to establish a new order in the violently fragmented archipelago.

Those charged with the responsibility of proclaiming and enforcing the *pax britannica* had laboured with repeating rifles and improvised scaffolds to cure the cannibals and head-hunters of their savage ways. They had succeeded in cowing a number of tribes on the south coast sufficiently to prevent major inter-tribal wars and attacks on plantations, trading posts and mission stations, and they had encouraged a number of unemployed warriors to accept indentures as labourers or domestic servants. Some progress had also been made with the more inaccessible inland groups in the south-eastern part of the mainland. Yet, after a generation of desultory and often misdirected effort, only a minute proportion of the total native population had been brought under either direct or indirect control. The diligent missionaries who established their stations in densely populated districts undoubtedly exercised a greater influence on native life and were a more potent force in pacification than the authority of the Government demonstrated by the scattering of permanent administrative posts and by sporadic patrols.

Because of its terrain and its almost unbelievable ethnic fragmentation, New Guinea proved the most difficult country in the world in which to subjugate savages and bring about permanent changes in their social order.

In the last fifty years or so, it has become increasingly popular among social moralists to challenge the right of civilized societies to impose their standards on primitive peoples, and to allege that the imposition is cruel, destructive, and motivated almost wholly by self-interest.

I do not believe that these critics of what one might loosely call militant civilization present a balanced case in support of their general condemnation of the morals of the colonialist era. It is true that self-interest—often the sort of self-interest rooted in pressing necessity—is and always has been the motive for migration. It is also true that migration has often involved the conquest and destruction of the weak by the strong; but it surely cannot be conceded that a conquering civilization invariably takes away from the vanquished savage more of human dignity and happiness than it confers on him.

If one is to understand the problems which confronted Hubert Murray when he became Lieutenant-Governor of Papua and to evaluate his attempts to solve them during thirty-one years of office, a sense of historical as well as moral perspective is necessary. One must not forget that the booze-sodden, pox-ridden bullies who debauched and depopulated Polynesia and parts of Melanesia in the mid-nineteenth century were the products of a society which condoned the use of its own children as beasts of burden in coal mines. The settlers who shot Tasmanian and Australian aborigines like vermin for killing sheep and cattle put to graze on their tribal hunting grounds also tolerated a penal system which flogged white-skinned convicts to death for petty misdemeanours, or drove them mad and blind by long incarceration in dungeons where light and sound never penetrated. The cruelty with which white colonists or itinerant exploiters of the Pacific treated indigenous peoples was fully matched by the cruelty with which the ruling classes treated the proletariat at home, and was perhaps excelled by the cruelty with which the indigenous people treated vanquished enemies of their own race.

In the days of the Yodda goldrush, patrols of native police led by British officers often repelled with unnecessary severity the attacks of frightened and resentful natives on whose lands they were trespassing. One patrol in the 1890s is reputed to have shot to death no fewer than 54 members of an attacking party numbering between 200 and 300. Such callous disregard of human life and rights is shameful; yet it should be remembered that some tribes who inhabited the district where this massacre occurred customarily confined prisoners captured on raids to compounds where they were forcibly fed and fattened for slaughter before being eaten. The Goiarabari men shot down in reprisal for the murder of Chalmers and his companions would, in the natural order of things, themselves have participated in sneak raids on the villages of their neighbours, attacking before dawn and clubbing or spearing to death the sleeping women and children before falling upon the warriors.

Though not commendable, it is at least understandable that the field officers of the British colonial service who attempted to establish the rule of law in New Guinea were untroubled by conscience when they found it expedient to meet savage aggression with brutality. They were the products of a harsh age in which truly humanitarian ideals were only beginning to build up the political support necessary to make them practicable in the metropolitan society itself.

In such an age, therefore, it is both noteworthy and commendable that during the last decade of Colonial Office rule in New Guinea the British Government—unlike the Germans in the north—gave native protection at least official priority over economic development for the profit of the white exploiter. Little or nothing was done to encourage the trader or planter, except to give him some assurance that the crime would be punished if he were set upon and murdered by the natives! Having yielded to the importunity of the Australian colonies by annexing south-eastern New Guinea as a bastion against German imperialism in the Pacific, the British showed no disposition to encourage large-scale European settlement of so formidable a country.

When Murray first took over as Administrator, the entire export earnings of the colony, mainly from gold, sandalwood and copra, amounted to only £60,000 a year. The failure of British policy to attract revenue-producing industry to Papua had been given considerable emphasis in the Royal Commission's findings and Murray's problems were soon defined. His tasks fell into four categories:

(1) To restore the decayed efficiency and morale of the public service.

(2) To consolidate control of the coast and such inland areas as had been opened up as a result of gold prospecting and mining; and to extend the controlled area by exploration and, thereafter, by pacification and supervision.

(3) To create a set of conditions which would encourage investment in primary production and commerce.

(4) To create and apply, within the framework of any overall directive he might receive from the Commonwealth Government, a native affairs policy which would afford the indigenous people protection from exploiters, hasten their social evolution, and improve their material condition.

Of the four prime aims, the first was easiest to attain, but even so, the attainment did not come quickly. Murray's evidence before the Commission had been bitterly resented by a large and influential section of the European community and he was, additionally, stubbornly opposed by Staniforth Smith, who in 1907 went to Port Moresby as Director of Mines and Agriculture and Commissioner for Lands and Survey.

Smith was a young West Australian who had won a seat in the Senate at the first Federal elections. He had interested himself in New Guinea affairs and resigned from the Senate determined to make a career in colonial administration.

Murray's position as acting Administrator was at that time by no means secure, and Smith set about undermining him through a vigorous campaign of correspondence with his friends and supporters in Parliament and the Commonwealth public service. Murray's energetic action to discipline the remnants of the Barton faction and to consolidate his authority over other resentful elements provided Smith with plenty of ammunition; but he would appear to have under-estimated Murray's capacity for counter-intrigue. The tactics of the protagonists, as revealed in official and private correspondence preserved from that time, were diverting—if unedifying except possibly as illustration of the truth that per-

sonal animosities and petty malice were even more part of
manoeuvre for political appointments in those days than they
are now.

Although Smith had said he would resign his posts in the
Papuan service if he did not obtain the lieutenant-governor-
ship, when it came to the pinch he did not do so. He remained in Port Moresby to head the bitter anti-Murray
faction comprising the defeated supporters of Barton and
those who came to feel themselves cheated and aggrieved by
the way in which Murray's policy was to develop.

In 1910 when Murray went to Australia on leave, Smith,
who in addition to heading the Departments of Mines and
Agriculture and of Lands and Survey held the redundant
office of Administrator, moved into Government House and
attempted to make capital out of the absence of his chief by
courting popularity with lavish entertainment. He also made
play for wider publicity by launching a major expedition of
exploration into the unknown country between the Purari
and Fly Rivers at the head of the Gulf of Papua.

Although Smith showed considerable imagination and
ingenuity in planning this perilous venture, bad luck and his
lack of experience in the New Guinea bush combined to turn
the whole thing into a fiasco. The would-be explorer took a
steam-launch and three whaleboats as far as possible up the
Kikori River—a point reached previously by Hubert Murray
on one of his routine tours—and then struck inland for fourteen days to Mount Murray, a feature reached and named in
1907 by an Australian geologist, Donald Mackay. From here
Smith, accompanied by two Europeans (Leslie Bell, Inspec-
tor of Native Affairs, and A. E. Bell, a surveyor), eleven police
boys and seventeen carriers, planned to travel westward in the
direction of the Fly and Strickland Rivers. The terrain, however, forced the party to the north of the proposed route and
they soon became hopelessly lost. The country was sparsely
inhabited and food, other than the concentrated rations on
which Smith depended for emergency, was unobtainable.
The carriers, all coast boys unaccustomed to cold and hill-
climbing with heavy loads, quickly lost both heart and physical condition. Smith could keep them going only by violent

abuse and liberal application of his walking stick to their bare backsides.

On 3 March, after nearly three months of appalling, blind travel in the wilderness, with only a faint idea of where he had been, Smith arrived back at the very spot on the Kikori River from which he had departed early in December! He had descended the Kikori in rafts and canoes for an unknown distance in the mistaken impression that he was on the Strickland.

The cost of this abortive attempt at exploration was excessive. Four carriers had died of pneumonia or exhaustion, and seven had been drowned in a whirlpool after a capsize while descending the Kikori. Search parties had been dispatched from Port Moresby to look for the missing Administrator.

Nevertheless, Smith and his European companions put the best possible face on the whole unhappy affair. Smith, who took his leave in England the following year, told such a stirring story of adventure in the Papuan wilds that he was eventually awarded the Patron's Medal by the Royal Geographical Society. This admirable feat of self-salesmanship was not destined, however, to advance his ambitions to unseat Hubert Murray. The inquests into the deaths of the carriers revealed only too clearly Smith's inefficiency and the harsh measures he had used to keep his carriers going. When the verdicts were recorded, Smith was formally reprimanded by the Department of External Affairs in Melbourne.

About twelve years later, there was an echo of the affair in Murray's Annual Report for 1922-3. Under the sub-heading 'PRESENTATION TO MR SMITH', he wrote drily:

> The most interesting incident of the year was the presentation to Mr S. Smith of the Patron's Medal by the Royal Geographical Society, in recognition of his Kikori exploratory trip in 1910, and also (apparently) of explorations by other members of the Papuan service which, so the secretary to the Royal Geographical Society says, were, in his opinion, less 'remarkable' but were (he thinks) prompted by the example of Mr Smith. It is no reflection on Mr Smith to point out that the secretary is mistaken, and that the expeditions undertaken by other members of the service were in fact part of a continuous

plan formed by the Papuan Government and approved by the Commonwealth.

Although Smith was to continue his efforts to undermine the Lieutenant-Governor for another twenty years, Murray's position was greatly strengthened by the Kikori affair. Thereafter he was able to devote more of his energy to solution of the colony's problems and less to outmanoeuvring his political enemies.

Once discipline had been re-established in the Papuan service by retirement of the worst inefficients and troublemakers, it was not difficult to complete and consolidate pacification of the coastal tribes and those dwelling on the banks of navigable rivers. Government influence was strong in any area which could be reached by steam-launch or whaleboat; but in the hinterland, control of savage tribes was a different matter. Exploratory or administrative patrols following tortuous and precipitous paths through dense upland forests, or wading through swamps at sea level, often took many days to cover a distance that might be traversed in a few hours by small ships.

Until 1913, Murray's exploration programme was modest. It was undertaken mainly to create a sort of buffer zone between the completely controlled population and the fierce hillmen whose habit it had been for centuries to mount sudden, bloodthirsty raids on the lowlanders. It was obviously impractical to outlaw war on the coast unless the Government could protect the people from such incursions. This Murray attempted to achieve by what may best be described as a low-density infiltration: patrolling as frequently as possible from strategically situated permanent Government posts, and winning the confidence and respect of the primitives by a judicious mixture of petty bribery with gifts of steel tools and of bluff that the white-skinned newcomers and their followers were invincible.

Murray and his field officers quickly accumulated a store of priceless experience, and perfected a system of exploration, pacification and government by patrol unique in the history of European colonization of tropical countries. For thirty-one years, throughout the whole term of his office, Murray never stopped trying to understand the minds and temperaments of the extraordinary hodge-podge of peoples he governed. His deep interest in the individual and social psychology of Papuans had important bearing on his theories of exploration, contact and pacification, for he soon realized a salient fact that had escaped his predecessors—namely, that perfectly natural fear was usually the motive for native attacks on European-led patrols *at the time of first contact*. He therefore instructed his officers to exercise the greatest care and self-restraint when they entered areas not previously visited by white men. Only in cases where attacks were stubbornly pressed and the lives of the patrol members gravely endangered were leaders permitted to fire on the attackers. In effect, Murray's advice was: 'Stick around, look as amiable as possible, and don't take offence at the "conservative" who lets fly the odd arrow at you. Tomorrow or the next day, they will have conquered their distrust of you if you do not behave nervously or aggressively.'

Yet another rule enjoined that generous payment be made for all food supplied by the local population, and that if dire emergency forced 'requisition' from native gardens even more generous gifts were to be left in compensation. In no circumstances were officers, native police or carriers to interfere with local women.

In 1925, when all Papua except relatively small pockets of country in the central and north-western mountains had been at least cursorily explored, Murray was able to write truthfully:

> The penetration of Papua has been made difficult by the diversity of language, but nevertheless it has as a rule been peaceful.
> It is not quite true to say that wild natives inevitably regard strangers as an enemy: they will always look on him with a certain amount of distrust; but it is an exaggeration to say that they will always be hostile.
> Certainly they will be hostile if they have been visited before and have been treated in the way in which Mr Jukes, the naturalist of H.M.S. *Fly* treated the people of the Ramu River whose pigs he stole; and d'Albertis the Fly River natives whom he defrauded of a number of skulls (probably of relatives). . . .

When Macgregor visited the Ramu 45 years later the natives were still hostile.*

In 1912, when the Commonwealth Government increased the grant-in-aid to Papua by £10,000 a year, Murray was at last enabled to begin a systematic drive to explore and pacify the whole of the vast area under his jurisdiction. He had from the beginning fortified the strength, discipline and efficiency of the armed native constabulary formed by Macgregor, and he was fortunate in having attracted to the service European officers capable of commanding the respect of native constables and NCOs and of welding them into a small but highly effective and flexible quasi-military force.

The exploratory work done by the European field officers and the native police in the Papuan service during the next twenty-five years was prodigious; and it appears the more so when it is realized that they made every effort to pacify and supervise every new area they explored. Murray's formula for peaceful penetration, evolved from his profound reflection on the emotional springs of primitive behaviour, worked almost magically.

The white man's conquest of Papua was a saga of courage, enterprise, patience and unremitting labour to overcome enormous physical difficulties, but from the time that Murray took over the element of racial conflict in it was reduced to a minimum. The adventures and fortunes of every expedition into the Unknown—and the Unknown was here the world's densest and most impenetrable jungles peopled by savages innured to almost continuous warfare—varied in every perilous detail; but in form all these expeditions were the same. A small force would assemble its stores and equipment at a base usually situated on the banks of a river at the highest point navigable for small boats or canoes, and from there quietly set out in the planned direction, following native paths or animal tracks where possible, or canoeing or rafting when favourable stretches of river were discovered.

There were rarely more than two or three Europeans in such a patrol. The rest comprised native police, ordinarily between ten and twenty, and a line of carriers whose numbers

* *Papua of Today* by J. H. P. Murray, King and Sons: London, 1925.

depended partly on the estimated duration of the expedition
and partly on the availability of fit, willing men capable of
carrying forty- to fifty-pound loads for eight to ten hours a
day, for weeks on end—and to carry them over high mountains, across wild rivers and through deep morasses.

For the European officers and their retainers alike, life on
patrol was cruelly hard. It became traditional in the territory
to measure distance not in miles but in hours of walking.
Sometimes days of exhausting travel would advance a patrol
only a mile or two in the desired direction. In the lowlands,
the explorers sweltered in heat and saturating humidity; in
the mountains they were drenched by bleak rains or cut by
icy winds; in limestone country the going was often so rough
that jagged rocks hacked to pieces the stout boots worn by
the Europeans and crippled the horn-hard bare feet of the
police and carriers. River travel in lower reaches was fraught
by very real danger of attack by crocodiles, and in higher
reaches, of capsize in rapids, cataracts and whirlpools. The
crossing of mountain torrents in narrow, deep canyons, by
way of log and vine bridges, was particularly perilous.

In unpopulated country or in districts where the population subsisted mostly on food gathered in the forest rather
than on garden produce, the patrols often went desperately
hungry, for practically every expedition had to be planned
on the basis that at least a proportion of the rations for police
and carriers could be obtained by barter with the local tribesmen after friendly contact had been made. No patrol could
hope to carry with it all the food it would require for a journey that might last upwards of three months. Only when the
aeroplane came into its own in the late 'twenties or early
'thirties, when pre-arranged supply drops could be made, did
New Guinea explorers stop worrying about the imponderable
factor of living off the country.

Added to all these hazards was the factor of disease. In the
lowlands malaria and dysentery took heavy toll of the health
of Europeans. In the highlands there was always the danger of
contracting scrub typhus, a lethal fever transmitted by small
red mites which abounded in the grasslands; and coastal
police and carriers were especially susceptible to respiratory
diseases in a climate much colder than that to which they

were conditioned. All travellers, native and European alike, were plagued by the fungus and bacterial infection of even trifling abrasions which under bush-living hardships often became deep-seated, stubborn tropical ulcers.

In essence, the men who conquered within the lifetime of a single generation one of the last great wildernesses left on earth, were threatened less by its fierce, primitive inhabitants than by the elements of an implacably hostile environment.

True, the patrols were sometimes greeted by showers of arrows from panicky bowmen scuttling through the long grass or the bush, or night raiders might creep up on camps and try to brain the sleeping intruders with stone clubs. Yet such initial encounters rarely caused fatal casualties. If the patrol made no violent retaliation, the primitives more often than not would within a few days be bartering food for knives, axes, salt, tobacco and sea shells, helping the carrier line and supplying the explorers, if an interpreter could be found, with valuable information—or colourful legend—about the country and the people over the next razorback.

Unhappily, a few of Murray's field officers lacked the iron nerve necessary to apply his formula of passivity in particularly trying or dangerous circumstances. They shot several of the hostile 'demonstrators'. In districts of Papua where such encounters occurred or where the memory of Macgregor's tactics lingered, the Administration subsequently met trouble in enforcing peace; and it was there that white men were attacked and murdered. When cannibals and headhunters were handled with genuine understanding and patience, even the most aggressive could soon be persuaded to abandon raiding for slaves, meat and trophies, although it was admittedly harder to discourage them from personal payback murder among themselves.

The system of conquest and government by patrol developed by Murray and his men proved almost unbelievably economical in terms of human life and money, however sorely it taxed the intellectual and physical resources of the mere handful of men who administered it.

It took Murray more than a quarter of a century to complete the second set of tasks he faced on his assumption of

ABOVE: *The primitives—out in the rain.*

BELOW: *The sophisticates—in school.*

ABOVE: *The pathfinders. A modern patrol in the trackless bush.*

BELOW: *The roadmakers. Highland villagers surface a motor track with shingle.*

office—that is, the extension and consolidation of control; but complete them he did. He was not fated to succeed in his remaining aims: the establishment of a sound economy in the colony and the discovery of a means by which the savages he had subdued could be integrated with the twentieth-century world.

It had been clear to Hubert Murray from the beginning that one of his besetting handicaps in governing Papua would be shortage of money for public works and services. When he took office he was determined to do everything possible to build up the colony's economy by encouraging European settlement and investment.

Under Colonial Office policy, acquisition of native land for agricultural development had been virtually impossible. Murray himself was also opposed to indiscriminate land-grabbing by whites, but he believed that native interests could be protected and investment encouraged through Crown purchase of waste or under-utilized land and by its allocation under long leasehold to Europeans prepared to develop it. He tried to perfect a system which would prevent natives irresponsibly selling tribal land which they needed or were likely to need for their own sustenance, but which would also give Europeans a chance to settle surplus land on reasonable security of tenure. So long as the Government retained control of land transactions, it could exclude settlers or interests which it considered undesirable. As early as 1906, a Land Ordinance was passed establishing this system, which has with a few modifications endured to the present day.

After the passage of the Ordinance, large numbers of applications were received for land, mainly from speculators who operated on the theory that once they had secured leaseholds they would be able to raise the capital to develop them. The theory rarely worked out in practice. There was now no shortage of cheap land in Papua for entrepreneurs, but there *was* a labour shortage which inhibited the growth of the planting industries. Although the value of the colony's exports in the first five years of Murray's rule increased from about £60,000 to £360,000 a year, this was due not so much to new developments under a progressive administration as to the full fruition of old enterprises begun under a previous conserva-

F

tive administration. The year Murray became Lieutenant-Governor, only 10,000 acres out of 350,000 acres allocated in European leases were under cultivation. Forfeitures of uncultivated holdings were increasing because the leaseholders were unable to meet the five-year development clause by which they were bound.

The scarcity and inefficiency of agricultural labour in New Guinea was the inevitable result of the pattern of conquest imposed on the indigenous people by the whites.

The first phase of conquest was the introduction of metal tools by traders. These were gradually disseminated along established native trade routes, and enormously decreased the time and labour spent on subsistence agriculture by those people into whose possession they came. It requires little imagination to envisage the changes wrought by the substitution of steel axes and knives for stone or wooden implements in building fences, houses, village fortifications and canoes. The introduction of efficient metal tools grossly disturbed the whole balance of employment in native society.

The second phase of conquest came with pacification by force or persuasion: the outlawing of inter-tribal war, feud-raiding and head-hunting. This further disturbed the balance of employment by making the fighting men redundant in all communities under the effective protection of the Administration.

The third phase of conquest was 'missionization'—a cumbersome term that is, however, preferable to 'conversion to Christianity' because relatively few natives received into baptism were in fact capable of accepting the Christian doctrine or comprehending Christian ethics. In missionized areas, the people abandoned the old magico-religious ceremonies which had previously occupied a great deal of their time and creative energy. In effect they substituted belief in the omnipotence of one set of ghosts and spirits demanding continual and elaborate propitiation for belief in the omnipotence of the Holy Trinity, a supernatural Power that was much less demanding on the time, resources and skills of the faithful.

The primary economic effect of conquest, therefore, was the creation of under-employment among the male population. Secondary social and psychological effects were even more important and will be discussed later, but for the moment it is sufficient to mention the naive belief of many early administrators, missionaries and planters, that native men who were freed of the burdens of petty war, superstitious ceremonies and inefficient tools would turn eagerly to employment in European-style industry. Nothing of the sort happened. Professional labour recruiters, successors to the old-time blackbirders, did manage to persuade thousands of bored, under-employed young men to leave their villages and contract to work in various menial capacities for white employers; but this occupation gave the men none of the social and emotional rewards they could have expected in the old, forbidden way of life. The dull routine of weed-chipping, copra-cutting or manhandling the white man's cargo, was poor substitute for the excitements of head-hunting and cannibal feasting! Security, superior shelter, regular rations, medical help in sickness or injury, and regular if small wages, could not possibly compensate for the emotional deprivation of the tamed savage, removed from his own disrupted community and set under duress to perform monotonous tasks for purposes he could not understand.

It was inevitable that labourers provided with so few meaningful incentives should be inefficient and lazy so that their work required continuous supervision. The situation was further exacerbated by the language difficulty. A dozen regional languages might be spoken in the labour lines of a single planter, and no really adequate *lingua franca* existed. When the employer gave a precise instruction, he could never be certain that he was understood.

So it was that labour rather than land problems were to foil Murray's plans to create a prosperous plantation economy in Papua. At first he had opposed the British policy of discouraging white settlement and had placed great hopes on raising developmental revenue from taxing the profits of Europeans; but before long he was forced to the conclusion that European prosperity and native protection could not simultaneously be achieved. He chose to give native protection priority, and succeeded in this cause because the Federal Government at the time was not particularly interested in the economic development of Papua and was content to leave policy-making to the man on the spot.

Murray refused to experiment with imported Asian coolies for plantation work, and he would not countenance the coercion and severe disciplinary methods with which the Germans were partly solving labour problems in their territory to the north. He enacted a Labour Ordinance which set strict conditions on recruiters and employers. The term of indenture was fixed at a maximum of three years. Minimum wages were 10/- a month. Hours of labour were set at fifty a week, with a nine-hour day and Sundays free (except in genuine emergency). Employers were required to feed, clothe, house and provide medical attention for their labourers on defined scales. Natives had the right to appeal to magistrates for adjudication of disputes or to test the merit of complaints. Civilian whites were forbidden to inflict corporal punishment on natives for misdemeanours or breaches of discipline.

The European commercial community bitterly resented the Ordinance, particularly the sections regulating disciplinary measures and hours of work. How, planters asked angrily, could a lone white man on a property which might be many days' journey from the nearest Government post get work out of lazy or insubordinate labourers if he were not permitted to inflict immediate corporal punishment on defiant loafers or troublemakers? If the law bound an employer to feed, clothe, shelter and pay natives during the period of their contract, should it not in equity allow him to exact a fair return for his outlay? Native labourers should be kept at work until they had performed a reasonable allotted task. Without supervision their work output was virtually nil. Furthermore, it was unreasonable to stipulate a ration scale based on expensive imported items such as rice, beef, sugar, tea and tobacco, when local produce of equal nutritive value was cheaply available.

Murray doubtless recognized the logic of these objections. The Administration could not possibly adjudicate every trivial dispute between employer and employee; native labour *was* inefficient and irresponsible; a balanced and satisfactory diet *could* more easily be achieved by the inclusion of locally grown foods in the ration. But Murray was unwil-

ling to alter the Ordinance to give the whites the discretionary power they sought. By now he well knew the moral and
intellectual calibre of the Europeans with whom he had to
deal. Some were fairly humane men, but most were not. They
were the successors of the Pacific freebooters whose behaviour
had strongly influenced the agitation for island annexations
a quarter century earlier, annexations aimed at preventing the
complete debasement of the free indigenes. A white drill suit
and a whisky bottle might have replaced the striped pyjamas,
revolver belt and rum demijohn which symbolized the Pacific
pioneer of the 'seventies and 'eighties, but the man behind
the uniform was little changed. Discretionary power in the
hands of such people would be used for the sole purpose of
exploitation.

Staniforth Smith, of course, allied himself with the most
rancorous critics of Murray's native labour policy and of the
severity with which he applied the law when he felt that the
case warranted it. Smith never failed to point out that labour
regulations were offsetting the effect of the liberalized land
laws, and he charged that in every dispute between whites
and natives Murray took the side of the Papuans.

The truth of the matter was that Murray was without resources to police his Labour Ordinance, and it was never
strictly observed by employers at any time during his term
of office. Even in the 'thirties, when I myself first had the
opportunity to observe plantation labour conditions in
Papua, employers often used a cane or their fists to deal with
minor insubordination or insolence in the labour line, and
the victim of the assault rarely took the trouble to invoke the
law unless he was labouring under a sense of intolerable
injustice. Similarly, variations on the ration scale were often
made without complaint being raised. The existence of the
Ordinance, however, gave the Administration power to deal
sternly with those who exceeded the limits of justice, decency
or commonsense in their behaviour with indentured labourers. Murray began a 'spot inspection' system as soon as his
little civil service was numerically strong enough to handle
the task, and in the early days the inspections revealed many
cases in which natives were being grossly exploited, cheated
of wages, inadequately fed and housed, and harshly beaten

for alleged breaches of discipline. The employers were heavily fined or their licences to employ labour revoked.

In time most planters with predilection for excessive brutality either mended their ways or left the territory. The objective of the Ordinance was attained, in spirit if not in the letter. Unhappily the humanitarian rationalization of the system did little to improve the efficiency of the average worker, whose comprehension of his tasks and the incentive to effort remained low.

The costliness of employing labourers was further increased by the three-year limit on the term of indenture, because perhaps one-third of that time was spent in transporting the recruits to and from their villages and in training them in the simple routines of their work. But Murray would not budge on this regulation either, for he was fully aware of the disruptive effect on native communities of a more prolonged absence of considerable numbers of young men. In heavily recruited areas during the days of longer indenture, birthrates had fallen and horticulture declined because of disturbance in the balance of population.

Throughout his term of office, Murray survived the intrigues inspired by the unpopularity of his policy partly by force of personality and his knack of dealing with politicians, and partly because influential factions in the Australian Parliament were at first indifferent and later opposed to vigorous development of the Papuan economy for fear that the territory would become a cheap labour competitor of tropical industries in Queensland.

Eventually, Murray's position became that of the complete paternal autocrat—although an autocrat forced by poverty to extraordinary improvisations, substitutions and economies. In the business of legislation and everyday administration he was assisted by an Executive Council of six official members and by a Legislative Council comprising the Executive Council and three non-official members representing mission and commercial interests. The Lieutenant-Governor, however, retained the power of veto and he was responsible only to the Australian Government through the Minister of External Affairs.

Nobody who knew Hubert Murray could doubt his earnest

desire to make a better life for the people he governed, but to the end of his life the resources of money, understanding and skill at his command were inadequate to attain the objectives he set himself. There is every reason to believe that he himself was keenly aware of his failures; and high among these failures, he ranked the inability to discover a way of integrating his tamed savages with civilization.

The system of government by patrol which he evolved achieved certain things. It suppressed inter-tribal warfare in most, if not all, of Papua, a suppression which implied the abolition of head-hunting, and some forms of sorcery. It diminished intra-tribal feud fighting and murder, and the observance of many primitive religious practices and rituals offensive to European morality: for example, ritual cannibalism in which certain parts or organs of dead relatives or friends were eaten in the belief that magic powers would be obtained, mourning and burial practices which involved the grossly cruel treatment of individuals or endangered the health of communities, and *tabu* observances which adversely affected regional order and economy.*

These achievements were negative. As we have seen, the advent of European government in the first instance implied *prohibition* of a great deal of activity which had hitherto been an integral and important part of the social order in most Papuan communities.

Provided one subscribes to a moral code which accords absolute priority to the welfare of the individual, these prohibitions must be regarded as beneficial. Their enforcement abolished not only much physical suffering but also much crippling fear. Murray himself was well satisfied that this achievement was worth while, but he was more and more convinced by experience that prohibitions were not enough. Papuans killed one another, ate one another, tortured or enslaved one another, for reasons not comprehensible to the civilized mind. Outlawing these acts must be accompanied by a substitution of reasons for *not* behaving in this way.

For thirty years Murray strove to understand the Papuan mind and temperament, concerned always with the problem

* Report to Administration, by E. R. Oldham, Resident Magistrate West District, 1922.

of integrating Papuan life with the demands of the dominant civilization whose agent he was. The annual reports which he submitted to the Australian Government, informative, unpretentious but colourful documents which can profitably be studied by anyone interested in the history of colonial administration or race relationships in the early twentieth century, continually reflect his struggle to 'think native' and his inevitable failure to do so. The effort, however, made him perceptive, tolerant and flexible in the exercise of his authority.

Murray's thinking about the sociological and moral aspects of colonization was succinctly expressed in a paper which he read to the Pan-Pacific Conference at Melbourne in August, 1923. The following excerpts are of particular interest because they describe problems with which administrators were still grappling forty years later:

> The two outstanding facts about European settlement of a country like Papua are the introduction of metals and the establishment of tribal peace. The immediate effects of these are that existence is thereby made much easier for the native, and that the chief activities of his life—the delight, for instance, of head-hunting and the joys of the raid—are lost to him for ever. At the same time contact with the white man inevitably undermines his confidence in his ancestral religion and the magic of his tribe, and makes his traditionary institutions appear rather absurd to younger men. . . .
>
> As I have already said, it is useless in most cases for the Government to fight against these facts; the true policy is to substitute some other interest in life for those which are going rapidly and, perhaps, are already gone.
>
> Such an interest is the interest to be derived from work—that is from manual labour. And by this I do not mean labour in the service of a European employer. I think that the native generally benefits from a term of service with a good employer . . . but I cannot bring myself to believe that manual labour in the service of a white man can add much zest to native life, or prove an efficient substitute for the interest and excitement of bygone days. . . .
>
> I do not think that the majority of Papuans will ever adopt a term of indentured labour as part of their ordinary existence. . . .
>
> To my mind the most obvious, and possibly the only, solu-

tion is to encourage or if necessary compel the native to work for his own benefit.
This is what we are attempting in Papua. . . . Personally I have no doubt of ultimate success, but it will be a long and difficult task.

In areas where control was firmly established, Murray attempted to stimulate substitute activities which would demonstrably raise material living standards. He continued Sir William Macgregor's regulation which required villagers in proclaimed areas to plant coconuts and other useful plants; he introduced rice cultivation in the Mekeo district and elsewhere (with only indifferent success); he proclaimed regulations requiring villages to improve their sanitation; and he made communities with time on their hands build bridges and improve tracks to encourage inter-tribal trade and facilitate patrolling.

But these measures did not synthesize a motive for peaceful industry. The natives did what the Government told them to do under pressure and not by preference. In 1919, Murray followed the German example of some twenty years previously and imposed a head-tax in sophisticated districts to test the theory that if natives had to earn cash to pay the Government demands they would be encouraged to extend their money-making activities to earn cash for their own use. From the seed of taxation new economic motivation, in tune with the ideas of the civilized world, might sprout. However, all that can be said is that if the seed survived, its growth was imperceptibly slow. The average Papuan was unable to abandon his ancient standards almost overnight and accept what the white man had to offer him—little more than the monotonous routine of agricultural labour—so that he might earn enough money to buy commodities for which he felt no urgent need, and for which he was never likely to feel an urgent need so long as he could still obtain subsistence from land of which the metropolitan power guaranteed him continued ownership. Boredom, curiosity or the urge to adventure, not desire to accumulate money or better himself according to European standards, provided the reasons which induced young Papuans to sign labour indentures. And when it came to the proof, boredom was not relieved, nor curiosity satisfied, nor adventure found.

From the beginning, the inability of the native labourer to share European motivations and accept European patterns of work poisoned the relationship between the races. Time and experience did not alter attitudes. To the great majority of white planters, traders and miners, their native employees continued to appear lazy, stupid and maddeningly irresponsible, at worst mere animals which could be trained to the performance of minimal tasks by the methods of the ring-master and at best children whose behaviour could be conditioned by simple consistency in reward and punishment.

Few white colonists showed the perception of the Assistant Government Anthropologist in 1921, a Mr Armstrong, who commented in his report to the Administration:

> This attribution of laziness to the native has, no doubt, arisen in the minds of employers from the study of their employees working under what are for them exceptional conditions. That the native, doing the eternal round of uninteresting work on a plantation for a mere 10/- a month, should try to dodge the work indicates intelligence rather than laziness. [In the natural life of the native] clearing of land for gardens, building of fences, making of canoes and fish nets, fishing and preparation for feasts . . . leave little room for laziness.

Murray himself thoroughly appreciated this viewpoint but the basic oddities of primitive psychology always baffled him. In *Papua of Today*, for instance, he illustrates the primitive incapacity to distinguish fact from fantasy by telling the story of a native who insisted that he had seen a monstrous snake near a village. Murray's inquiries convinced him that no such snake existed, but he was curious to know why the man had lied and cross-examined him very closely. The man persisted with his story and was indignant because he was disbelieved. Murray, with a flash of inspiration, got to the bottom of the affair by asking: 'Were you awake or asleep when you saw this snake?' The man replied with some surprise: 'I was asleep, of course, taubada.'

Similarly Murray was puzzled by savages' lack of inhibition, the behaviour of men who would burn down their own houses to relieve a passing mood of ill temper or depression. To the end of his life he was disappointed by the failure of both his own Administration and the missionaries to weaken much the belief in sorcery which persisted in the minds of even the most intelligent and sophisticated natives.

Although he was not himself a religious man—some who knew him well claimed that he was an agnostic—he was always willing to give credit to the missionaries for their indispensability, even though on numerous occasions he was at odds with them on specific issues, such as the admonition to natives to 'cover their nakedness' with European clothes. He was the first to acknowledge that the missions, and the missions alone, could do something about the moral disturbance caused by the destruction of old ways of life. He once wrote:

Moral disturbance is a matter for missionary influence and not for Government action. . . . It is precisely here that the influence of the missions can be so extremely valuable . . . so valuable as to be indispensable. Unless the missionary is there to help him, the native is left like a ship without a rudder, and will run a great risk of being wrecked in the sea of an alien civilization.

In the Papua of his time, missions consolidated the work of the patrol men and provided what health and education services they could. They carried out work of mercy at the village level and enormously accelerated the taming of the people. But it is doubtful that they dealt with the matter of moral disturbance nearly as effectively as Murray (perhaps with deliberate diplomacy) claimed they did, or that such aspects of Christian doctrine as they could inculcate provided an adequate substitute for what in native life inevitably had to be destroyed by white domination.

In the light of problems which were to perplex policy-makers and administrators of the next generation, it is interesting to note Murray's views on the higher education of New Guineans. As he repeatedly emphasized in his annual reports to the Australian Parliament, he opposed the creation of a native élite.

In one report he wrote:

I prefer the native 'conservative' . . . to the type of native who wears trousers, a bowler hat, smokes a clay pipe and affects to despise his fellow countrymen.

And in an address to the Australasian Association for the Advancement of Science, as late as 1928, Murray said:

It would be unwise to give the Papuan a first class education unless we can also provide him with the opportunity to use it.

So do the progressives of one era come to be regarded as reactionaries of the next!

4

The Intractables

IN German New Guinea the historical background to annexation, and the policies and practices of administration which developed after it, were entirely different from the historical background and administrative pattern in the Australian part of the island. Whereas the Australian colonies had agitated for action to circumvent German ambitions in the Pacific on strategic grounds, the Germans had been interested in extending their sphere of influence in the region simply because it seemed economically profitable to do so. They sought to make money from trading and ventures in tropical agriculture, and they were concerned with native welfare only in so far as pacification and control of the tribes advanced their commercial aims by providing a supply of manageable labour and security for German exploiters.

This philosophy of colonization was to produce in German New Guinea a relationship between the governors and the governed totally dissimilar from that which pertained in Papua, particularly after Murray's reforms came into effect. The difference accounts for many of the anomalies which confounded the administrators of the combined territories more than half a century later.

When the German Government annexed the north-eastern segment of the mainland and the islands of the Bismarck Archipelago in 1884, it made no effort to establish a direct administration. Instead it entrusted the New Guinea Company, a commercial organization which had its genesis in von Hansemann's South Seas Syndicate, with the business of administering German law throughout the newly acquired territory.

Godeffroy and Sons were already firmly established in a trading station on Mioko in the Duke of York's group off the coast of New Britain and 'Queen Emma' (Mrs Emma Forsayth, a legendary figure in the history of the Pacific copra industry) had already laid the foundation of her plantation empire which was destined to grow eventually into island estates totalling 150,000 acres of bearing coconut palms.

No doubt von Hansemann's backers felt that if a half-caste Samoan woman like Mrs Forsayth who started with practically no capital could make millions out of copra and shell in New Guinea, a rich syndicate with unlimited Government support could pay fabulous dividends. Unhappily for the shareholders, the board of the New Guinea Company made two prime errors: they decided to establish headquarters on the mainland instead of the healthier offshore islands and, like the British settlers in the south, they underestimated the difficulty of handling native plantation labour.

The Company sited its first capital at Finschhafen on the Huon Peninsula on 5 November, 1885, and set about purchasing land from the local tribes on which to build trading posts and later plant coconuts.

From the beginning the enterprise was mismanaged. The climate of Finschhafen was oppressive and the whole district infested with mosquitoes which carried a lethal type of malaria. The local natives showed no disposition to accept trivial wages for hard physical labour, and when recruits from other parts of the coast were brought in they could be 'persuaded' to work only by the most brutal disciplinary methods.

In desperation the company tried the expedient of importing Chinese and Javanese coolies. But these, too, were almost useless as workers. They were terrified of the savage New Guineans, disease sapped their vitality, and they died in droves. Deserters who were recaptured often committed suicide rather than go back to the labour lines. Finally an outbreak of plague stopped the importation of more Chinese. The Dutch, by no means noted for mollycoddling subject peoples, heard such shocking stories of conditions in the German colony that they forbade the recruitment of more Javanese to serve there.

Even the German 'masters' themselves found life nearly

intolerable in the dreadful little outpost. They were plagued by fever, frustrated by continual bureaucratic interference from Berlin, exasperated by the appalling slowness with which any enterprise requiring physical effort progressed, and so bored by the routine of their tiny community that most of them became alcoholics. The casualty rate among management, from malaria, blackwater fever and suicide, was scarcely lower than in the labour lines.

After four years so many men had been lost, so much money spent on ill-advised and fruitless schemes, and so little achieved, that the Company asked the Berlin Government to relieve it of its administrative duties so that personnel might concentrate on trying to establish payable trading posts and plantations. This the Government did for a period of four years. It then handed authority back to the Company which, despite the breathing space, was still not strong enough to run its own affairs efficiently, let alone carry out the work of exploration, pacification and control that was essential for effective white colonization.

In 1892, headquarters were removed to Stephansort (later called Bogadjim) in the hope that this site would prove more healthy. But in 1897 a severe epidemic of smallpox occurred and the administration transferred to Frederick Wilhelmshafen (later called Madang), where malaria was almost as prevalent as it had been at Finschhafen.

By 1899 the climax had been reached. The charter of the New Guinea Company was cancelled by the Imperial Government, which then assumed full responsibility for the administration of the colony. Shareholders were paid a compensation of four million marks and given liberal grants of land from which they might in future recoup the heavy losses incurred in the establishment period. Governor Rudolf von Benningsen assumed office in April, 1899.

There were at this time only 200 Europeans in the whole of German New Guinea, and of them only ninety-three were German nationals. The population was concentrated mainly in the islands of the Bismarck Archipelago. There were only thirty white men resident on the north coast of the mainland.

Von Benningsen energetically set about cleaning up the administrative mess he had inherited, and from the turn of the century business began to look up. The capital was again transferred, this time to Kokopo, and finally in 1910 to Rabaul. By 1914, more than 630,000 acres of land had been purchased from the natives, 85,475 acres had been planted in coconuts and the value of the copra exported annually had reached £300,000—more than eight times the value of the product from European plantations in Papua. Bird-of-paradise hunting, one of the most profitable minor industries in the colony, in 1913 yielded skins to the value of £54,000. Purchase was a Government monopoly and the proceeds were ploughed back into the copra industry.

At no time, either under the rule of the Company or the Imperial Government, were the Germans inhibited about the alienation of native land. Nor did humanitarian considerations much enter into their dealings with the population.

Regulations governing the employment of native labour did not stipulate a ration scale, and the term set for indentured labour was seven years. Minimum wages were fixed at the equivalent of 5/- a month (half the Papuan rate), payable at the end of the labour term and convertible into trade goods. Recruiting methods were considerably more flexible than in Papua, and although blackbirding had been banned in the rest of the Pacific there can be little doubt that tens of thousands of unsophisticated primitives were tricked into signing indentures in German New Guinea which virtually bound them in slavery for seven years.

Licensed employers were permitted to flog, fine and imprison their labourers for disciplinary breaches, and the legal power to cane recalcitrants was even extended to lay brothers of the Christian missions.

In time, of course, experience taught the German colonists, too, that terrorism alone could not assure the subservience and efficiency of the native labour force. The more intelligent —and therefore more successful—planters and traders realized that it was good business to feed and house their recruits adequately and to use discipline which stopped short of arrant brutality. They learned the 'trick' of handling kanakas, of gauging accurately the amount of work that could be extracted from them without provoking rebellion or desertion, and of adapting the whole economy of copra production to this limit.

Although failure resulted from the early attempts of the New Guinea Company to grow crops other than copra— cocoa, cotton, sisal and kapok—and to establish beef cattle and timber industries, the pioneers at least succeeded in building a number of permanent settlements, a few miles of passable roads, and minimal port facilities. The little colony was well served by a monthly steamer service run by the North German Lloyd Company from Singapore via Batavia. The policy of both the Company and the Imperial Government was to consolidate in the settlements first, and thereafter gradually to extend influence in the surrounding countryside. Exploration and pacification therefore progressed much more slowly than in Papua; and the impact of white settlement, though geographically limited, was much more severe on the native population.

As in the British territory, a native police force was recruited, quarantine and postal services established, and traffic in firearms, alcohol and opium forbidden. But the Germans were quicker than the British and Australians to apply pressure on the population in the effort to force them to work for money.

In 1901, von Benningsen imposed a head-tax of five marks (which could be raised to seven or ten marks 'if necessary') on all communities under Government control. Failure to pay was punishable by forced labour on the roads or on Government plantations. In the same year, he forebade the use of the traditional green snail, cowrie and pearl shell currency in all trade transactions, and made it unlawful for traders to buy whole coconuts from natives. The idea was to inculcate 'the habit of industry' upon these slothful people by compelling them to cut copra and thus earn cash—if only to stay out of gaol or avoid a flogging!

There was an almost immediate increase in native copra production, and in native attacks upon isolated plantations and mission stations.

There can be no doubt that the application of these methods of direct rule and the increasing alienation of land

G

were bitterly resented by all New Guineans who were unfortunate enough to live in the vicinity of any white settlement. In 1902, a year after the administration had removed from Madang to Kokopo and come into conflict at close hand with the veteran independent planters who had been established on New Britain and New Ireland, repeated raids by alarmed and angry hinterland tribes drove Marist missionaries from their station at Kieta on Bougainville Island.

About the same time, von Benningsen retired and was replaced by Dr Albert Hahl, a much more humane and liberal man who was inclined to admire the more subtle and persuasive methods of colonization adopted by the British. However, Dr Hahl was unable to improve noticeably the relations between the whites and the natives. The memory of twenty years of labour impressment, shootings, hangings, burnings and floggings cannot be quickly obliterated, and during his entire term of office Hahl could not free himself from the previous policy of reprisal for attack on lonely missions or trading outposts. It can only be accounted lucky for the natives that the means of reprisal at his disposal were relatively ineffective. The Germans, like the British, found that naval forces were not efficient in subduing jungle-dwelling savages, and their ground forces were far less experienced and capable in the bush than Sir William Macgregor's men.

In 1904, five male missionaries and fifteen nuns were slaughtered by raiders on the island of Aua in the northwestern corner of the territory. Community reprisals were taken, but it is doubtful that the actual murderers were punished. In June the same year, three tribes near Madang, alarmed by European land purchases and fearing that forcible acquisitions were in the offing, entered into a crude conspiracy to steal firearms, attack the settlement by night, and kill all Europeans in it. Accounts of the affair are fragmentary, emotional and contradictory, but it seems that the plot was betrayed by the native mistress of a German official. Groups of conspirators were raided and dispersed by the police, and at least some of the ringleaders were arrested. Reprisals and inquisition kept the whole district in a ferment for two years. The Germans were then satisfied that the last embers of rebellion had been stamped out, but they remained vigilant on this section of the coast for a long time for they realized that something unique and highly dangerous had happened—New Guineans of different tribes had for the first time sunk their differences and made common cause against the white invaders. Had the conspiracy succeeded other groups would have followed suit, and the tiny European settlements throughout the islands might have been exterminated.

A somewhat similar plot against the Germans at Kokopo, by hill tribes in the Gazelle Peninsula of New Britain, was discovered in 1905. The leaders were banished to forced labour on the mainland. On Bougainville Island, where the people were particularly warlike and vigorous, hostility to Europeans was so active that in 1906 seven punitive expeditions had to be dispatched from the settlement at Kieta alone.

Between 1885 and 1910, fifty-five Europeans were killed by natives in German territory, and more than one in five died of disease—figures which assume significance when it is remembered that at the latter date the resident white population of the colony was only 230.

Dr Peter Worsley, whose study of millenarian cults in Melanesia* most accurately summarizes race relationships during this period comments:

> In New Guinea . . . a tradition of Black-White hostility and of the violent enforcement of European domination persisted into the Australian era.

In these circumstances, it is not surprising that white influence in German New Guinea was not nearly as widely disseminated as it was in Papua, and that exploration was not regarded as a routine function of administration. It was something undertaken only by carefully planned scientific expeditions.

Nor did German theories of direct rule have much place for native co-operation in law enforcement. In 1897, however, in an attempt to lighten the burden on junior officers of trivial supervision and administration in controlled areas, the New Guinea Company appointed village headmen, or

* *The Trumpet Shall Sound* by Peter Worsley, Macgibbon and Kee, 1957.

luluais, who were charged with the responsibility of keeping the peace, adjudicating minor disputes and seeing that Company edicts were obeyed.

From all accounts the system was not at first very successful. When the Imperial Government appraised its operation after taking over the administration, it was noted that many *luluais* were lazy, corrupt, and grossly abused their authority. Nevertheless the system was continued for want of an alternative and eventually began to work reasonably well as the native communities accepted the idea that the whites had come to stay.

By 1910, after twenty-five years of sordid and often bloody fumbling and bungling, the colony was at last on its feet administratively and economically, and it was attracting immigrants. The copra industry was thoroughly established and profitable, a relatively docile labour force had been built up, and attacks on outlying missions and plantations diminished. A mild boom developed, and scientific experiments in diversified agriculture were begun.

When war broke out in 1914 between Germany and Great Britain, there were 1,273 Europeans in German New Guinea, including 690 in New Britain, 333 on the mainland, and 60 in the Solomon Islands. There were also 1,800 Asiatics, mainly Chinese and Japanese, who had a virtual monopoly of small trading and who made up the artisan class of the territory. Of the Europeans, 135 were Government officials and 400 were missionaries.

By this time revenue raised locally—from copra export tax and import tariffs (levied in 1910), licence fees and head-taxes—exceeded the grant-in-aid of the German Government. The more efficient planters and traders were enjoying considerable prosperity. On the other hand, the administration still did practically nothing for the betterment of the indigenes generally. It was interested in the pacification of only those districts which supplied labour regularly or which seemed to offer prospects for pioneer planters.

As in Papua, rudimentary health and education services, and the substitution of new beliefs and motives for those destroyed with the old social order, were left entirely to the missionaries, who also often preceded Government patrols into virgin territory.

Broadly speaking, the work of the missions followed a pattern similar to the work of the various denominational groups in Papua. Perhaps the missionaries operating in German territory were more openly authoritarian in dealing with their flocks, had fewer qualms about the liberal use of the cane to correct backsliders, and were more diligent in their efforts to achieve economic self-sufficiency. Yet it may, I think, be fairly said that many of them won the lasting affection and respect of the segments of the population with which they made contact. Virtually all other whites were feared, hated and resisted to the limit of the native capacity to resist the physical and psychological forces brought against them.

In Papua, the tradition of Black-White hostility was the sort which derived from insidious interference rather than from overt physical domination. As labourers and servants, 'New Guinea boys' from the area under German rule tended to be more obedient, taciturn and, indeed, reliable. They learnt in a hard, brutal school to conceal their feelings and yield to the white man's will. Papuans, on the other hand, were inclined to affect stupidity as a form of defence; they were relatively indolent, devious, insubordinate and soft. The difference of attitude was to puzzle both administrators and employers of labour when in later years administration of both territories was combined. It lessened only when exploration of the remote hinterland, from the 1930s onward, brought into the fold of the Administration, and into the labour lines of planters, miners and contractors, great numbers of primitives who had no memories at all of gunboats, punitive expeditions, public hangings or chastisement with the cane.

Strangely enough, the blood and iron theories on taming savages which were put into practice by German administrators did not seem to be shared by the men who explored the territory of the New Guinea Company. Gavin Souter in his colourful outline of exploration* shrewdly suggests that the

* *New Guinea: The Last Unknown* by Gavin Souter, Angus and Robertson, Sydney, 1962.

comparatively peaceful way in which the Germans made the first surveys of their newly acquired property was due to the fact that the expeditions were led by scientists rather than by adventurers, soldiers or policemen.

In 1884-5, Dr Otto Finsch, who had been prominent among those who persuaded Bismarck that New Guinea was worth annexing, made five journeys along the north coast and discovered and entered the mouth of the Sepik River, a great waterway which like the Fly gave relatively easy access to the heart of the country. In 1886, Vice-Admiral von Schleinitz, the first Governor of the new colony, took the steamer *Ottilie* 200 miles upriver, and the following year Dr C. Schrader took another small steamer, the *Samoa*, 380 miles upstream. Neither of these expeditions, which did for German New Guinea what d'Albertis had done for British New Guinea, was attended by the lethal fireworks which the flashy Italian naturalist was so fond of using to demonstrate the white man's superiority.

In 1888, Hugo Zoeller led an expedition, sponsored by the newspaper *Kolnische Zeitung*, into the Finisterre Mountains, again without any spectacular clash with the fierce inhabitants of the region.

Now, however, the first flush of adventurous enthusiasm was over, and the colonists struggled with the miserable business of trying to establish their settlements and the industries to support them. No gold strikes served to speed penetration —or to diminish financial losses.

Eight years later, in 1896, Dr Carl Lauterbach, a botanist who had previously carried out minor explorations in the hinterland of Astrolabe Bay, headed a New Guinea Company expedition to determine the sources of the Markham River in the Bismarck Mountains. In a patrol lasting more than three months, his party crossed into the upper valley of the mighty Ramu River, where it was attacked by natives although without suffering casualties. But it was now running short of food and retired to the coast. Lauterbach suspected that the river he had discovered might be the same river which reached the sea in a large estuary east of the Sepik, and which von Schleinitz had discovered ten years before and named the Ottilie. This was proved correct when one of the land party,

Ernst Tappenbeck, took a Company steamer to the Ottilie in April, 1898, and travelled about 200 miles upstream into the country that had been discovered after the mountain crossing in 1896.

Three years before Lauterbach and Tappenbeck made this highly important contribution to knowledge of the island's geography, a professional adventure-seeker and travel writer, Otto von Ehlers, made a heroic but abortive attempt to cross New Guinea from north to south. Unfortunately, von Ehlers chose a route through some of the most heartbreaking country in the entire island, lying south and south-east of the Huon Gulf. Here the peaks of the Kuper and Central Ranges rise to heights of more than 11,000 feet and are clothed in dense rain forest to within 1,500 feet of their summits. The terrain is contorted into a series of endless razorbacks, the bush is infested by myriad insects and parasites, and the natives are mostly nomadic cannibals, the so-called Kukukuku tribes.*

Von Ehlers was warned by experienced Company officials at Madang not to attempt the journey, but in August, 1895, with W. Piering (a European officer in charge of native police) and forty-one carriers, he left the mouth of the Francisco River near the site of the future Salamaua and struck southward.

After five weeks' struggling through the razorbacks, the food supply ran out and the carriers began to die of hunger and exhaustion. The white men were weak with malaria, dysentery and ulcers caused by leech and tick bites. They abandoned most of their equipment—which had been inadequate from the start—and laboured on until they had reached the southern watershed of the dividing range, where they came upon the headwaters of a tributary of the Lakekamu River which flows into the eastern end of the Gulf of Papua.

Here von Ehlers and Piering ordered the strongest of their carriers to build a raft on which they hoped to float down to the coast. Two Buka Islanders, Opia and Ranga, revolted. They shot the white men, flung their bodies into the river and, after overawing the surviving carriers who were recruits

* In 1942, the author traversed the same route in the reverse direction. The country was still virtually uncontrolled.

from New Ireland, continued the journey downstream to the coastal village of Motu Motu. The Bukas reported that their masters had died of hunger and exhaustion and, with eighteen other survivors, were eventually repatriated to Madang by the British authorities. Here the New Irelanders informed. The Bukas could not stand up to cross-examination and were arrested. While awaiting trial they broke out of gaol, stole firearms, 'went bush' and began to preach insurrection in villages close to the capital. The Administrator, Kurt von Hagen, led an expedition in pursuit of the fugitives and was shot dead, probably by Ranga. The pair again escaped, but were killed a few months later by the warriors of a tribe subservient to the Germans. Their heads were cut off and taken in to the authorities in Bogadjim.

The tragedy of von Ehlers and Piering was probably the sole example of a useless adventure in exploration to occur in New Guinea under the German regime. It could not have contributed to scientific or geographical knowledge since neither man was a geographer or naturalist, and neither had instruments to locate accurately any important topographical features that they might have chanced to discover. It was undertaken solely to provide material for another of von Ehlers's colourful but misleading books of travel and adventure.

In the decade that followed the turn of the century, the pace of major exploration slowed considerably on the German side of the mountains. Few major Government patrols were undertaken, and it was left mainly to enterprising missionaries to extend white knowledge of the interior and spread white influence. After 1910, however, there was revived interest in filling in the enormous blank spots on the map as the colony started to become really profitable. Lutheran missionaries explored the tangled ridges and ravines of the Finisterres, crossed into the valleys of the Bulolo, Watut and Waria Rivers, and learnt to know the Markham Valley fairly well.

In 1910, a combined Dutch-German expedition, organized to delineate the boundary between the two territories, surveyed the vast swamps and declivities of the Upper Sepik to a point 600 river miles from the sea, and crossed the 141st meridian. Two years later, a large and excellently equipped scientific party under Dr Walter Behrmann made a survey of the Sepik basin, as distinct from merely following the river itself. The outbreak of war in 1914 interrupted an ambitious programme of further work.

What should, however, be clearly understood about most German exploration of this period is that it was rarely undertaken with the objective of pacification and control. Hubert Murray's patrol officers were forerunners of Government posts, however thinly scattered and scantily staffed. They were the harbingers of permanent change. Hahl's men satisfied their curiosity and passed on, leaving little behind them but a legend. Only when missionaries or recruiters followed in the footsteps of the explorers was the native way of life deeply affected.

5

Conquest and Mandate

GERMAN rule in New Guinea ended soon after the declaration of war on 4 August, 1914. On 11 September a small Australian expeditionary force landed near Kokopo in New Britain and captured (and senselessly destroyed) the new wireless station recently installed by the Government at Bitapaka a few miles away. In a brief, brisk fight five Australians, one German officer and about thirty native soldiers were killed. The following day the invaders entered Rabaul, the German forces withdrew to Toma, twenty miles westward, and negotiations for surrender began.

The battle for the wireless station was the only armed clash of any consequence. Within the next few weeks, Australian forces occupied all the other small German settlements in the islands without resistance.

Only one German managed seriously to embarrass the 'conquering' Australians—a short, slightly-built man who was employed as a patrol officer and surveyor on those parts of the frontier with Papua which could then be reached. He was Captain Hermann Detzner whose exploits as a one-man army over the next four years have never been surpassed in the history of Pacific adventuring for courage, endurance and intelligent adaptability to environment.

In a mountain camp near the southern limits of German territory, Detzner was making preparations for an ambitious journey westward to explore the sources of the Sepik River when he received news that war had been declared and a demand from the mining warden at Bulldog on the Lakekamu goldfields that he should cross the watershed and surrender to avoid unnecessary loss of life. Detzner decided not to accept

94

the word of the enemy that all was lost, so he reconnoitred the coast and tried to organize resistance to the Australians at settlements not yet occupied. Finally he was forced to flee to the bush—and in the bush he remained until December, 1918, travelling among the tribes, preaching the doctrine of German invincibility, inviting pursuit by contingents of the Coconut Lancers (as the Australian occupation forces were rather contemptuously known) and generally making a thoroughgoing pest of himself.

During these years, Detzner undoubtedly travelled through extensive tracts of territory to which explorers of the late 1920s and early 1930s laid claim of discovery; but as it is quite clear, from his subsequent account of his journeyings, that he seldom knew exactly where he was, his contribution to geographical knowledge of New Guinea can be rated as negligible. But militarily he did a magnificent job for his fatherland, tying up large numbers of enemy soldiers who might have been used in other theatres of war to guard against the chance that he might organize a full-scale native rebellion.

Detzner's exploits are worth attention from any student of New Guinea history because they indicate how physically tenuous was white control of the hinterland in those early days, how strongly the factor of personality counted in dealings with primitives, and how completely those primitives were at the mercy of even a lone white man's 'magic'.

After the German defeat in 1918, Detzner—then in the vicinity of Sattelberg on the Huon Peninsula—surrendered to the district officer at Finschhafen and was taken to Madang and Rabaul. After brief internment as a war prisoner, he was repatriated to Germany. In 1921, he published an account of his adventures which, for some inexplicable reason, has never been translated into English.

The Australian occupation did not have much impact on native life. German planters and missionaries carried on as usual, German civil law was retained, and all land transactions were frozen. Civilian immigration was forbidden and overseas remittance of funds blocked. Head-tax remained unchanged, but export tax on copra was raised from ten shillings to twenty-five shillings a ton. Despite Detzner's activities in uncontrolled areas, discipline was maintained on the coast where law was firmly established.

In 1915, Australia's first military administrator, Major-General W. Holmes, promulgated new native labour regulations already drafted by the Hahn Administration. They forbade flogging by private employers, but empowered them to impose fines and terms of imprisonment as disciplinary measures. Courts were still permitted to order flogging for minor offences, a power that was not withdrawn until 1919, and Field Punishment No. 1—hanging by the wrists—was retained until 1922. The Military Administration retained the right to conscript labour for road construction and maintenance and, at discretion, to order natives to work on Government plantations for four weeks a year.

During the seven years of military rule, the territory's economy continued to flourish. Copra and rubber production increased, partly because pre-war plantations were now coming into full bearing and partly because the Administration demanded and got efficiency from German planters producing strategic war materials. Labour recruiting was stepped up. In 1914, 17,500 labourers were under indentures. By 1921, the number had grown to more than 31,000. In the same period, 20,000 acres of native plantations were established under Administration supervision. But there was slight change indeed in the lot of the ordinary native. Veterans of the occupation claim that many native leaders expressed joy at the overthrow of the Germans, but the motive behind this verbal jubilation may have been tact rather than conviction that better times were ahead. In any case, years were to elapse before the natives of ex-German New Guinea could enjoy the protection and privileges of their fellows in Papua under Murray.

After the Treaty of Versailles stripped Germany of her colonies in 1919, the Australian Government appointed a Royal Commission to examine the position of German property owners in the islands. The Commission recommended expropriation. The German Government was to pay compensation in German currency to the owners of expropriated properties, and the total payout was to be credited to Germany as part payment of war reparations. In September, 1920, the Expropriation Order was issued, and in 1921 almost all German planters were deported. Today it is hard to see either justice or wisdom in this course—unless one takes the view that the Germans had been particularly cynical and harsh in their native dealings, and therefore their financial ruin by the currency inflation that followed the war was no more than fair retribution.

In December, 1920, Australia received its Mandate from the League of Nations to administer North-East New Guinea, New Britain, New Ireland, the Admiralty Islands, Lavongai, Bougainville and Buka. The territory must be governed in the interests of the indigenous inhabitants who were to be protected from exploitation and accorded all natural human rights. These were the conditions of mandate.

For Australia, it had been easy enough in 1906 to express high-minded intentions towards the population of Papua, a territory of doubtful economic potential, but it was not so easy in taking over German New Guinea to renounce an established system of management that had proved itself capable of returning satisfactory profits. For these practical reasons, and because of some convenient legal complications, the administrations of Papua and of the Mandated Territory remained separate. Many years passed before the regulations governing all aspects of native affairs in the two territories were matched. Actual enforcement of paper reforms generally was delayed still longer in the Mandate, where German methods were in part retained even in the 'thirties.

The German plantations were taken over by the Public Trustee and managed by an Expropriation Board. They were eventually re-allocated to Australian citizens, mostly ex-servicemen entitled to repatriation benefits. Many of these men had no experience of tropical agriculture or the management of native labour. Their financial casualty rate was high, and the effect dismal even on the undemanding copra industry. The situation became more difficult when primary produce prices fell after the war and the rival whaling industry competed strongly with producers of vegetable oil. Many smaller island plantations faced ruin when the Australian Government decided to apply the provisions of the amended Navigation Act of 1921 to all island ports. Under this Act—

primarily designed to protect high-cost Australian coastal shipping from low-cost British and foreign competition—the direct export of copra and other produce from Papua to foreign ports became illegal, and so did the direct importation of food and other consumer commodities. All cargoes to and from Papua had to be shipped through an Australian port. In most instances, this meant an extra haul of 2,000 miles to Sydney—a perquisite eagerly snapped up by the single Australian shipping company which operated a subsidized service between Papua-New Guinea and Australia. The immediate effect of the Act was a 25 per cent reduction in imports and a sharp rise in retail prices at all European settlements. Increase in freight charges severely cut profit margins on copra and other products.

After yet another Royal Commission to study the economic problems of the colony and the Mandate, the Commonwealth Government in 1925 freed island ports from the restrictions of the Navigation Act, but the copra industry had not fully recovered from the reverse when the Great Depression struck in 1929. By 1932, the price of copra at island ports had fallen to £5 a ton, less than one quarter of what it had been before and during the war. In Papua Murray tried his best to help the stricken industry by allocating, from his own already inadequate treasury, funds to meet the freight costs on copra from plantation loading points to the pick-up ports of Moresby and Samarai. The Commonwealth Government also came to the aid of the colony with supplementary grants and loans.

The Mandated Territory, however, escaped the worst privations of depression. While Papua starved, the Mandate boomed on gold mining.

Papuan gold mining in the Yodda Valley and on the offshore islands had for many years been profitable enough to yield in taxes a significant proportion of the colony's internal revenue. When the fields in the south-east were almost worked out, new discoveries in 1909 on the Lakekamu River, north-west of Port Moresby, gave the industry a fillip which lasted over the war years. In the first two decades of the century, Papuan gold production amounted to about £1,500,000 —small sum enough, but important to a colony in which the white population never exceeded 1,000 and the white civil service never numbered more than 100.

The Germans were not so lucky with prospecting their territory. They discovered no payable goldfields anywhere in the colony until just before the war.

As early as 1906, prospectors based on Kokoda, near the Yodda fields, crossed the frontier into German territory and discovered and worked profitable deposits in the valley of the Waria River. News of their poaching reached the German Administration, which had reserved all mineral rights in the colony, and a patrol post was established at Morobe, near the mouth of the Waria River, to discourage the illegal infiltration. In 1913 and 1914, German prospectors made small strikes along the Markham and Watut Rivers, and plans were formed to explore and develop the area further. The war intervened.

Meanwhile, three especially persistent pre-war poachers, Australians named Matthew Crowe, Arthur Darling and William ('Shark-eye') Park, had made—and kept secret—rich gold discoveries when they were roaming the wild mountains and valleys at the back of Morobe in the guise of bird-of-paradise hunters. All three men were extraordinary characters—tough, jungle-wise and cunning. They were capable by sheer force of personality of commanding respect from the savages among whom they lived and travelled, singly or together, sometimes for months on end.

The outbreak of war, of course, put a stop to any plot the three may have concocted to work their finds secretly or negotiate a deal with the German authorities. But when the Mandate was granted and prospecting could be resumed under Australian law, Park returned and re-located a strike on Koranga Creek, a tributary of the Bulolo River, which had been made originally by his partner Darling.

Park did everything to keep the find quiet. By the end of 1921, with the help of a few native labourers and carriers he was taking about 120 ounces of gold weekly from his small alluvial workings. Then the strain of travelling alone to make consignments and obtain supplies at Morobe began to tell on him. The terrain between his claim and the coast was truly horrific, and the tribes who inhabited it—among the fiercest in the territory—were getting restive about Park's continual coming and going.

The lone miner took a partner, John Nettleton, largely to improve the security of his lines of communication. The partnership was successful. The output of the Koranga workings rose so much that the size of gold shipments from Morobe began to attract attention. Other tough and experienced old-timers forced a way through the mountain jungles and made strikes of their own in the rich gravels of the Bulolo tributaries.

By the end of 1923, about a dozen miners were working profitable claims in the area, using only the most primitive sluicing methods, but still a full-scale rush did not develop. Living and travelling conditions were so abominable—all the way from the swampy, malaria-ridden coast over the bitterly cold mountain passes to the wild and precipitous gorges in which the gold had been found—that only the most courageous and hardy prospectors were willing to try their luck on the new field.

To add to the hardships and dangers imposed by the terrain, the local natives became more and more disturbed by the influx of white men and their 'foreign' labourers. Government influence had not reached this inhospitable region, and doubtless the men who followed Park lacked his uncanny understanding of native mentality. The mountain tribes, fearful for their land and provoked by the arrogance of the white men and the petty thievery of their retinue, began to raid the miners' camps and to attack the carrier lines between Morobe and the diggings.

The history of the Yodda rush a quarter-century earlier repeated itself. The casualty rate among the miners' labourers grew. Pneumonia, dysentery and exposure took heavy toll of the wretched procession of coastal natives who lugged supplies and equipment over the narrow ridge-top tracks. The tribesmen, moving in country they knew intimately, stalked stragglers, shot them to death with arrows or speared or brained them with stone clubs, and dismembered the bodies for cannibal feasts. Sometimes war parties risked open attack on parties led by white men.

By the end of 1925, about fifty miners along the Bulolo

River and tributary creeks were taking a good deal of gold, but for small return because of the high cost of maintaining supply lines and recruiting labour for work on the field. But early in 1926, two prospectors, W. G. Royal and R. M. Glasson, made a tremendously valuable strike on Edie Creek, where pockets of gravel yielding £200 worth of gold to the cubic yard were not uncommon.

The new field lay at an altitude of 6,500 feet—3,000 feet higher than the original strikes—in country so steep that it was difficult to find enough level ground to pitch a tent. The normal rainfall in this area aggregated hundreds of inches a year, and at night the thermometer dropped to freezing point. Mortality among indentured labourers was high and the hardships of life for white miners almost unimaginable. Nevertheless, a full-scale rush developed. Hundreds of prospectors began flooding into the tiny settlement of Salamaua, at the mouth of the Francisco River, from which carrier lines set out on the eight-day journey of forty miles to Koranga Creek, or the ten- or twelve-day journey to Edie Creek. The Administration moved its post from Morobe to Salamaua, and a mining warden was borrowed from Queensland in an effort to sort out the incredible confusion at the beachhead and along the track to the fields.

Many of the gold seekers who arrived at Salamaua by all kinds of ships, large and small, from Rabaul, Moresby and Queensland ports, were inexperienced in New Guinea and had little money to pay and provision carriers. Probably a majority of starters never reached the field, but for all that more than 200 white miners had more or less established themselves by the end of 1926 in the vicinity of Wau, a settlement which had grown up near the Koranga Creek discoveries, and at Edie Creek.

Early next year, a severe epidemic of dysentery broke out and decimated white men and natives alike. The situation was completely beyond the control of the few available Administration officers. The tribes, particularly those centred on the large stockaded villages of Lambura, Salinkora and Kaisenik, east of Wau, were by now waging continuous guerrilla warfare on the carrier lines. After one particularly bloody raid in which a score or more carriers were killed and

H

eaten by the Kaiseniks, the patience of the white men was exhausted. Miners and Administration officers quietly organized a 'private' punitive expedition with the deliberate intention of breaking the spirit of the savages harrying them. They mobilized all the constabulary available, issued arms to the more reliable carriers and personal servants, and moved on the village of Lambura. The population had been warned of the impending attack and had fled into the bush, but defiant bowmen sniped and jeered at the punitive party all through the next day as it advanced on Kaisenik, a populous village not only strongly stockaded but surrounded by fighting ditches and hidden man-traps furnished with sharpened, fire-hardened stakes.

There are no detailed and reliable accounts of the battle which followed, but it would appear that Kaisenik fell to concentrated rifle fire and dynamite bombs, and was then burned to the ground. Scores of natives were killed and wounded, and the survivors were pursued for some days by vengeful parties led by whites and native police.

After the Kaisenik massacre, attacks on the miners' lines of communication ceased and the white men were firmly entrenched in the valley of the Bulolo. Crude public health measures policed by the Administration gradually brought the dysentery epidemic under control, although conditions on the field remained dangerous and highly uncomfortable until an air service linked Wau with Lae, the old German settlement at the mouth of the Markham River, twenty miles west of Salamaua.

The year 1927 was a turning point in New Guinea's economic history. Among the pioneers of the Morobe goldfields was a widely experienced and far-sighted ex-Administration officer, C. J. Levien, who had resigned the public service in 1923 to become a prospector. Levien, although he was moderately successful in the early days of the diggings, realized how wasteful were the methods of the alluvial miners. He knew that really big money would be won only when up-to-date, scientific techniques were employed. After a couple of years accumulating basic capital with shovel and dish, he set about organizing the industry as a large-scale operation.

The rich alluvial fields of Edie and Koranga Creeks were on the headwaters of the Bulolo River, and it therefore followed that large quantities of gold would have been washed down in sediments from which it could be recovered by mechanical dredging. Levien went south with this information and money to attract speculative investment. He and associates in Adelaide, South Australia, formed Guinea Gold N.L., which applied for and obtained large dredging leases in the Koranga and Bulolo areas. Tests showed that gold occurred in considerable quantities in the gravels, but the problem remained of how to bring in heavy mining machinery from the coast and supply the many hundreds of workers who would be required to operate it. Road-building in such terrain seemed out of the question.

Levien was not discouraged. Commercial aviation was still in its infancy, but he conceived the idea that the field could be supplied by air. Despite ridicule, he located, marked and cleared sites for landing strips at Lae and Wau, and bought an old de Havilland 37 aeroplane in Melbourne. This aircraft was crated and shipped to Lae where it was assembled and tested. It was flown into Wau for the first time on 18 April 1927, by Captain E. A. Mustar.

The next few months and the arrival of other aircraft owned and flown by men who realized the profits that could be made from air transport in such a country proved two things: the goldfields could be supplied by air, and the overhead costs of working the mines could be substantially reduced.

The pioneers of aviation in New Guinea were not only pilots of skill and daring but also brilliant improvisers and mechanics. They adapted their aircraft to carry such parts of heavy mining machinery as batteries and dredges, and for a time they operated the busiest commercial air service in the world, Guinea Airways Ltd, a subsidiary of Levien's Guinea Gold N.L. which eventually was incorporated in the internationally financed Bulolo Gold Dredging Company.

Further tests on the Bulolo gravels showed that they were even richer than at first estimated. The field attracted South African, English and Canadian investors as well as Australians. Sizeable settlements grew up at Wau and Bulolo. All building materials, machinery, equipment, furniture, stores and other supplies were air-freighted from the coast on twenty-minute flights which covered the same ground that had taken the carrier lines of the early miners at least eight days to traverse.

By 1935, gold production from New Guinea exceeded £2,000,000 annually, and the white population of the Territory had risen from 1,800 in 1927 to about 4,300 in 1938. The subsequent exploration and development of the hinterland was to be influenced profoundly by the techniques of commercial aviation.

Throughout the years of the depression, the Mandated Territory rode high on the prosperity of the gold boom, while Papua barely managed to scrape along on its grant-in-aid and the revenue from its hard-hit copra industry. Prosperity in the Mandate, however, was very little reflected by expenditure on native welfare projects. In 1938-9, internal revenue amounted to £400,000, of which £21,000 was raised in head-tax. Only £8,000 was spent on native education. Only 385 pupils attended day or elementary schools supported from public funds, and there were only 100 pupils receiving technical training at a school run by the Administration. Certainly this was something of an advance on the situation in 1921, when the annual report of the Administration to the League of Nations solemnly records an expenditure of twelve pounds on native education during the financial year!

The missions still carried the weight of providing whatever formal education the indigenous population received. They claimed to have established 2,290 village schools, but these were mostly run by native teachers who themselves had achieved only minimal literacy in Pidgin and the vernacular. The education offered in the schools was rudimentary. Pupils learnt a few Bible stories, the symbolic significance of which they failed to understand, picked up a little Pidgin, and were perhaps taught how to write their names in Roman characters. Brighter—or more fortunately located—pupils might graduate to one of 150 elementary schools run by the missions, where they received instruction which approximated that given to the first two grades of Australian primary schools. There were fifty-six high, intermediate or technical schools producing a small proportion of 'graduates' who had reached roughly the equivalent of fifth or sixth grade education in Australia and were thereby enabled to train as teachers, medical orderlies or lay preachers, with some skill in such trades as carpentry, or sail-making and painting. In the Mandate as in Papua, the mission education programme was financed in no small part by commercial enterprises: plantations, sawmills and trade stores in which labour conditions for native workers were rarely better, and in some cases worse, than in industries operated by the laity. German nationals comprised about two-thirds of the total of 690 missionaries resident in the Territory.

In public health the record of the Administration was somewhat more impressive. By 1938-9, the annual expenditure on medical services had risen to £99,000, or a little more than 20 per cent of internal revenue. There were twenty-two qualified medical practitioners in the Territory, of whom thirteen were employed by the Government and five by the missions. They were assisted by a small force of European medical assistants and by about fifty natives trained as orderlies. At this time there were fifty-two institutions, the majority of them small and crudely equipped, which were classified as hospitals, and 199 district aid posts or dressing stations carried medical supplies and were visited periodically by patrols.

The relatively high expenditure of public funds on health services was undoubtedly motivated by a desire to sustain a level of efficiency in the native labour force. Staff and facilities were concentrated in areas where maximum service could be given to natives numbering 41,000 who were under indentures to European employers at the outbreak of the Second World War. Of these men, about 20,000 were working on plantations, and 7,100 in mining. Labour was still scarce and still rated as expensive, with recruiting costs averaging from £20 to £25 a head.

Public works in the Territory were, inevitably, undertaken almost exclusively in the interests of the European population—to house and provide amenities for public service employees whose salaries by now amounted to more than

£200,000 a year, and to set up port facilities for such settlements as Lae, Rabaul, Kavieng and Madang. In more than fifty years of colonization, the Germans and Australians built only 139 miles of vehicular road on the mainland, most of it in the immediate vicinity of the larger settlements. About 580 miles of vehicular road served the gentler coasts of New Britain and New Ireland where the copra industry was very profitably established.

In the years between the wars, Papua and the Mandated Territory went separate ways with as little liaison as there had been in the days of the German colony. There was minimal interchange of administrative staff, or even of plantation labour, between the two territories. A wide gulf existed between the Murray Administration and the Mandate Administrations headed successively by Brigadier-General A. E. Wisdom (1921-32), Brigadier-General Thomas Griffiths (1932-4) and Brigadier-General Sir Walter Ramsay McNicholl (1934-8). Murray, although still starved of money, persisted with his native welfare programme. He still depended mainly on the missions for health and education services, but as early as 1919 introduced in more sophisticated districts a head-tax varying between five shillings and twenty shillings a year. The proceeds he devoted to education by subsidizing mission schools. It is worthy of note that the natives paid their taxes willingly, and some communities exempted from tax protested vigorously at the slight on both their public spiritedness and their economic status!

In 1941, however, thirty-four years after the Commonwealth took over from the Colonial Office, Papua's budget provided for an expenditure of only £189,000 a year. The European population had then grown to just over 3,000, and the value of imports still substantially exceeded that of exports.

In the Mandate, administrative effort was largely bent towards regulation of the Territory's thriving economy, in which the native population was by no means a partner. It is nevertheless true that the work of exploration and pacification was speeded up under pressure of a combination of factors, chiefly the search for gold or other minerals stimulated by the Bulolo-Edie Creek strikes and facilitated by the use of aeroplanes for reconnaissance and supply. Prospectors now pushed boldly into the interior in what was to prove a vain endeavour to discover a second Edie Creek—or, even better, a commercial oilfield. Oil exploration had been going on sporadically but hopefully since 1912. By the 1930s, it had assumed considerable proportions in the Gulf of Papua and along the lower reaches of the Sepik River.

The Administration was of course obliged to establish some control of areas penetrated by the gold and oil prospectors, and if possible stay a little ahead of them. Murray's methods had proved effective, and patrols in the Mandate came to resemble in technique those conducted by his officers in Papua. European influence spread more rapidly under these conditions than it had hitherto.

Early in the 1930s, explorers from both Papua and the Mandated Territory broke into the true New Guinea Highlands, an area roughly 600 miles long and 300 miles wide, ringed about with great mountain ranges, which were later proved to contain almost half the mainland population.

In 1929, two Papuan officers, C. H. Karius and Ivan Champion, succeeded in crossing the island from Upper Fly to the Sepik, mapping sources of these great rivers and that of the Fly's biggest tributary, the Strickland River. By mere chance they missed the heavily populated areas of the Great Papuan Plateau.

Discovery of the high valleys of Central New Guinea, closely inhabited by tribes very different from the coastal peoples, was left to explorers in search of gold probing the unknown country north and west of the Bulolo fields. In 1932 and 1933, the three brothers of a renowned prospecting family, James, Michael and Daniel Leahy, and an equally renowned patrol officer, J. L. Taylor, explored with the aid of light aeroplanes the headwaters of the Markham and Ramu Rivers. They pushed on into the vicinity of 13,000 foot Mount Hagen, and crossed into the watershed of the Kikori and Purari Rivers which discharge into the Gulf of Papua. Thus they discovered the existence of a chain of open, grassy valleys inhabited by a tall, intelligent, warlike people whose culture was appreciably more advanced—or, perhaps, just more compatible with European ideas—than that of the low-land Melanesians.

In 1935, two Papuan patrol officers, J. Hides and L. J. O'Malley, examining the country east of the route taken by Karius and Champion, penetrated the Great Papuan Plateau and approached the sources of the Purari from the south and west. Here too were numerous tribes of the highland type, a people cut off from contact with the outside world since the days of the first migrations. The entire region was sealed from the south by an enormous barrier of limestone peaks, gorges and ridges, and from the north and east by the less formidable but nonetheless rugged cordilleras of the dividing range.

The Murray Administration reacted strongly to the discoveries of Hides and O'Malley, and during the next few years sent a number of patrols into the region. In 1936, Champion and Hides on an aerial reconnaissance discovered Lake Kutubu, a body of water some ten miles long suitable for landing amphibious aircraft. Soon afterwards the Administration established an advanced police post there and supplied it by air.

The work of bringing the white man's civilization to these New Guinea 'Shangri-Las' was begun in the south. But in the north the Mandate Administration was slower to act, and Government influence was hardly established in the highlands when the Second World War broke out.

In West New Guinea, after more than a century of indifference, the Netherlands Government began to take interest in the economic potential of its territory, stimulated, no doubt, by the rich gold discoveries in the east and by the mounting tempo of oil search. In 1932, a group of merchants and publicists in The Hague formed the New Guinea Committee to promote a survey of resources. In 1934, the Government allotted several oil exploration leases in the Vogelkop peninsula, and experiments began in colonizing arable areas near Manokwari with Eurasian migrants from Java. But here also ambitious plans for agricultural development were frustrated by the scarcity and inefficiency of native labour.

From 1935 onwards, the search for gold and oil stepped up exploration of the interior. Scientific interest in the country also revived. In 1938, the Richard Archibold Expedition made extensive aerial reconnaissance of the central mountains in the giant flying boat *Guba*. This expedition discovered the Baliem Valley, a continuation of the chain of hidden valleys revealed by the explorers in Australian territory. The inhabitants were ethnically related and equally advanced tribes.

The Dutch authorities, however, made little serious effort to extend their influence inland, except along the navigable Digoel River. Coastal communities which came by accident of commerce into contact with Europeans evolved new attitudes and relationships as best they could. Nine-tenths of the indigenous population were completely undisturbed and lived precisely the same lives as they had lived when Holland laid claim to the western half of the island in 1828. Even the missions—although long established in the extreme west on Geelvink Bay and its adjacent islands, and in the south-east—were neither as numerous nor as active as they were in Eastern New Guinea. In 1941, the vast territory west of the 141st meridian was as little touched by influences from the outside world as Australian and German New Guinea had been in 1910.

6

Cargo from Heaven

THE devastating changes wrought in the New Guinea social order by the coming of white men have so far been examined only in general terms. To understand the sociological and political problems of the contemporary scene, we must study those changes in greater detail and try to reach some realistic assessment of their effect on the native mind and spirit.

When war broke out in 1939, about half the native population in the eastern end of the island and the Bismarck Archipelago was under direct or indirect Government influence, that is to say, the tribes had been pacified and their work patterns altered by the introduction of steel implements and other trade goods. In most of the controlled districts, white or native missionaries were active and new, disruptive ideas were being disseminated by men who had returned home after years of service as indentured labourers. European law was now applied in an approximate sort of way. Cases of murder, rape and abduction were tried before the superior courts. Lesser offences were in the main dealt with summarily by the Administration's officers in the field. Imprisonment was the punishment for major transgressions.

Superficially the people lived much as they had always lived, eating the same foods obtained or grown in traditional ways, dwelling in the same kind of houses, observing the old domestic routines. But in those areas of communal activity connected with religious beliefs or tribal solidarity, the times were cataclysmically different.

As a means of appreciating in modern European imagery just how different the times must have seemed to New Guineans, let us suppose the earth today has been invaded by a race of men from outer space: men 10,000 years ahead of us in technical achievement and, because of that, ultimately invincible. Within a few months, the invaders usurp all major functions of government, decree total and universal disarmament, and by a few exemplary demonstrations convince us that they are capable of enforcing the decree. At the same time they give us machines fabricated of an unknown element and driven by power which renders all conventional fuels obsolete. They inform us firmly and kindly that we must prepare to abandon all our religious beliefs and practices as a first step towards emulating their superior philosophies and skills.

If such an event is within compass of our imagination, we can perhaps comprehend something of the impact made by the first European civilization on the Stone Age tribes of New Guinea. In our case, sudden enforcement of complete universal disarmament—that consummation of reason so devoutly to be wished—would alone result in such great economic disruption that it would tragically affect millions of people whose skills and livelihood depend upon designing, making and using weapons of war. Pacification had—and has—comparable effect upon New Guinea society. The tragedy within the situation was, however, imperfectly understood by even the most perceptive and humane among the early administrators and missionaries. They believed that emancipation from the fear, pain and insecurity of a savage existence by far outweighed in its blessings the undermining of tribal life which inevitably accompanied it. They believed they would be able to replace what was undermined with a slightly modified version of the institutions and motivations which supported their own society. They were destined to disappointment and failure on almost all counts.

The under-employment of males was only one aspect of change in the economic relationship of the sexes which followed the suppression of inter-tribal fighting. Pacification struck more deeply than this, for it destroyed much of the system of activity by which men achieved status within their community. It weakened the magico-religious beliefs which New Guineans had evolved to explain natural phenomena and keep their equilibrium in the mystery of existence. But it did not dispel those beliefs.

The dominant race attempted to effect crude substitutions for the institutions and customs it felt it had rightfully destroyed, and the first area of re-indoctrination was religious. Early missionaries found that many natives could be persuaded to profess faith in Christian dogma, to recognize the divine authority of the Holy Trinity, and to accept as history the lore of the Old and New Testaments. But later missionaries were to discover that acceptance of Christian doctrine did not at all imply a significantly wide practice of Christian ethics, nor necessarily imply loss of belief in the existence of ghosts and spirits or the efficacy of magic. In this respect the attitude of the New Guinean differed merely in degree from that of many backward Europeans, or Asian converts to Christianity. Duality of belief created confusion and tension in the individual. The tension was not emotionally insupportable, but it meant that Christianity was not a complete or quickly effective substitute for animism.

The second substitution on which the early administrators placed great reliance was changed economic motivation. They thought that the native would envy the white man his possessions and soon see that the obvious way to get similar goods for himself was to earn money to buy them. Work would thus procure for the individual the status he had previously attained by waging successful war or in the honourable business of payback for old wrongs.

Contrary to expectations, the New Guinean did not react according to this pattern. True, he envied the white man his possessions, although untroubled by desperate need for them, but he was totally unable to perceive the connection between those possessions and the unpleasant type of work and minute wages offered him by white employers. He had not the slightest idea why the whites wanted such vast quantities of dried coconut kernel, rubber, shell or gold, or how such produce could possibly be converted into metal tools, canned food, calico, glass beads or intoxicating liquors. The processes of manufacture and the real significance of money in a complicated technical economy were utterly beyond his ken, exactly as the micro-organic causes of disease were beyond it. He therefore inclined to attribute the possessions of the whites to their 'magic', and to regard their goods as the product of that spirit world in which he still instinctively believed even though he might profess Christianity.

The primitives naturally began to resent and dislike their conquerors as soon as the exciting novelty of their arrival had worn off. Not even the material benefits that the newcomers brought with them—the miraculous trade goods and protection against long-feared enemies—could compensate for the puzzlement, helplessness and frustration which the ordinary native felt in the presence of the white man and most of his works.

This unhappy state of mind was for decades fortified by the behaviour of a number of low-grade whites who were attracted to commercial and administrative employment in the islands. As we have seen, many of these arrivals were brutal in their dealings with natives. Even worse, almost all were offensively arrogant, as people of inferior intellectual calibre usually are when given authority in societies less sophisticated than their own. Yet, for all their growing resentment, the New Guinea tribes could make no effectual common cause against their conquerors. The fate of the Madang conspiracies against the Germans had shown that. In the absence of political organization strong enough to unite small tribal groups with different languages and customs, dislike and a humiliating sense of inadequacy had either to be sublimated or to find expression non-politically.

The majority settled for sublimation. Some groups however, particularly where mission and Government contact had been sporadic, attempted sub-consciously to resolve their bewilderment in forms of hysterical mysticism, millenarian in character, which have in recent years been loosely described as 'Cargo Cult'.

The earliest Cult outbreak authentically recorded in Eastern New Guinea occurred in the Milne Bay area in 1893, five years after Sir William Macgregor had led an expedition there to arrest the murderers of a white trader. He had taken hostages from suspect villages, and had hanged four men tried and found guilty of complicity in the crime.

A young native named Tokeriu from Gabagabuna village

began to preach among the people that he had visited the
spirit world and been told of events to come. He prophesied a
great storm and a monstrous tidal wave which would sub-
merge the whole coast. Only those who renounced the white
man's authority and goods, and returned to the ways of their
ancestors, would be saved from this disaster. Believers, he
said, must burn down their houses and retreat inland. After
the storm had subsided, the south-east trade wind would blow
continuously and crops would thrive in all seasons. Eventually a huge ship, much bigger than the Government steamer,
would arrive from the south bearing the spirits of the tribe's
dead ancestors. Tokeriu assured his followers that he would
then form a government of his own which would be as powerful as that of the white men. The times would be so prosperous that the people now could cease work in their
gardens, and kill and eat all the village pigs.

Despite the fact that pigs were the most precious of the
villagers' possessions, Tokeriu's orders were obeyed. A party
of missionaries, supported by warriors from a rival and dis-
believing village, Wagawaga, visited the Gabagabuna people
on the site of their new village inland and attempted to
reason with them, but were received with such hostility that
they split up and retreated to the coast where they boarded
their boats and canoes just ahead of their angry pursuers.

Eventually, of course, Tokeriu was discredited and his
deluded followers threatened to kill him. The Government
intervened, put him under 'protective arrest', and gaoled him
in Samarai for two years.

The Milne Bay incident was apparently the first occasion
on which a New Guinea tribe expressed by crypto-political
action and not by direct physical resistance, their dissatisfaction with white domination.

As the years went on, similar outbreaks of millenarian
hysteria occurred in many other parts of the country. One of
the most widespread and serious was the 'Vailala Madness',
first reported from the Gulf Division of Papua in 1919. Here
the symptoms were eerie and sensational. Whole village populations were affected by the delusion of being possessed by
spirits, bending, swaying, jigging, tottering, rolling the eyes,
and mouthing gibberish or 'speaking with tongues'.

The Cult had many leaders, but its originator was probably an old man of extraordinary personality named Evara who began falling into trances and prophesying the coming of a steamer manned by the spirits and carrying a cargo of rifles, flour, rice, tobacco and other 'trade'. Evara declared that the cargo rightfully belonged to the people of Papua, but that to obtain possession of it they would have to band together and drive out the whites.

The movement developed and the promises were embellished by other 'prophets', at least one of whom declared that the Cargo would be delivered by aeroplane. No aeroplanes had been seen in Papua at this time, but the prophet had seen one pictured on the cover of a paperback novel! Many converts to Christianity defaulted, swearing that they had had visions of God or Christ and received messages from them. In some villages, ingenious leaders set up 'wirelesses' made of bamboo poles, pumpkins and lawyer cane, to take messages from the ship or aeroplane bringing the Cargo.

Unlike Tokeriu, the prophets of the 'Vailala Madness' did not counsel a return to the old ways and a rejection of the white man's goods and ideas. They strove rather to invent origins for the goods which would entitle them to their possession without work, and to modify the white man's ideas into forms compatible with their own social or individual psychology. This Cult tended towards puritanism. It forbade fornication, smoking and chewing betel nut, enjoined strict Sunday observance, and imposed an early curfew on its followers. Even 'education' had its part in this tragic little world of make-believe. Evening 'schools' were set up, at which prayers were led by Cult leaders and illiterates sat with Bibles in their hands, trembling, twitching and muttering meaningless phrases. At the same time, resentment of the whites was expressed by many leaders who advised young men not to sign on as indentured labourers, by the insolence of the hysterically 'possessed' people to missionaries and recruiters, and by the rejection of Government-sponsored development schemes.

In the five years that followed Evara's 'revelation', the Cult spread rapidly until it covered the entire area of the Purari delta. Murray's Administration was greatly embarrassed. A threat of famine developed in the district because of continuous feasting and the cessation of work in the gardens. Numbers of badly affected natives were forcibly brought in to the Government stations, where they were put to work and liberally fed. Some radical prophets were fined small sums for spreading lying reports, but Murray was unwilling to undertake more vigorous repressive measures. Eventually the Government and the missions succeeded in containing the movement. Effluxion of time, and of hope that prophecies would come true, weakened it; but it was not until the early 'thirties that the last overt traces of the 'madness' vanished.

Throughout the 'twenties and 'thirties, Cargo Cult outbreaks spread—or, more accurately, occurred spontaneously—all along the New Guinea coast and in the islands of the Bismarck Archipelago. The details varied but the pattern of the phenomenon remained constant. A prophet or leader arose claiming the power to communicate with the spirit world, as the witch-doctors had done in the old days. The spirit world revealed the origin of the white man's goods and indicated that, if the people followed instructions, Cargo for all would be sent in a ship or aeroplane manned by ancestral ghosts. Usually delivery would be preceded by some natural disaster in which believers would be preserved, and unbelievers, including white men, were to be destroyed. In most instances, Christian teachings, fantastically distorted, were incorporated in Cult ideology. Prophets insisted that they were 'Jesus men' and not pagans, and they preached not a return to the old life but an acquisition of new ways which would entitle them to equality with or superiority over white men. In the heavily populated Sepik district, where native religions had assumed highly complex forms and involved the manufacture and ceremonial use of sacred artifacts, Cult outbreaks were frequently associated with mass destruction of the artifacts. Millenarial prophecies as a rule were followed by disruption of work in the gardens and continuous feasting which consumed the people's wealth of pigs or stored food.

The outbreaks embarrassed the Administration of the Mandated Territory in Rabaul almost as much as they embarrassed Murray in Papua, but there was very little that could be done about them by direct Government or mission intervention. They burned themselves out after a few months or years, leaving hardly any perceptible change in the native way of life or thinking.

Among Europeans, the cause of Cult remained a baffling enigma until the ideas of anthropologists began to win some acceptance. The outbreaks were generally considered as just one more symptom of savage stupidity and instability—of the 'childish' or 'animal' nature of New Guineans which was incomprehensible to any civilized intelligence. Even early anthropologists like F. E. Williams thought that Cult showed a 'weakness' in the native character and failed to detect in it any connection with similar manifestations which occurred in other parts of the world, including Europe and America, where a frustrated mass of people from time to time reacted in comparable ways to the problem of making difficult social adjustments. The intelligent and relatively unrepressed Maoris had their Hau Hau movement after defeat by the British in the wars of last century, and the 'poor whites' of America's southern states worked off their feelings in revivalist camp-meetings where the forms of mass hysteria were scarcely less startling than they were in the Gulf of Papua. Modern European history is full of references to outbreaks of religious hysteria in times of acute economic difficulty or painful social upheaval.

In New Guinea, however, Cult had particular significance because it was virtually the *sole* practical way in which the indigenous people found it possible to express their resentment of conquest and their aspiration of regaining independence. It might perhaps be regarded as a normal and inevitable phase of their social evolution. As we shall see later, Cult outbreaks after the Second World War were of much more sophisticated character in areas where there had been brief but massive contact with foreign invaders, and in later years the link between these mass hysteria manifestations and proto-political organization was discernible to greater extent.

So far we have looked at the roots of Cult only from the intangible aspects of race relationship: the psychological effects upon natives of seeing their structure of society destroyed by civilized prohibitions, and the results of inadequate substitutions offered by administrators and mission-

I

aries. The actual inadequacy of those substitutions is easier to describe in concrete terms.

Recruitment of indentured labour to exploit the country's natural resources in European fashion was, from the beginning, economically unavoidable. Even the most altruistic administrators considered it desirable. Murray himself did not fight the indenture system. He attempted only to ensure that it was governed by regulations which protected the labourer from gross brutality and exploitation. People who had the welfare of New Guineans genuinely at heart believed that a period of disciplined labour in plantations, mines and public works projects was a potent civilizing influence. They were able to point out with justice that if recruits did not succumb to imported diseases, they benefited physically from the regular food, medical attention and comparatively hygienic housing. They were cured of the skin disfigurements which afflicted almost all coast kanakas and they rapidly put on weight in the labour compounds.

Recruiters did not find it excessively difficult to tempt under-employed young men to sign up as labourers once harsh disciplinary sanctions had been outlawed and employers had grown accustomed to the low output of their work. But labour was still in such short supply that some districts soon became over-recruited, with unhappy consequences. In the absence of a large percentage of the young men, a disproportionate burden of work to maintain the native economy fell on women, children and the aged. The pattern of marriage customs was deranged, and the birthrate began to fall.

In Papua, as we have noted, Murray recognized what was happening and was quick to legislate against it. He limited the indenture period to a maximum of three years, enforced repatriation of time-expired men at the employer's expense and made it illegal for them to sign on again without spending a year or more in their villages. These measures were not wholly effective. Many men accepted indentures to accumulate bride-price, but because they could convert their wages to trade goods in plantation stores only the most provident managed to take back enough money to buy themselves a wife. They had acquired an outlook which made them impatient of village customs and yet they had not acquired actively progressive attitudes or skills which could create a durable new order in place of the old one they had been taught to despise.

It is patently true that the New Guinean of the period between the annexations and the Second World War was only willing to work within the frame of a European-organized economy when compelled to do so by threat of punishment or by dire want or boredom. But it is also true that Europeans were singularly inept in the methods they used to convince the people that cash cropping was worth while.

Violent fluctuation in the market price of copra was one factor which New Guineans could never understand. Between 1906 and 1939, the world price see-sawed irregularly between £35 and £5 a ton, the variation being as much as £8 to £35 in a single year. The mind of the untutored primitive, unable to cope with the abstractions of the law of supply and demand, could discern no logic or justice in such a state of affairs. Not unnaturally he suspected the white man of cheating him. Even if it had been possible to diversify agricultural production as many authorities urged, price fluctuations at the time would still have been so great that the suspicion would have remained.

The entire system and performance of government must have seemed without rhyme or reason. The Government outlawed inter-tribal fighting, but had fought and expelled the Germans. The Government proclaimed the sanctity of human life and disapproved payback, and yet it mounted punitive expeditions to arrest and hang murderers or to punish by imprisonment those who broke laws which seemed meaningless. The Government enforced or encouraged tedious and equally meaningless public health rules, but at the same time it did not prevent the introduction of new diseases more deadly than the old. The Government proclaimed new laws against white men flogging or physically assaulting their labourers, but, in the Mandate particularly, it made no serious or effective attempt to enforce them. Missionaries proclaimed the equality of all men in the sight of God, but jealously preserved the colour bar. Simple theft was sternly punished, but the rankest cheating by white and Asian

traders was condoned. White doctors worked miracles to preserve the lives of sickly children, the aged and the hopelessly
crippled, yet white miners were licensed to drive carrier
lines of strong young men to death from exhaustion, exposure, dysentery and pneumonia in the hills.

Magic, the superior magic of the white man, was surely
the only explanation for the irresistible domination exercised by such an illogical and inconsistent race, a race which
clearly lacked the wisdom of those ghostly ancestors for whom
it had at first been mistaken!

Cargo Cult movements were, in one aspect, an appeal
to the supernatural to resolve the intolerable paradoxes of
white rule, yet by no means all native communities generated or fell victim to them. A more general reaction was hope
that equality would be achieved not by supernatural intervention but by discovering the secrets of the white man's
magic. Literacy was commonly regarded as the key to this
discovery, and consequently the early missionaries found
their flocks as eager for education as for baptism.

Such a reaction might have appeared progressive if there
had been any indication that the people as a whole compre-
hended the uses of literacy. There was no such indication.
The standard of scholastic education provided by the missions
before the Second World War did little more than enable the
average school product laboriously to read or write a simple
message in Pidgin, Motu or the vernacular, to cope with
infant-grade arithmetic, and to use the printed word as a
mnemonic aid to the recollection of biblical mythology. No
real effort was made to teach standard English, to standardize
Pidgin or to provide a significant and useful literature in any
of the more widely used indigenous languages.

A few exceptionally gifted New Guinea children, usually
those who had been for one reason or another removed
entirely from the familial or village environment at an early
age, achieved some fluency in English and attained a scholastic standard which enabled them to be employed as clerks,
storekeepers or ordained clerics. In attaining this status they
became, of course, completely detribalized and, in the estimation of their ingenuous compatriots, living examples of the
potency of the white man's educational magic. Having learnt

the spells and incantations in their books well enough, they were now and forever relieved of the need for tedious and exhausting physical labour. They had become apprentice white men: arrogant, superior, patronizing, remote and untrustworthy. In the field of technical education the picture was not quite so dismal. The better mission schools had modest success in teaching elementary trade skills, but generally speaking the New Guinean carpenter, plumber or mechanic was markedly inferior to his expatriate Asian counterpart. The people were not ambitious to become tradesmen. The work was too hard. There was little 'magic' in it. The man who worked with chisel or plane enjoyed nothing of the repose and status of the man who worked with mystic written words and symbols.

In agricultural education progress was also modest. Coconut growing, and cutting and drying copra, made small demands upon initiative or skill. Probably the greatest advance lay in persuading the people to grow new varieties of edible plants in their gardens. Maize, potatoes and beans were successfully introduced into the highlands by some of the earliest patrols, but the cultivation of grain crops such as rice required continuous, organized and monotonous labour that the native temperament could not sustain.

Thirty-six years after Australia assumed the metropolitan power in Papua and twenty years after it accepted the League of Nations Mandate of ex-German New Guinea, very little positive progress had been made towards preparing New Guineans to take their place in a twentieth-century world. The achievements, such as they were, had been negative: a partial destruction of savage institutions and traditions among perhaps half the total population, without adequate substitutions; a taming without training; a consolidation of white domination without measurable consolidation of native opposition. Technically, politically and scholastically, the controlled tribes of New Guinea were as ignorant as they had been on the day they saw their first white man. The gulf between the races was just as great and mutual understanding just as remote.

Yet it should not be forgotten that demolition is often a prerequisite of rebuilding, and three or four decades is not a long time in history. The Australian record in Eastern New Guinea was certainly better than the record of the Dutch in Western New Guinea or the Portuguese in Timor or the French in New Caledonia. It was certainly no worse than the record of the British in the Solomon Islands or the Condominium of French and British in the New Hebrides. Valid comparison with the record of colonial Powers in Africa and South-East Asia is impossible because the evolutionary status of subject peoples in other continents was vastly different.

It is now the fashion to deplore European colonialism, and influential sections of modern educated populations tend to feel guilt for the sins and omissions of their empire-building forbears. This surely is a peculiarly narrow neurosis, for the morals of each civilization and each age are absolute within the exigencies of their time. Moral change and moral evolution usually await the upsurge and resolution of great political and economic crises. The tidal wave of such a crisis —the greatest in modern history—was to sweep over New Guinea in 1942 when the Japanese entered the Second World War and within months had conquered practically the whole of South-East Asia.

7

The Cataclysm

NEW GUINEA was plunged into the Second World War with paralysing suddenness. Neither civil nor military authorities were prepared for the speed of the Japanese advance after the surprise air attack on the United States naval base at Pearl Harbour on 7 December, 1941. The majority of natives in the controlled areas of Papua and the Mandated Territory did not know that war had been declared, and even those who heard the news knew nothing of the reasons for the conflict. They certainly had no cause to suspect that the all-powerful government of white men which had for so long ordered their lives was soon, in the Mandate at least, to be ousted by invaders whose ways and motives were to prove even more puzzling than those of the whites.

On 4 February, 1942, Japanese bombers attacked Rabaul airfield and killed twelve natives. Thereafter air attacks were so frequent that there could be no doubt that the enemy intended invasion. On 21 January, after a devastating 100-bomber raid on Rabaul, the Japanese extended their air offensive to Bulolo, Lae and Salamaua on the mainland and to Kavieng in New Ireland. Two days later, after token resistance by a small Australian garrison, Rabaul fell to an amphibious assault. European civilians who had already been evacuated were either captured and interned, or fled west along the south coast of the island.

Panic spread through the European communities on the mainland. Lae and Salamaua were abandoned the day after the first air attack, and soon afterwards Wau was evacuated of all civilians. Men over military age who could not escape by air or small ships fled overland by way of the wild mountain

tracks to the south coast. Even in Port Moresby the civil
administration ceased to function. The town was deserted by
civilians and looted by a dispirited and poorly disciplined
Australian garrison. On 12 February, a military administration under Major-General Basil Moorhouse Morris, general
officer commanding New Guinea Force, was set up at
Moresby and martial law was declared. On the north coast,
small groups of white men, native police and militia withdrew into the hinterland to act as scouts and wage guerrilla
warfare against the Japanese when they landed.

By the middle of March, enemy troops had occupied key
points on the islands of Buka and Bougainville, were in complete control of strategic coastal settlements in New Britain,
and had established themselves on the mainland in Lae,
Madang, Finschhafen and Salamaua.

Considering the humiliating rapidity and panic of the Australian collapse before the onslaught of overwhelmingly
superior Japanese forces, it is not perhaps surprising that
many New Guineans received the invaders with friendliness
and accepted their assurances that Nippon had come to
liberate them from the white men. Large numbers of natives
co-operated willingly with the enemy during the early days
of invasion under circumstances which indicated clearly that
they felt little loyalty or love for their former masters. A
minority either fled south or remained sceptical of Japanese
blandishments, but these were mainly police or veteran servants who had enjoyed privileges above their fellows. It
would probably be accurate to say that the vast majority
were simply bewildered by the collapse of the authority that
had governed their affairs, and were not stirred by emotional
partiality for one side or the other.

In assessing the effect of Japanese invasion on the New
Guinea population as a whole, however, it should be remembered that massive contact occurred only in coastal areas. The
invaders did not deeply penetrate the hinterland except
during the campaigns over the Owen Stanley Range and in
the Markham Valley. Even so, they touched the lives and
thinking of an infinitesimal percentage of the mountain
peoples.

New Guinea's 'fortress' terrain was to contain the land

forces of the Japanese Army in the South-West Pacific. By the end of March, 1942, the first fury of the assault had spent itself. The Japanese were compelled to pause and regroup. The Australians, now receiving air and sea help from the Americans, were enabled to marshal what small defensive forces they possessed in the vicinity of Port Moresby. American bombers began to strike back at enemy land, sea and air concentrations in the occupied settlements of the Bismarck Archipelago and the north coast.

The Allied Command of General Douglas MacArthur, who was charged with direction of the war in the South-West Pacific area when he escaped from Corregidor to Australia, envisaged the probability of prolonged jungle campaigning in New Guinea and realized the great importance of native work forces in such operations. Early in April, 1942, the Australian New Guinea Administrative Unit was established under the command of General Morris. This organization absorbed the younger and more competent field officers in the civil administrations of both territories, and it quickly set about re-establishing control of native affairs in all accessible areas not effectively occupied by the enemy. The objective now, of course, was no longer the extension of civilization but the maximum exploitation of native population for the purpose of waging war against the Japanese. All available males were conscripted for labour on military works, or for service as carriers, stretcher-bearers or workers on the coconut and rubber plantations which had assumed new importance as a modest but by no means negligible source of strategic raw materials.

ANGAU contributed very substantially to the eventual defeat of the Japanese in New Guinea. It managed to maintain a sketchy continuity of administration in most of the hinterland, and even in the face of apparent enemy ascendancy a more than sketchy assertion of European authority. In the difficult months of 1942 and 1943, carriers and stretcher-bearers who were supplied, organized and controlled by ANGAU officers played a valuable part in the campaigns fought along the Kokoda Trail and in the mountains of the Morobe district. Commando and guerrilla units fighting in the Lae-Wau-Salamaua area were supplied for some months mainly by carrier lines. ANGAU's retention of prestige and control over bush natives made possible much of the inestimable work done by the naval intelligence organization—popularly known as The Coastwatchers—which operated in wild country far behind the enemy lines and gave early warning of troop and naval concentrations and impending air attacks. Bush natives kept obedient by ANGAU patrols helped many Allied airmen forced down in the jungle, concealing them from the Japanese and often caring for the wounded for long periods until they could be taken out to the coast by rescue parties. Both Papuan and Mandate Territory natives selected for combatant units served with gallantry and distinction as scouts, guides and guerrilla fighters.

By the end of 1942, the Japanese in New Guinea were in serious trouble. From 6-11 May, an invasion fleet they had dispatched to attack the still lightly defended Allied bases on the south coast had been defeated and turned back in the Battle of the Coral Sea, an engagement decided by carrier-based aircraft in which the surface units at no time sighted one another.

Despite this grave reverse, and an even heavier setback in the Battle of Midway Island about a month later, the Japanese persisted in efforts to consolidate their positions on land. On 22 July, they landed a strong force at Gona mission, near Buna on the northern coast of Papua, and began almost immediately to advance across the island towards Kokoda and Port Moresby. The Australian command at once sent a battalion of poorly trained and equipped infantry to delay the advance and defend the 'passes' of the Owen Stanley Range. But this force, outnumbered and on dangerously extended lines of supply and communication, was driven back through the northern foothills along the old forest track, subsequently known as the Kokoda Trail, which was used for many years by native runners to carry mail overland to and from the northern stations. Three more infantry battalions reinforced the defenders. Two comprised veteran troops recently returned from the Middle East, but the Japanese, especially equipped and long trained for jungle warfare, defeated them in detail, more by ability to travel rapidly on foot and manoeuvre in such terrain than by sheer force of arms.

The Australians were pushed back to within forty miles of Port Moresby, but this time it was the Japanese who outran their communications and supply. It was their turn to be defeated by the terrain rather than by the enemy's firepower. The Australians had breathing space to regroup and, heavily reinforced by supply aircraft which were able to take over the job of native carrier lines as dropping techniques were developed, they pursued the exhausted, starving, disease-stricken Japanese columns back to the north coast. There, early in 1943, the remnants of 15,000 crack troops who had been committed to the attack were trapped and annihilated by the weary Australians and by fresh American airborne troops advancing along the coast from the south-east.

In August, 1942, another invasion force was wiped out at Milne Bay by an Australian brigade. In January, 1943, Australian airborne troops repulsed on the outskirts of Wau a Japanese column dispatched from Lae and Salamaua, and inflicted heavy losses. Thereafter the Allies regained almost complete control of the inland and confined the invaders to their coastal bases where they were under constant air attack.

The Americans had by now established undoubted air supremacy and the Allies began a series of campaigns to destroy the Japanese expeditionary force. In March, American and Australian planes intercepted and wiped out in the Bismarck Sea a convoy of ten warships and twelve transports bound for New Guinea. More than 15,000 of the enemy were killed. Thereafter the Japanese abandoned any determined attempt to reinforce their beleagured garrisons.

In September, 1943, Allied troops recaptured Salamaua, Lae and Finschhafen, and began the long, bitter, bloody business of clearing the rest of the north coast.

By April, 1944, the Americans had seized Hollandia and Humboldt Bay in Dutch New Guinea, and moved on to capture Biak, a strategic island off the coast. The Australians had recaptured Madang, and the Japanese garrison at Rabaul had been cut off by American landings on Manus Island and the capture of the Momote airfield, an area which was then built up into a gigantic base for further operations in the

Central Pacific. Strategically the war was now over in New Guinea, but bloody and destructive fighting to mop up pockets of fanatically resisting Japanese continued for more than a year afterwards. The land battles were confined mainly to the coastal strip from Buna westward on the mainland, to the regions of Rabaul and Cape Gloucester on New Britain, and to the immediate vicinity of enemy-held bases in the Australian Solomon Islands.

Although very large areas and relatively large populations during the struggle were not affected, the destruction of property and displacement of native peoples were almost total in those areas where the fighting raged. Tens of thousands of New Guineans were dragooned into the service of the combatants, and tens of thousands more were either forcibly evacuated from enemy-threatened territory or fled tribal lands after their villages and crops were destroyed. In a matter of months, 'civilized' warfare wrought greater material damage than had centuries of tribal fighting and raiding for heads, slaves and meat.

ANGAU contrived a maximum mobilization and use of native labour. At the critical period, its method of conscription was even more arbitrary than German recruiting in the early days. In some villages every able-bodied male over the approximate age of sixteen years was rounded up, transported to the clearing centres, and thence drafted to whatever type of work had priority in the immediate emergency. Brutal disciplinary measures had often to be taken in the field; but when the first and worst crises of invasion were surmounted, ANGAU did what it could to conserve the life and health of its native levies and to maintain the viability of native communities depleted of 40 or 50 per cent of their able-bodied men. Under military rule, the labourers' health was more carefully considered and their diet in general better than under private employers before the war. ANGAU was fully aware of the value of native labour and co-operation to the Allied effort.

As the danger of a complete Japanese victory receded, the more far-sighted officers of the administration realized that their work might be fraught with strong political implications.

During and after the Owen Stanley campaign, war correspondents gave great publicity to the part played by carriers and stretcher-bearers on the Kokoda Trail. They emphasized the endurance, gallantry and loyalty of the natives, and the consideration with which they treated wounded Australian soldiers making the long and cruelly arduous journey back to Port Moresby by foot or on litters.

While it is true that some natives did show the qualities for which they were praised, it is equally true that the majority did their work only because the white men in command bullied them into doing it. Few if any were serving voluntarily and most would have deserted if possible. At this stage they knew of no reason and felt no desire to fight on the side of the Australians against the Japanese; but the habit of obeying white men, inculcated by about sixty years of colonization, was hard to break. In some cases, of course, loyalty *was* a factor, but it was usually a matter of personal attachment between master and servant, not a spontaneous expression of gratitude by the brown race for benevolent leadership and protection by the whites.

At the time, of course, such unromantic realities could not have been either reported or discussed. The Australian public was in a highly emotional state, alarmed and humiliated by the ease with which the Japanese had swept through the Pacific and threatened the continent with invasion. It was in desperate need of some reassurance that it was fighting on the side of the angels—an alignment which is presumed to ensure eventual victory. Failing the apparition of celestial angels in the New Guinea stormclouds, to match the reported phenomenon at Mons when the Germans were carrying all before them in the First World War, terrestrial angels would have to suffice. A sentimental soldier with a bent for versification wrote some lines of doggerel which described native stretcher-bearers on the Kokoda Trail as 'Fuzzy Wuzzy Angels'. The phrase caught on. Almost overnight even the most sullen, reluctant New Guinean employed on the military supply routes became in the minds of a large section of Australians a heroically faithful underdog offering proof by gallantry and devotion that he was not only a Christian gentleman at heart but he was also profoundly grateful for the benevolence of Australian policy and performance in the past. The speed with which the public image of a New Guinean was transmogrified from that of a bloodthirsty cannibal with a bone through his nose to that of a dusky-skinned, mop-headed, sexless Florence Nightingale must forever remain an inspiration to political propagandists.

The new image did not quickly fade. It endured through the war and long into the peace, and it provided a favourable political climate for expensive experiments in education and 'hothouse' social development undertaken by the Commonwealth Government from 1949 onwards. However, it must be conceded to the credit of ANGAU that long before the invaders were cleared out of the islands, it laid the foundations for the much-publicized New Deal for Papua-New Guinea which began soon after the Japanese capitulation and the creation of the United Nations Organization Trusteeship. While the war was still in progress, the Australian Government for the first time moved with relative vigour into the fields of education and public health. A large secondary education establishment was founded at Sogeri near Port Moresby, and medical patrolling was stepped up.

The Japanese were of course in no position to woo the co-operation or exploit the usefulness of the native population once the tide turned against them. Early in the invasion, they had been at some pains to foster anti-white sentiment and indeed had gained considerable support among the tribes west of Lae particularly, but they were unable to maintain the face of benevolence for long. They too conscripted carriers and labourers, but as soon as supply difficulties increased they could no longer feed these workers adequately. Their disciplinary measures were brutal in the extreme and, even more important, they lacked Anglo-Saxon talent for preserving even in defeat the mystique of racial superiority. As time went on they lost the support even of those elements which had at first welcomed them with enthusiasm, so that they tended more and more to leave the local people out of their calculations. They simply requisitioned guides, labour or food as the need arose and otherwise let the population fend for itself.

Even in the Gazelle Peninsula, where a large force remained beleaguered until the end of the war, the Japanese showed little gift for handling the indigenous people. New Guineans who could not flee the areas of occupation suffered far more acutely than even the most expendable carrier lines of the Allied army during 1942 and 1943. Starvation and disease wrought more havoc than fierce air bombardment. But at least the omnipresent wilderness was friendly to a primitive people. In extremity it offered them concealment—and a modicum of food which the invaders had not the wit to find and appropriate for themselves.

In Dutch New Guinea, however, where the invaders were by comparison dispersed and where the fighting never matched in intensity that which devastated parts of Australian New Guinea, the impact of war upon the natives produced significant reaction in places where the seeds of Cargo Cult had been sown. The greater part of Dutch New Guinea was unexplored and therefore remained untouched by foreign influence, but in large populous islands like Biak and Japen and in adjacent areas of the north coast, traders and missionaries had been entrenched for many years. White contact had sparked off Cult movements of which the political implications were much clearer than in the eastern half of the country. Outbreaks here were almost always associated with the Mansren Myth, a story of the Creation which originated in Biak and spread in numerous variant forms through regions of the coastal mainland. According to the myth, all surviving branches of the family of man sprang from a common ancestor, Manamakeri or Mansren, who took prisoner the Evening Star and exacted from that heavenly body a ransom of magical powers and immortality. Mansren, irritated by the faithlessness and disobedience of his many offspring, eventually sailed away in a canoe and was never seen again; but prophets foretold his return and with it the coming of a Golden Age.

Mansren prophecies were noted by Dutch missionaries in Biak as early as 1855. Through the years a succession of prophets rose and fell from influence among the tribes, but in the late 1880s the movement began to develop anti-mission and anti-white characteristics. In 1911 a prophet named

Mangginomi roused the tribes to such fervour with his pre-dictions of the imminent return of Mansren, the expulsion of the Dutch and Malays and the arrival of Cargo, that village riots occurred and Mangginomi was arrested and sentenced to five years' gaol.

Similar Cult outbreaks happened with increasing fre-quency during the next thirty years, all the while gaining in political significance and borrowing from and distorting mis-sion teachings. Just before the war, all Biak was thrown into uproar by the preachings of a leper woman, Angganita, who openly advocated revolt against the Dutch. She and her disciples claimed that the missionaries had concealed the 'magic' in the Bible from them by tearing out the first page; that the whites had stolen Cargo sent by Mansren to his New Guinea children; that Mansren was returning to help them by way of Germany or Japan.

The Dutch gaoled Angganita when she became too trouble-some, but the movement she had begun continued to gain impetus. Rioters attacked native police, killing one and wounding several. Great feasts were held to express faith in the coming of Mansren the Redeemer. There is, indeed, evidence that Mansren was regarded as the true Christ, and that the natives believed the missionaries had deliberately and dishonestly distorted the myth of Mansren to their own advantage.

The arrival of the Japanese in 1942 strengthened the move-ment. The energetic military works of the invaders and the landing of large numbers of trucks, aeroplanes and other machines at Biak and Hollandia impressed the natives deeply. Cult leaders began to accuse the Dutch Administration and the missionaries of having concealed from them not only the fact that Mansren was Christ but also the true nature of the modern world. They greeted the Japanese as liberators and forerunners of Mansren's coming, and began to organize themselves on quasi-military lines, adopting for themselves grandiose and fantastic titles such as 'King of America' and 'Prince of Peace'. They appointed 'doctors', 'ministers', 'radio operators' and 'apostles'. Some prophets even proclaimed the imminent magical arrival of a war-plane factory and prom-ised the faithful that when Mansren came, their knives and home-made dummy weapons would be changed into modern arms and the bullets of their enemies turned to water. The Japanese were at first quite unaware of what was going on. They promised the New Guineans partnership in the Co-Prosperity Sphere in East Asia, but as the course of war went against them they became even more arrogant and demanding than the Dutch had been. Cult sentiment swung violently. The leaders who had headed murderous attacks on Dutch missionaries and officials in the early days of invasion, now preached the expulsion of all foreigners. Ambonese informers alerted the Japanese that the natives were planning a rising, and suppressive measures were taken quickly. In July, 1942, a captured Dutch gunboat was sent to bombard one of the more truculent villages. Mansren fanatics attacked it in canoes, waving their knives and dummy rifles. But even the slaughter that followed did not kill the movement in other areas. It survived the systematic arrest, torture and execution of every Mansren prophet the Japanese could identify and a number of punitive expeditions which wiped out whole communities.

When the Americans expelled the Japanese from Biak and Hollandia in 1944, they were in turn hailed as the true deliverers and precursors of Mansren. Cult followers still firmly believed that the mountains of food, clothing and miraculous equipment that the Americans brought was merely a first instalment of the great Cargo to come. When the Americans went, the true believers would inherit all this vast wealth. Disillusion came only when the Americans did go—and bulldozed into useless wreckage most of the equipment they did not take with them. Nevertheless, sporadic small outbreaks of Cult occurred in the area even after the return of the Dutch, although the Mansren Myth itself now appeared to have been utterly discredited.

What is particularly interesting about Cult on the north coast of Dutch New Guinea is the course of its evolution from passive escapism and protest against interference into a relatively well planned inter-tribal organization with a political objective, the expulsion of all foreigners—an organization which survived every Japanese effort to smash it by brute force.

K

The deep and abiding effect of the Second World War on the minority of New Guineans who experienced it at first hand stemmed less from the tremendous material destruction, loss of life and physical suffering inflicted on the coastal tribes than from profound psychological and social trauma. Between 1884 and 1942, the gradual intrusion of a handful of white administrators, missionaries and commercial exploiters had wrecked the cultural and social structures of perhaps a million primitives, and forced them to attempt painful adjustment to a totally new conception of the meaning of life. But between 1942 and 1945, several million foreigners flooded into the country and demolished what little sense of fresh purpose and security the tamed savages had been able to build up in the wreckage of their old order. The men who had preached peace and the sanctity of life, pressing acceptance of their ideas with rifles if necessary, were suddenly engulfed in an orgy of bloody fighting such as the cannibal islands had never experienced nor the cannibals dreamed possible. The few noisy little aeroplanes which the natives had regarded as the acme of the white man's beneficent magic, in a trice and without warning, proliferated and grew horribly into fleets of flying monsters which rained death and ruin on the earth below. Ships bigger than any seen in a Cult prophet's vision sailed in from the sea and debouched on the narrow beaches armies of fighting men who brought with them instruments for killing at which the native mind boggled. Not even the most garrulous white master boasting to his houseboy or cook in a lonely drinking bout in a lonely plantation house had ever revealed the enormity of the magic commanded by his kind. The priests of Mansren were right— the white man had concealed from the people of New Guinea the true nature of the modern world!

Paradoxically, the more magical and incomprehensible the works of civilization seemed to those unfortunate New Guineans trapped in the battlefields and forced to participate in a conflict not of their making, the less superhuman the authors of those works appeared to be. Europeans and Asians alike had been mistaken on their first appearance in some primitive areas as ancestral ghosts returned to earth and bringing with them the powerful magic of the spirit world.

Later they had been regarded as terrestrial but infinitely superior beings to whom unquestioning deference must be accorded. War revealed the overwhelming power at the command of the foreigners, but it also revealed their essential mortality. It dispelled, in the case of white men especially, the mystique of inimitable superiority upon which their influence had so largely depended.

The pre-war white population of the islands had assiduously cultivated the airs of a master race. Physical labour was beneath them. Even the rough miners disdained to dig their own pay-dirt and wash their own gold. 'Boys' did it under supervision. Even the drink-sodden beachcomber, contemptuously dismissed by his compatriots as having 'gone native', granted no social equality to his dark-skinned mistress. On ceremonial occasions, or in emergencies, a European might deign to eat food with natives in the village, but a European never invited a native to his table.

With breathtaking speed, war demolished all elaborate structure of discriminatory custom with which the whites had surrounded themselves, partly for reasons of venial selfishness but chiefly as a measure of self-protection. When white soldiers arrived in force they seemed hardly to belong to the same race as the aloof Government officials, planters, missionaries and commercial men whose 'magic' had exempted them from vulgar toil. Stripped to the waist, whole battalions of troops sweated under the sun, carrying loads, shovelling earth, tackling a multitude of menial tasks. These strange white men were not aloof. They did not bother about custom in race relationship. They were busy, breezy, egalitarian, and often recklessly generous. The abandonment of the established 'etiquette' in handling natives at first gravely worried ANGAU officers, who feared that their authority might be undermined by the unconventional behaviour of the troops; but as things turned out their fears were unwarranted. The all-too-visible *force majeure* of the army assured obedience without the aid of trivial forms and observances evolved to meet the needs of a day forever gone.

The thousands of New Guineans who came into close and prolonged contact with the Allied soldiery devised new yardsticks by which to measure European worth—the yardsticks which gauge worth by material possessions. Thus the Americans were, in the native mind, incontestably a superior breed. The whites who had been in the country before the war possessed very few aeroplanes, trucks, guns, tanks and wireless sets. Therefore they were of a low order. Their arrogant manners had been mere bluff. They were commonly called 'the English'. They were parsimonious because they were poor by comparison with other white men. One might respect them, largely from habit, but they were on the whole not a people to be loved. By contrast, the Australian troops had many possessions. They were warm-hearted, free and easy fellows who did not forever keep reminding a native of his hopeless inferiority. But even they were obviously No. 2 white men compared with the Americans, whose possessions overtopped the wildest dreams of affluence. Their planes, guns, tanks and trucks were infinitely bigger and better. They were better clothed, better fed, better housed. They were more than just free and easy. Without a moment's hesitation they might offer a native pay for some trivial service which exceeded that given for a month's labour by 'the English'. Their gifts were fantastically generous.

So profound an impression did the wealth of the Americans make upon the New Guinean mind that in 1963, eighteen years after the war ended, the spokesman for a rather backward group of Sepik tribesmen asked members of a visiting United Nations Mission why America didn't help Australia to do all the things it said it wanted to do in New Guinea and could not afford.

The generosity and egalitarian attitude of the Australian and American troops towards the local population affected the emotional and indeed intellectual factors of race relationships, but did very little to help New Guineans in a practical way to sustain the shock of war or bridge the gap between the capabilities and performance of modern civilizations and the Stone Age. The confusion of 1942 was doubly confounded by 1945. In the longest possible view, it may be contended that the tragedy of war greatly accelerated the basic education of the tribesmen directly or indirectly involved, and that its hardships increased the capacity of those who survived to come to terms with global realities. Massive foreign invasion may have done a great deal in breaking down old tribal animosities and making at least some natives feel that the people on the north side of the mountains shared common cause with those who lived on the south side. The importance of these factors in contributing to the emergence of a national outlook among New Guineans is, however, imponderable. Nevertheless war undoubtedly speeded the opening up of the country. Scores of military airfields and hundreds of miles of military roads and tracks were constructed. In innumerable ways the need to maintain large armies in New Guinea hastened solution of formidable problems of public health, transport, supply, communication and topographical reconnaissance. War's urgent demands perfected techniques which white men required to cope with the country's implacably obstructive terrain.

Reliable estimates of native war casualties and property loss have not been made, but at least 15,000 people were killed by military operations of both sides and tens of thousands of others died from disease and starvation. Populations in Bougainville, the Gazelle Peninsula of New Britain, the Huon Gulf area, and the coastal strip westward of it to the Dutch border (through which the defeated Japanese retreated in 1944) suffered most heavily. More than 20,000 dwellings were destroyed, and 100,000 pigs—high-denomination certificates of affluence—were eaten by the hungry Japanese invaders, annihilated by Allied bombs, or given the chance of going bush.

The hurricane of war blew away even the ruins of the ancient order which had been shattered by some sixty years of more or less peaceful and on the whole benevolently intentioned white penetration. For perhaps a million New Guineans, the war marked the point of no return. They were from then on hopelessly compromised and committed, flushed out of their ethnic backwater into the torrential mainstream of twentieth-century history.

8

On the Side of the Angels

SUDDEN peace proved almost as bewildering to coastal New
Guineans as sudden war. The years 1942-5 had brought them
a terrible revelation of the mighty forces at the command of
technological civilization and removed any lingering doubts
that white men had the material strength to enforce their
edicts, but they had added little to comprehension of white
motives or the realities and complexities of the civilized
world.

To the native mind, Australian and American servicemen
seemed a different breed from the 'masters' who had run
away when the Japanese invaders came. These people were
more approachable, human and generous, and they manifestly
possessed the real power in the lands beyond the sea. It was
they who had fought and annihilated the Japanese. Then
suddenly all the soldiers departed, leaving behind them vast
dumps of stores, arms and equipment. Almost overnight the
parsimonious 'English' had become the Government again—
but a Government far less paternally authoritarian and effective than it had previously been.

In October, 1945, the Provisional Administration cancelled
without warning the indentures of between 30,000 and 40,000
labourers employed on military works and rubber and copra
plantations, and told them to go home. The given explanation was that the villages in devastated areas needed the help
of all able-bodied men to rehabilitate them. It made no odds
that thousands of the labourers had been so long away from
home that they were virtually detribalized and accustomed to
working for regular rations of food and clothing, accommo-
dation and cash pay. The abrupt termination of the

traditional employment system, signalling almost complete cessation of plantation and construction work throughout the two territories, caused utter confusion and bewilderment. In 1946, only about 4,000 natives were still in paid employment. Thereafter economic recovery was painfully slow. With the exception of Port Moresby, every European settlement had been wiped out by bombing. The battlefields were strewn with the garbage of war. The fighting had done tremendous damage to coconut plantations, big and small. Gold mining in the Bulolo Valley had ceased. Ninety per cent of the trees in young cocoa plantations, established on New Britain and elsewhere in the Bismarck Archipelago, were dead. Military sawmills were shut down. As soon as the Army and Navy withdrew their small craft, essential shipping services ceased. Military roads, airfields and port installations, constructed at a cost of many millions of pounds and many millions of man-hours, fast began to deteriorate for want of maintenance.

After the restoration in October, 1945, of a provisional civil administration (at first restricted to those areas cleared of the remnants of the Japanese armies) civilian planters, miners and businessmen started to drift back to see what could be salvaged from the ruins of their old properties. They met dispiriting conditions: the labour famine, a severe shortage of materials needed for reconstruction, and incredible political and administrative confusion. A Government which had been able to solve the logistical problems of keeping large military forces on the New Guinea battlefields for three years was now seemingly unable to set up an efficient public service or to organize the resumption of essential services and productive industries upon which depended the long-term welfare of the natives just as much as that of the whites.

One of the extraordinary anomalies of the time was the way in which surplus war material was disposed. Much of it was suitable or adaptable for peacetime use, notably earth-moving machinery, engineering and generating plant, vehicles, building supplies and prefabricated structures of all kinds. With the exception of vehicles—New Guinea depended on military jeeps and trucks to provide land transport for many years after the war—and a few Quonset-type prefabricated huts requisitioned for administrative offices and stores, little of this surplus was retained to help in reconstruction. It was auctioned by the Commonwealth Government's disposals authority, often for absurdly small sums, to speculators who shipped it out of the country and re-sold it at enormous profit. A peculiar situation arose in which the civil administration, when at last sufficiently organized to concern itself with the practicalities of reconstruction, was forced to buy back essential equipment and materials from the scrap merchants, and to pay prices hundreds, and in some cases thousands, per cent higher than the speculators had paid.

Until the early 1950s, the only really profitable post-war business conducted in New Guinea was buying and selling junk. Individuals and syndicates made great fortunes wrecking thousands of abandoned planes, salvaging instruments and non-ferrous metals, and smelting the scrap aluminium into ingots. Others bought for a song the salvage rights to enormous vehicle parks or equipment dumps left forgotten in the bush. Tens of millions of pounds worth of material which should have been conserved and utilized in the rehabilitation of the country and its people was borne away by the salvage dealers, with the full knowledge and approval of Australian Federal authorities in Canberra.

Meanwhile the labour shortage was exacerbated by the cash payment of war-damage compensation to the natives, whose claims to have lost anything from a productive coconut grove to pigs, fowls and trivial articles of domestic equipment were accepted after only cursory investigations often conducted by inexperienced officials. The only people to derive much permanent benefit from these payments were the indestructible Chinese trade store proprietors, who set up business in shacks when the military departed and soon did a roaring business in soft drinks, gaudy calico and cheap jewellery. While the war-damage windfalls lasted, the village men were reluctant to go back to the dreary routines on plantation, mines or construction sites, and indeed reluctant to toil in the gardens while they still had the money to buy white bread, sugar, rice, tinned fish and tobacco.

In such circumstances it is small wonder that Papua-New Guinea was slow to regain even the indifferent economic stability it had achieved in pre-war years. The political wrangles that had bedevilled Papua forty years previously broke out again, and with greater acrimony. Which target would the metropolitan authority choose this time—a blanket protection of native interests, or economic development by Europeans offered what were considered adequate profit incentives?

Inevitably the cause of native protection prevailed. Now native policy was the concern of more than a fraction of missionaries and humanitarians, more than a remote moral issue. Australia set a course dictated by pressure of world opinion as well as domestic sentiment.

The Second World War had ended European-style colonialism in Asia with stunning speed. The British, Dutch and French empires in the East were to be totally dismantled within a decade. The old formula of colonialism no longer worked. Two catastrophic wars had proved it to be intolerably dangerous to world peace in the rivalries and resentments it provoked. A concordance of war-chastened nations enunciated the principle that all peoples had an inalienable right to choose the form of government they preferred. Although events were soon to show that the principle could not be put into practice, at the time the expression of high ideals in high places was reassuring to the weary masses which, as usual, had footed the gambling debts of the power élite. The obvious fact that political and economic self-determination accorded to people who were unready for it after centuries of subjugation would cause great hardships and exacerbate rather than reduce inequalities, was conveniently ignored. In the liquidation of obsolete empires, necessity all too often assumed the mask of virtue and weakness the guise of generosity. Behind the four freedoms of the Atlantic Charter lurked a spectral fifth, the freedom of newly liberated nations to starve and degenerate out of sheer political and administrative ineptitude.

For all this, the demand for immediate freedom was expressed vociferously and violently throughout all Asia, and the demand was naturally exploited by Soviet Russia, which sought to achieve a position of dominance in world affairs by the process of ideological ingestion rather than by the outmoded technique of overt military conquest.

For better or for worse, India, Pakistan, Ceylon, Burma, Indonesia, the provinces of French Indo-China and the Philippines emerged as sovereign states soon after the war's end. All were jubilant at the retirement or expulsion of the arrogant Europeans who had dominated them for so long, and all pledged themselves to help the cause of independence in other colonial territories which had not attained it. Anti-imperialist sentiment was at fever pitch.

The position of Australia in relation to its new neighbours was difficult. The war had brought home to the Commonwealth the unpleasant truth that it could no longer count upon the naval and military power of Great Britain to protect it from attack by a hostile nation. The United States was traditionally anti-colonialist. Prudence demanded the friendliest possible relations with both the United States and the new Asian nations, and friendly relations depended upon Australia being able to convince them that it had neither colonialist ambitions nor sentiments. New Guinea was therefore a grave embarrassment. On the one hand, there were apparent strategic advantages in maintaining control of this still wild frontier, and yet on the other hand the danger existed of Australia being left holding the last colonial 'baby'. An equal danger of Asian condemnation might also arise if the baby were dropped too soon, before it was viable.

While the war was still going on, a skeleton post-war policy for New Guinea was hammered out in Canberra by the Labor administration, whose advisers had accurately forecast the direction from which the winds of change would blow. In 1942, the Government created a Directorate of Research which included among its duties that of advising ANGAU on how to handle native affairs behind the lines in New Guinea. The Directorate made extensive if rather hasty anthropological investigations in the field. In 1944, it became the Directorate of Research and Civil Affairs, and from its reports and recommendations a new policy course for New Guinea was set. The Government founded a School of Civil Affairs to instruct young ANGAU officers. This subsequently became the Australian School of Pacific Administration at Mosman, Sydney, where all officers of the district services were required to take instruction: a short induction course, two years study supervised by correspondence while in the field, and a year's academic work at the school itself, covering such subjects as colonial administration, anthropology, law and government, elementary medicine, tropical agriculture, Pidgin and Motu languages, animal husbandry and entomology.

In addition to training the administrative field service, the Government also resolved to supplement, immediately after the war, the health and education services provided by the missions, to reform the labour laws, to guide and encourage the natives in economic enterprises and to give them an opportunity to participate actively in government, first at local and later at the territorial level.

In 1945, the Minister for Territories, Mr E. J. Ward, speaking before the House of Representatives to a Bill enabling the establishment of the Provisional Civil Administration, foreshadowed the New Deal and made clear the Government's intention to promote native welfare on a scale never previously contemplated.

On 13 December, 1946, Australia entered into a Trusteeship Agreement approved by the General Assembly of the United Nations which largely reiterated Australia's old Mandate responsibilities and amplified them.

Article 5 of this Agreement stated:

It is agreed that the Administering Authority . . . will be at liberty to bring the Territory into a customs, fiscal or administrative union or federation with other dependent territories under its jurisdiction or control, and to establish common services between the Territory and any or all of those territories if (in its opinion) it would be in the interests of the Territory and not inconsistent with the basic objectives of the trusteeship system to do so.

Article 8 stated:

The Administering Authority undertakes that in the discharge of its obligations . . .

(1) It will co-operate with the Trusteeship Council in the discharge of all the Council's functions under Articles 87 and 88 of the United Nations Charter.

(2) It will, in accordance with its established policy:
  (a) Take into consideration the customs and usages of the inhabitants of New Guinea and respect the rights and

safeguard the interests both present and future of the indigenous inhabitants of the Territory, and in particular insure that no rights over native land in favour of any person not an indigenous inhabitant of New Guinea may be created or transferred except with the consent of the competent public authority:

(b) Promote as may be appropriate to the circumstances of the Territory the educational and cultural advancement of the inhabitants:

(c) Assure to the inhabitants of the Territory as may be appropriate to the particular circumstances . . . a progressively increasing share in the administrative and other services of the Territory:

(d) Guarantee to the inhabitants of the Territory, subject only to the requirements of public order, freedom of speech, of the press, of assembly and petition, freedom of conscience and worship, and freedom of religious teaching.

Between the wars, the Australian Government had been able to interpret very liberally the undertakings it had given to the League of Nations. Although from time to time criticism was expressed, no voice of much importance in world councils was raised in complaint about the way the affairs of the Mandate were administered.

But from 1946 onwards, the Australian Government had to treat its commitments to the United Nations much more seriously than it had treated its commitments to the League of Nations. Critics in the Trusteeship Council were quick to point out the grave deficiencies in health and education services, the fact that no New Guinean had been given political or administrative responsibility, and that no direct taxation was levied on European enterprises in the Territory which had in the past earned substantial profits. It was apparent that the New Deal would have to take precedence over economic development by private capitalists, and that the Australian taxpayer would for many years be required to foot the bill for the appeasement of the highly critical anti-colonialist bloc.

In 1945, Colonel Jack Keith Murray, a former professor of Agriculture at Queensland University who had been Chief Instructor at the School of Civil Affairs the previous year, was appointed Administrator of both Papua and the Mandated

Territory, pending determination of the Mandate's new status. Both territories were in effect administered as one until 1949, when Australia legalized the *de facto* administrative union by invoking Article 5 of the Trusteeship Agreement and passing the Papua and New Guinea Act.

Colonel Murray was not related to the late Sir Hubert Murray, but like his famous predecessor he was a man of strong humanitarian convictions. He thoroughly approved the New Deal principles, but on assuming office soon learnt the vast difference between the mere enunciation of principles and their practical application. He was beset by complex and formidable difficulties: reconstruction during a time of acute labour and material shortage, pressing demands that he should lay at least the visible foundations of the projected Government health and education services, sporadic native unrest, confusion and inefficiency within his own reconstituted public service, and the responsibility of pacifying and bringing law to newly discovered, heavily populated areas in the highlands.

Murray's burden was increased by pressures brought to bear on him by the local commercial community, pressures substantially the same as those brought to bear on his namesake from 1906 onwards. Once again the planters, traders and miners raised the old grievances: 'How can we get ahead with exploiting the resources of this country if the Government makes it almost impossible for us to get new land even under leasehold, fixes wages and conditions which make the employment of native labour excessively expensive, and then denies us the legal right to discipline that labour so that it will be reasonably productive? Is it the policy of the Government to make things so difficult for white enterprise in this country that Europeans will be forced to withdraw?'

Once again the Administrator had to steer a stormy course between extremes. A stocktaking in New Guinea showed that the New Deal was bound to prove costly. In some way private enterprise must be enabled to carry on. The revenue it generated, even without direct taxation, could substantially reduce the amount of grant-in-aid, which in any case was to rise to more than £3,000,000 a year by the end of Murray's term in 1952. The problem therefore was to keep Europeans

in the country by offering them profit incentives and at the
same time to put on a good show of honouring pledges that
Australia would safeguard native landholdings and respect
native 'customs and usages'—short, of course, of condoning
tribal fighting, payback murder, sorcery, cannibalism and
head-hunting!

J. K. Murray's administration, however confused and incompetent it may have appeared in the chaotic circumstances, at least preserved a middle course. Some leasehold
land in the highlands was made available to carefully selected
Europeans, but in general the policy of discouraging sales
of native land to the Crown continued. A modified system of
indentured labour was re-introduced, but with the proviso
that it should be replaced by a contract system within five
years. Indentures were limited to one year, and penalties for
natives who broke the terms of agreement were removed. A
wage minimum of fifteen shillings a month, with increased
ration scales and improved conditions, was fixed for both
territories. Weekly hours of work were reduced from fifty-five
(fifty in Papua) to forty-four. Professional recruiting, under
which recruiters received a lump sum for each 'boy' they
delivered to employers, was abolished. The minimum age of
recruitment (sixteen years for labourers and twelve for
domestic servants under the old system) was set at sixteen
years.

These reforms aroused furious protest from the majority
of the old-timers who had returned to New Guinea, but it is
notable that only the most inefficient among them went out
of business. Some capital and a small number of new settlers
planning to grow coffee were attracted to the highlands which
enthusiastic explorers were then describing, with unconscious
irony, as 'another Kenya'. The relatively fertile soils and
pleasant climate of this region did, indeed, offer a prospect
of great development in tropical agriculture, but the dense
indigenous population left little land surplus for Europeans.

What to do about the highlands and their million or so
primitive inhabitants was one of Murray's greatest head-
aches. He was under strong pressure, because of the labour
famine, to permit recruitment of highlanders for employment on the coast. Some highlanders had, in war emergency,

been illegally recruited and brought to the coast to work, but the mortality among them from malaria and dysentery had been very high. There was also the danger that traffic between the areas would introduce malaria and other diseases endemic on the coast into districts which had hitherto been free of them.

Realistically enough, the Murray regime acknowledged that the clock could not be stopped, nor the highland tribes forever remain locked away from the world in their mountain-ringed valleys. Medical teams began a vigorous campaign of BCG inoculation against tuberculosis in the eastern highlands, the area most exposed to the dangers of contact. The Administration then approved limited recruitment of highland labour subject to rigorous health controls. The use of modern drugs prevented a repetition of the disaster which followed the impressment of highlanders during the war, but it was impossible to prevent the introduction and spread of malaria when infected labourers returned home. The Administration did not have the resources to carry out mosquito control measures in a region so extensive and rugged.

Meanwhile, Murray's field officers pressed on with exploration and pacification in the Western and Southern Highlands, adding almost daily to the perplexities and burdens of an Administration which already had responsibility for far more people than it could effectively govern. It proved impossible to break all this new ground and at the same time to re-establish and strengthen influence in areas which had been either grossly disturbed or neglected during the war.

Recurrence—or perhaps continuance—of Cargo Cult troubles on the Rai Coast east of Madang and in the Admiralty Islands between 1946 and 1951 was undoubtedly due to under-government when civil administration took over from the military. Both districts had been under white influence for many years, and Cult prophets would have won little support had the Government been able to give the people the sympathetic reassurance and firm leadership they needed in the difficult period of reconstruction and readjustment following the expulsion of the Japanese.

Cult was by no means confined to these two districts. It became a major problem for the Murray Administration and the subject of a special report to the Trusteeship Council in 1950-1. It was spread in the highlands by coastal natives employed by white explorers and settlers. Fresh outbreaks occurred on the Lakekamu River in Papua, in the Morobe district, on New Britain and in many other intermediate areas.

For the most part the outbreaks took the familiar pattern —the rise of a prophet who proclaimed the imminence of supernatural intervention to resolve the natives' frustration and incomprehension of the outside world; elaborate mystic rituals; mass hysteria and interruption of normal productive work.

The movements on the Rai Coast and in the Admiralties were especially noteworthy, however, because they brought forth action and leadership which could for the first time in Australian New Guinea be recognized as clearly political.

The Rai Coast people had received the Japanese invaders gladly and believed them to be genuine liberators. When they were disillusioned, they took refuge in fantasy. Millenarian prophets flourished in the Madang district from 1942 onwards. When the Japanese were defeated in 1944, Cult leaders began to tell their followers that it was really the white men who were stealing the Cargo sent by their ancestors in the other world. As the war moved westward, they set up mock-military organizations in the unsupervised areas behind the front.

At first the most influential Rai Coast prophet was a man named Kaum, a former police-boy from New Britain, who preached that those who followed him would soon miraculously shed their black skins and become white men. Kaum set up headquarters on an old American camp site near Madang and drilled his believers with dummy rifles. Eventually the Cultists began stealing grenades and other equipment from dumps, and in 1944 at the village of Bagsin mutinied against the ANGAU team trying to restore the authority of the Government in the area.

Kaum was arrested and sent to gaol for nine months, but his movement did not die and he resumed leadership of it when he was released towards the end of 1945. Again he was arrested and gaoled, this time for six months. A third gaol sentence was imposed on him in 1949. By this time his followers had lost faith in his extravagant prophecies but turned eagerly to other seers. The whole coast became a hotbed of millenarian fanaticism.

The link between these flights into fantasy and a dawning political consciousness, a rational rather than an irrational attempt to resist white domination, was provided by a man named Yali. Yali had served with the Army during the war and risen to become a sergeant-major, the highest rank which could then be achieved by a New Guinean. He was discharged in 1945 and returned home to Madang, where he was greeted as something of a hero. He was a man of high intelligence, and forceful personality, and although illiterate knew a great deal more about the outside world and its ways than the rest of his countrymen. He had visited Australia and seen a number of war factories at work.

Yali appreciated the need of his people for unifying leadership and he was at first disposed to support the Administration, going about the district advising obedience to the law and co-operation with the missions which had established stations as soon as the Japanese fled. He also spoke strongly against Cult. This however did not prevent Cult leaders approaching him with the suggestion that he himself should take over leadership of the whole region and unify the people against the whites.

Yali did not accept, but on the other hand he did not reject these overtures outright. He reflected deeply on the plight of his people, yet was undecided what course of action he should take personally. The Cult leaders took advantage of his indecision and began preaching that Yali had been killed during the war, that he was really a ghost, and that he had visited the King in Australia and God in Heaven who had told him how the Cargo would be sent to the people.

Yali's reflections evidently led him to the conclusion that the missionaries were humbugs, not true men of God, and that they were concerned only with the exploitation of the natives and lands that rightly belonged to the tribes. No one knows exactly why he suddenly adopted an anti-mission attitude, but it is safe to assume that he had heard disparagement of missionaries in the army and had had leisure to ponder

L

over the relative luxury in which they lived while preaching the doctrine of Christian brotherhood to people who were desperately poor.

In 1946 and 1947, Yali walked from Madang to the mouth of the Sepik River spreading reports that the Government wished to abolish the indentured labour system and do many things to help the people, but that the missionaries were resisting the reforms—a charge not entirely unfounded at the time because the missionaries, like all other white men trying to re-establish productive industries, were handicapped by the labour shortage and the ferment among the tribes.

Yali's reputation was enormously enhanced by his Sepik tour. Cultists started to preach so many subversive ideas in his name that the Administration became alarmed. It summoned him to Port Moresby for 'orientation'. There he was lectured by numerous officials who explained the illogicality of Cult and promised that the Government would help the people by promoting co-operative cash-cropping, village councils, and native-run trade stores, and by establishing schools and hospitals independent of the missions. Unfortunately for Yali, anti-mission elements—reported by some to be sophisticated Papuans—also explained to him the theory of evolution and showed him a book purporting to outline its principles. He was deeply impressed, the more so because he associated these crude expositions of Darwinian belief with his own people's old totemic religion, a religion which he had renounced in favour of Christianity.

The disturbed and disillusioned hero returned home fanatically anti-Christian, and set about preaching expulsion of the missionaries and a return to the old ways of life. The more immoderate his pronouncements, the greater the support he received. Cult leaders climbed on the bandwagon and Yali himself lost all control of the movement. Rejecting the biblical myths on which it had hitherto been based, it now turned violently pagan. Traditionally hostile tribes were temporarily reconciled, missionaries were threatened, and illegal taxes were levied to finance *sing-sings** and the construction of 'Yali Houses' to replace the old spirit houses in which the ghosts of the dead were believed to reside.

* A ceremonial dance meeting accompanied by feasting.

The Yali Cult spread rapidly up the Ramu River and as far west as the Torricelli Mountains. The whole of the coast from Finschhafen to the Dutch border was ripe for rebellion. In 1950, the situation forced the Administration to act. Yali was arrested, charged with extortion of money and incitement to rape, the latter charge resulting from sex elements in Cult preachings, and sentenced to six and a half years' gaol. So completely had the whole movement depended on the personality of this remarkable man that it began to collapse almost from the moment of his arrest. The Administration released him from prison in 1955. Today he is an influential but retiring figure in the legally constituted councils of the Rai Coast tribes (but he was defeated as a candidate in the 1964 House of Assembly elections).

A movement founded in the Admiralty Islands by another extraordinary natural leader, Paliau, is of even greater interest and significance. The Admiralty Islanders (or Manus as they are more commonly known) were among the most advanced of Melanesian tribes when the first Europeans arrived. Specialized occupations and a complex trading system were far better developed in the archipelago than elsewhere in New Guinea. Economic stratification was more pronounced, both between village and village and within individual communities. Though the tribes were divided by language and dialect differences, and had evolved no real cultural or political affinities, they had on their own initiative taken the first step towards urbanization. Their talents as traders had emancipated them from complete dependence upon garden lands and hunting grounds.

The Manus felt the impact of European colonization very early. They were acquisitive, industrious, healthy—and unhappy under the strains created by their extraordinary economic system.* The younger people were ripe for change, for escape from wearisome tradition, and they were far more ready than other New Guineans to accept employment by Europeans and to explore European money incentives. For this reason, early settlers sought Manus recruits eagerly, even though they were incorrigible individualists, often rebellious

* See Margaret Mead's definitive studies of the south coast and offshore island people, *Growing Up in New Guinea* and *New Lives for Old*.

and difficult to handle when they felt they had been affronted or dealt with unjustly. Their vigour and intelligence outweighed their faults.

Manus men made excellent police-boys. They enjoyed responsibility, status and authority, and they were prepared to settle down permanently in white employ. Before the war, reform movements within the tribes were already breaking down traditional social structure in the villages, and young men were beginning to challenge the tyranny of their elders and to advocate a new order in tune with European ways.

The impact of war on the Admiralties was profound. When the Americans expelled the Japanese in 1944, they set about building an enormous base from which to supply further campaigns in the west and in the Central Pacific. More than 1,000,000 United States troops, including large numbers of negroes, were staged through Manus during the next year, a demonstration of might unsurpassed in the New Guinea theatre. By 1945, considerable numbers of Manus were employed by the United States forces, liberally paid and rationed, and treated as equals—at least of the negroes.

The wealth and egalitarianism of the Americans dazzled the islanders who soon came to regard their former Australian and German masters with dislike and contempt. The anti-climax of peace and rapid military withdrawal left them in a state of confused shock and disillusion which the tentative re-establishment of frugal Australian civil government did little to alleviate.

In 1946, Paliau—who had been a prominent advocate of inter-tribal co-operation and the 'new life' in the late 1930s— was repatriated from Rabaul where he had been a police-boy before the invasion. Like Yali, Paliau was endowed with exceptional adaptability and personality, qualities which the Japanese rewarded by making him responsible for the behaviour of all village officials in the Rabaul area. Paliau did his job efficiently for the Japanese. He escaped prosecution as a collaborator after the war only because, as a native of the Mandate, he owed no allegiance to the British Crown. In any case, many Administration officials in the New Britain district had before they fled advised the natives to obey the Japanese rather than risk victimization.

When Paliau went home, he began again to preach inter-
tribal co-operation, and urged abandonment of the traditional
economy, burial feasts, bride-price and polygamy. He attracted a considerable following among landless people, young
men who could not afford a bride-price, and defectors from
the Roman Catholic missions. There can be little doubt that,
in the beginning of his campaign at least, Paliau used the
technique of Cult prophets to win audiences, claiming inspiration from dreams, visions and supernatural revelation; but
at no time did he promise the coming of Cargo as a solution
to the people's problems. He attempted instead to convince
them that they would find a solution for themselves in unity,
reform and economic reorganization. However, he made the
grave tactical mistake of openly preaching expulsion of both
whites and Asians, and of organizing a boycott of the Administration whose weakness he despised and whose promises he
distrusted.

In 1947, Paliau was arrested and brought to Port Moresby
for orientation with a number of bothersome lesser leaders.
Officials explained, or tried to explain, the workings of the
new Government and spoke of their plans for social development, plans which could not, of course, be put into practice
for many years. Paliau was unwilling to wait. When he returned to Manus he attacked the Cult prophets who had been
causing trouble and embarrassing him with offers of support,
but he proceeded even more energetically to organize communal agriculture and resettle displaced or landless people
in new village sites. The success with which he persuaded
mainland Manus tribes to co-operate with the people of the
offshore islands was without precedent. Under his guidance
the production of food increased, housing improved and the
standard of village sanitation and cleanliness was greatly
raised.

Paliau's enforced visit to Port Moresby had taught him a
lesson. He now refrained from anti-Administration propaganda and formed a number of unofficial village councils
which inexperienced officers of the District Service attempted
to advise. There is good evidence, however, that Paliau still
distrusted both white intentions and white capacity to help
his people, and that his real decisions were taken after clan-

destine discussion with his lieutenants and independent but minor leaders. He banned the use of money, instituted a system of barter, and encouraged a tacit boycott on both Government and mission schools.

The Murray Administration was now thoroughly alarmed by Paliau's steadily increasing influence, the more so because it had to report favourably to the United Nations on his movement. The movement demonstrated genuinely a capacity for progress among the indigenous tribes and it could not be repressed overtly without pungent criticism. Progressive elements in the Administration were sympathetic with Paliau's aspiration, but felt he was moving so fast that trouble might lie ahead if he tried to extend the sphere of his influence beyond the south coast of the island; or if other leaders, less balanced and without his capacity for organization, were to emulate him. Reactionaries, of course, denounced him as a fanatical upstart plotting subversion, a cunning, savage libertine who aimed to set himself up as a black dictator and whose real aim was to dispossess the whites.

The Administration concentrated upon bringing about Paliau's downfall by political manoeuvre. It appointed him *luluai*, or Government sponsored chief, of his home island Baluan and of adjacent islands. It promised to institute a local government council of which he would be the head. Thus it hoped effectively to limit his activities by denying him official status on the mainland of Manus where the majority of his adherents lived.

The manoeuvre did not work. Paliau had an intelligent and active lieutenant, Samol, who continued to propagate his ideas across the water. So the Administration then changed its tack. It delayed establishment of a legally constituted council on Baluan to see how Paliau would react. Paliau went on imperturbably with his task of economic and social organization according to his own formula. The mainland people, who had also been promised an officially approved local government council, became restive and demanded that the Administration honour its pledge.

Agitated by the implications of the situation, the idea that any native could possess the intelligence and competence to deal effectively with native affairs, the Administration decided on drastic action. Paliau was arrested and charged with spreading false reports that he had legal powers which he did not possess. He was sentenced to six months' hard labour. Numerous deputations to the District Commissioner protested, but to no avail. Native spokesmen in 1950 even expressed their dissatisfaction to the United Nations Visiting Mission, but its members were so unversed in the complexity of New Guinea affairs that they gave little evidence in their subsequent report of having understood any of the issues involved in the dispute.

Paliau served his sentence. He remained in Port Moresby for several months after his release for a polite brain-washing during which he was lectured by an anthropologist and taken on a tour of the more orthodox Papuan local government councils, infant and maternal welfare centres and agricultural co-operatives. Like Yali, he was intelligent enough to bow to *force majeure*, and returned to Baluan where the Administration had hastily formed a council in which both supporters and non-supporters of Paliau were represented. He was elected chairman of this council and devoted his organizational talents to making it work for the betterment of the people—within, of course, the white man's cautiously limited terms of reference. The next United Nations Mission in 1953 praised the orderly and progressive character of the communities it served.

Some anthropologists have severely criticized J. K. Murray's Administration for frustrating and sidetracking Paliau and for harsh treatment of Yali, but it should be remembered that neither of these men, however commendable their capacity for regional leadership, had the capacity to contribute much to the solution of the New Guinea problem as a whole. Progress and social reorganization in the Territory needed a broader base than limited, indigenously evolved autonomy on Manus or the Rai Coast. It would be ingenuous to believe that Paliau and Yali, even with the fullest support of the Administration, could have created within their lifetime communal order of a type which would have been practical or acceptable in other parts of New Guinea. Understandably enough, Murray and his advisers felt that if their job was to lay the foundations of a future nation, the first step was education to achieve wider political and economic concepts than those held by the two exceptionally gifted but troublesome visionaries from Baluan and Madang.

In practical matters the New Deal got away to a sluggish start. The Papua and New Guinea Act did not become law until March, 1949. It provided for an Executive Council comprising the Administrator and not less than nine officers of the public service (just as in the provisional government); and a Legislative Council of sixteen officers of the public service, three nominated Europeans, three nominated mission representatives, three nominated native representatives and three elected Europeans. Thus for the first time New Guineans had in theory a voice in the government of their country as a whole.

At a lower level, political apprenticeship for natives was provided by appointment to the District Advisory Councils, all the members of which were nominated, and to the Native Village Councils, the members of which were elected by a somewhat vague system of popular concurrence. The Asian residents, now numbering 2,000, were represented by nominees to the Town Advisory Councils.

In point of fact, none of these bodies exercised direct political power of any consequence. They existed as a gauge of reaction to the directives of the Department of Territories, and to help formulate ordinances and regulations in locally practicable terms.

The Papua and New Guinea Act made no changes in the judicial system set up by the Provisional Administration Act. This had provided for a Supreme Court with judges appointed by the Australian Governor-General; district courts in which Stipendiary Magistrates, Magistrates, District Commissioners, District Officers and other ex-officio members might preside; and Courts for Native Affairs of which District Commissioners and District Officers were ex-officio members. The police were amalgamated as the Royal Papuan and New Guinea Constabulary. The force comprised European officers employed wholly on police duties, an auxiliary of District Service officers, and a native constabulary, one third from Papua and two thirds from New Guinea.

An acute shortage of trained personnel retarded Government health and education services during J. K. Murray's term of office. There was difficulty in recruiting doctors and teachers for service in New Guinea, where salaries and conditions were still almost as unattractive to professional people as they had been before the war. The shortage of doctors was in part met by permitting migrant European medical graduates who did not possess qualifications for Australian registration to be appointed medical officers of the Health Department. By 1950, about fifty doctors were practising in the Territory, about one to every 40,000 of the population. Of an estimated 500,000 children of school age, somewhat less than 100,000 were attending mission or new Administration schools.

In the General Election of 1949, the Labor Government in Australia was defeated and the Liberal-Country Party administration of Robert Gordon Menzies (later Sir Robert) took office. The European commercial community expected a radical change in—or at least substantial modification of—the Labor policy of 'natives first'.

The new Minister for Territories, Percy Claude Spender, held the portfolio for only fifteen months. He reaffirmed the priority of native welfare in New Deal terms, but at the same time promised concurrent opportunity for European settlement and investment. How this was to be achieved without large-scale alteration of the land and labour laws was not clear, although at first the Europeans were hopeful.

In 1951, Mr Spender (later Sir Percy) retired from politics to accept the post of Australian Ambassador to Washington. Another election, following a double dissolution of Parliament, again returned the Menzies Government to office. The new Minister for Territories, Paul Meernaa Caedwalla Hasluck, soon made it amply plain that he intended no overall policy change at all. Private enterprise in New Guinea would be encouraged, but only so long as it did not in any way compromise Australia's position before the Trusteeship Council.

Paul Hasluck, an ex-journalist, university lecturer and diplomat, had been returned to Parliament in 1949 and had had time to study and assess the errors and inadequacies of the experimental years of the Provisional Administration. A man of formidable intelligence and industry, he brought to his Ministerial post much erudition and many firm convictions. Soon after assuming office, he retired Murray and appointed as his successor Brigadier (later Sir) D. N. Cleland, who had been appointed Assistant Administrator the previous year.

Murray's dismissal aroused furious controversy. Under appallingly difficult conditions he had achieved a great deal and his qualities were just beginning to be appreciated. In a statement to the House of Representatives, Hasluck indicated that in his estimation Murray no longer had the physical or mental vigour to cope with a task which would become more rather than less exacting. He further indicated that in future very little discretion would be accorded the New Guinea Administration in determining broad policy. Policy would be the prime concern of Federal Cabinet. The men in the field would be required to steer the course set by Canberra, no matter what local difficulties arose. The New Guinea autocracy had been removed permanently from Port Moresby to Canberra.

By the time Hasluck had been in office two years, the way ahead was clear to detached students of the New Guinea scene. Australian politicians of all parties were committed to a native protection and development policy much more radical than any dreamt of before the war. New Guinea was to become truly a showpiece of benevolent administration. The sins and neglect of the colonialist era were to be expiated. Australia's windy boasts of 1906 were to be made good. And incidentally—as a bonus for virtue—Australian influence was to be consolidated in a strategically important area adjacent to the new Asia.

9

Dispensers of Magic

UNTIL the early 1960s, no fair-minded critic could seriously question the honest purpose of Australian policy in New Guinea during the preceding fifteen years. The Commonwealth earnestly wanted and tried to discharge in both letter and spirit the obligation it had accepted under the United Nations Trusteeship Agreement—namely, to prepare the indigenous people as rapidly as possible for a durable political independence.

On the other hand, many critics became aware of a distinction between intention and performance. They questioned the wisdom of the Australian approach on several counts. First, could Western-style education superimposed upon these primitive societies greatly and permanently modify their basic characteristics? Secondly, could education of the scope envisaged by the policy-makers be financed from the surplus resources of Australia, and, if not, what foreign or international aid could be obtained? Thirdly, could education of this kind prove a prime factor in creating economic viability, the viability without which, in the words of Paul Hasluck, political autonomy would be 'a hollow mockery'?

Except in matters of minor detail, the Menzies Government elaborated the educational policies of its Labor predecessors. The objective was the synthesis in the Western Pacific of a new, small nation which could be compatible both in political structure and social character with the philosophy of Western democracy.

In theory at least, the formula for this synthesis was simple and logical. The fragmented primitive societies which comprised the natural human order of the region must first be disciplined to observe the tenets of civilized law as a fundamental step towards unification. They must then be taught a common language and educated through it in modern political, industrial, technical and administrative skills. Simultaneously, they must be encouraged to exploit the natural resources of their country in order to pay for the enormously increased volume of goods and services they would consume when they had adopted civilized living patterns.

The practical worth of this formula, in so far as it could be applied by a nation with Australia's limited resources, could be measured only by the speed of progress made towards the objective.

Government patrols did not complete even superficial exploration of the Territory until 1963 when parties based on Kiunga, a small station on the middle reaches of the Fly River, penetrated the fastnesses of the Star Mountains on the border of West Irian, formerly Dutch New Guinea. By then it could fairly be claimed that some 90 per cent of the Territory's population observed the white man's prohibition on outright tribal warfare, even though occasional feud fighting and payback murders still occurred in inaccessible districts. Perhaps 75 per cent of the population had otherwise modified their regional customs as a result of white influence. Only small areas in the central mountains, inhabited mainly by nomadic or semi-nomadic tribes, remained uncontrolled.

The accelerated programme of exploration and pacification undertaken since the war produced no new, miraculous technique for transforming savages overnight into civilized men. It went forward on the lines developed by Hubert Murray nearly half a century before, and was still eminently successful. Most native communities peacefully accepted the rule of law soon after the Administration established patrol posts and set up a system of supervision. Significantly, the Australians made it the responsibility of the individual to observe the law and applied no sanctions against communities as such. If fighting broke out, those who had promoted the quarrel or taken part in it were arrested, tried, and if found guilty committed to gaol for a term.

Fear of gaol acted as a deterrent against transgression but, particularly in post-war years, there was far less emphasis on the punitive element in the penal system than upon education. Prisoners were substantially better fed, clothed, housed and doctored than they had been as free men, and almost always were released in improved physical condition. The more intelligent were also taught skilled or semi-skilled trades, so that a gaol term tended to help rather than hinder men who wanted paid employment after release. They had become accustomed to regular routines, had acquired cleanly habits and been taught how to work persistently. Little if any stigma attached to men who had 'done time'.

However, experience of law enforcement in New Guinea emphasized one inescapable fact: that obedience to prohibitions had as yet no roots in the social emotions of the people. If they refrained from crimes they refrained not because of moral considerations but because of their respect for white authority, a respect which amounted to superstition. Proceedings in the courts showed that even criminals who came from districts pacified for upwards of fifty years rarely felt remorse for their offence, however much they may have come to regret the indiscretion of law-breaking.*

This attitude was so general in the courts that it can reasonably be supposed to have reflected the inward morality of the communities from which the offenders came. A New Guinean may experience the deepest mystical remorse for an act which he believes has affronted the ghost of his uncle, or for having risked retribution upon himself and his family by breaking a clan *tabu*, but he is seldom morally perturbed if he has yielded to primitive impulse and buried an axe in the skull of his unfaithful wife or her lover. Civilization may stamp a pattern of docility upon the surface of a savage society, but it cannot thereby create a new personal morality.

This practicality was quickly realized by a new generation of civilizers. They put their faith in formal education rather than in religio-ethical conversion by missionaries as an instrument of change. The kind of education provided by mission schools before the war had proved virtually useless, and the Administration started vigorously from about 1950 onwards

---

* Interesting comment on the attitude of natives convicted of crimes against European law can be found in *Itambu!* by Judge David Selby, Currawong Press, Sydney, 1962.

to establish its own schools. Mission schools were still encouraged and subsidized, but now only if they conformed to approved scholastic standards.

The Hasluck policy aimed at mass literacy. Hasluck himself believed that democratic institutions could prosper only if backed by a literate electorate. But the difficulties of creating a literate electorate soon became painfully apparent. This was a conundrum which had puzzled the educators of Hubert Murray's day.

In the first place, what language was to be used? Schooling could hardly begin until the point had been decided, for it was obviously useless to teach the population to read and write in local languages which were understood by only a few thousand people. A common tongue must be chosen, and taught throughout the region.

The choice now clearly lay between Melanesian Pidgin and English. Pidgin had several disadvantages. It had practically no established literature, was ludicrously clumsy and imprecise, poor in vocabulary, and unsuitable for the communication of abstract ideas. On the other hand, it had evolved almost spontaneously as a *lingua franca* from a vocabulary of a few hundred meaningful English, German and Malay words strung together on Melanesian grammar patterns. It could be, and was, learnt speedily by both adults and children of all indigenous linguistic groups. Within weeks it could be used as a means of simple communication between Europeans and natives, and between natives of disparate tongues. It was, furthermore, steadily improving in efficiency as its use became more widespread.

Ideally speaking, English was immensely superior, for it was a rich and precise language with a vast cultural and technological literature available immediately to anyone who had mastered it. Unfortunately, New Guineans had great difficulty in learning it—a difficulty perhaps comparable with the task faced by Europeans learning to read and write Chinese ideographs. Many of the commonest English words had no meaning for New Guineans. They described objects, situations and ideas which had no part in the island life. English grammar and idiom reflected thought processes and associations of ideas completely foreign and belonging to a people thousands of years ahead on the evolutionary scale. The indissoluble connection between a living language and a contemporary social state became perplexingly clear. Nevertheless, bitter controversy raged between the theorists on the question of which language should be adopted in schools. At the official level, the idealists, who heatedly damned Pidgin as undignified, inadequate and degraded, won the day. From the late 1950s, the Administration decided that all classes above Standard Two should be taught in English. This step was taken despite the evidence of experience that New Guineans could handle the language only if they began to learn it at the age of seven or eight years and continued without interruption to the secondary level, at which stage brighter students might become facile in use of its simpler forms.

Away from the Government schools, however, Pidgin went on spreading and developing, even in Papua where disapproval of it had for many years been most vehement. A new generation of missionaries, more concerned than the old with the temporal welfare of their flocks, regarded it as the true vernacular and taught it to thousands of children who had no chance of learning English because they could not continue their education to the secondary level. When New Guineans were appointed to the Legislative Council, most of them made their speeches in Pidgin. Court evidence given in the vernacular was ordinarily translated first into Pidgin and then from Pidgin into English. Administrative orders and pronouncements were published in Pidgin, and it was the language used in the great majority of newspapers, news-sheets and broadcasts disseminated for the information of natives.

Should authority have set the sights uncompromisingly on a far distant but desirable target—effective literacy in English? Or should it have compromised for the immediately practical? Would it not have been more realistic to have acknowledged the merits of Pidgin and have keyed elementary education to its use, providing it with a hastily translated literature of a utilitarian kind, rather than to postpone for two or three generations the hope of attaining genuine mass literacy in a better language?

These questions will be answered only by the outcome of the New Guinea experiment. If political considerations permit Australia to continue as a Trustee Power for another fifty or sixty years, then the decision to educate in English will undoubtedly prove right. But should the Australian trusteeship be truncated, as seems much more likely, a good deal of the effort expended in both primary and secondary education will have been wasted. Far more practical results could have been achieved by teaching in a language which, however inferior in the absolute sense, came easily to the tongues of children and adults alike.

The lessons learnt by the people who made and administered post-war educational policy in New Guinea were salutary. They demonstrated how difficult and time-consuming it is to teach Stone Age natives to speak, read and write a modern tongue. More important, they made it clear that true education begins far below the level of literacy, and that ability to read and write is an asset only in a society sufficiently advanced to have genuine use for the skill. In thousands of villages and hamlets living by subsistence horticulture, literacy in English was (and is) of little everyday value. It would acquire value only when another sort of education had introduced smallholder cash-cropping and small-scale commerce into the New Guinea way of life, or when the services of a clerkly caste were needed by indigenous society and not solely by the expatriates.

Nevertheless, the Government persisted in giving high priority to formal schooling. Formal schooling could be recorded statistically, and the figures were impressive to those who knew nothing about local conditions.

In 1950-1, from a school-age population of about 500,000 in both Territories, 132,000 pupils were receiving instruction in subsidized mission schools and about 4,000 in the new Administration schools—a total of 136,000. Ten years later the total had risen to 134,000 in mission schools and 73,000 in Administration schools, amounting to 217,000.*

---

* The numbers of children receiving both primary and secondary instruction of a standard considerably lower than that of Australian schools has since been substantially increased as a result of the accelerating crash education programme.

ABOVE: *Health. Medical patrol sprays insecticide to kill malarial mosquitoes and flies.*

BELOW: *Justice. Hillmen, subsequently convicted for the murder of two Australian patrol officers, on their way to trial.*

ABOVE: *How many acorns make twelve? A Kukukuku scholar carries out research.*

BELOW: *"The figures speak for themselves!" John Akunai, a candidate for the Legislative Council, produces documentary evidence.*

Of course, this rise in school population was not nearly as significant of achievement as the figures might seem to indicate. The great majority of pupils left school before they had acquired *effective* literacy of any kind. Life was little changed by the fact that thousands of youngsters learnt how to spell 'rat' and 'mat', and how to print their names. Only those in closest contact with Europeans showed any true comprehension of the practical value of scholastic education or how it achieved its results. The general population was enormously enthusiastic about schools only because it still regarded reading and arithmetic as white man's magic, a manipulation of occult forces rather than a key to the mastery of physical skills and intellectual techniques by which life could be made richer and more secure.

For reasons which we shall examine later in detail, the policy-makers were forced by the end of the decade to acknowledge the impracticability of the ideal of giving all tribes equality of educational opportunity and of building the putative nation on a foundation of universal literacy. Possibly influenced by Murray's ideas, Hasluck had tried to avoid deliberately training an élite from the native groups who happened to have closest contact with Europeans; but as time went on he was compelled to divert more and more resources to post-primary and secondary education, the levels of schooling that could be opened only to the very few.

Even so, only 564 native children by 1961 were attending secondary schools in either the Territory or Australia, and none had yet qualified for university entrance. This tardiness in educating youngsters for administration, commerce and the professions was criticized in the United Nations' sessions. By the end of 1963, the secondary school population had increased to about 1,000, and seven matriculants had passed entrance examinations and were enrolled at Australian universities. Despite this paucity of material, that year a Commission was appointed to investigate the possibility of founding a university in New Guinea itself, and after extensive studies recommended the immediate establishment of an Institute of Higher Learning as the 'seedling' from which an

M

autonomous university might eventually grow.* But obviously these plans were for the distant future.

Education officers estimated that within five years—by 1968 —about 10,000 children would be receiving post-primary or secondary schooling. They could not, of course, estimate how many of these children would complete their courses, or how many would go on to universities and qualify in professions. Optimistically one might guess that New Guinea high schools by 1970 would be producing about 100 matriculants a year, of whom perhaps one-sixth would finally graduate in arts, science, law, medicine, engineering, commerce, architecture, etc. At this relatively rapid rate of progress, one could scarcely expect the indigenous people to staff even by the end of the century the professional services essential in a civilized community.†

For propaganda reasons, the Australian Government was now giving considerable domestic and United Nations publicity to its 'crash' education policy, the drive for mass literacy in the villages and the preparation of young people for skilled employment; but the results of the policy though it was pursued with zeal by a dedicated teaching service, made meagre contribution towards attainment of the objective: the creation of a new society. The Commonwealth's publicists pointed out with pride that the Administration by 1963 was spending some three million pounds a year on education in the Territory—more than the total grant-in-aid for all purposes ten years previously. They did not point out that this sum, on per capita basis, represented only about one-fourteenth of the expenditure in Australia itself.

Obviously it cannot be suggested that Australians, however seriously they regarded their role as trustees, were in a position to step up the Territory's education grant fourteen times. But it is also obvious that an effort so limited could not accomplish a great deal for the New Guinea peoples as a whole. No more could be done than preparatory work—and then only preparatory work of an elementary kind.

* In 1965 the House of Assembly passed a Bill authorizing the establishment of a Papua-New Guinea 'university' with several decentralized 'colleges' or departments. The Commonwealth Government stipulated that it should be financed from revenues raised within the Territory.

† In 1965 John Natera, B.Sc. (Sydney) became the first native graduate.

The obstacles against educating even a handful of children to matriculation standard were enormous. The adoption of modified Australian teaching techniques and examination levels proved frustrating for both teachers and pupils. Moreover, experience had shown that a European-type secondary education for natives was possible only if the students could be removed from the environment of family and village life, and accommodated in boarding establishments where isolation from the distracting influences of their own culture could be ensured. Even this did not wholly remove the handicap of cultural incompatibilities. Students in senior classes found the greatest difficulty in coping with the Australian curricula, not because they lacked innate intelligence but because they were working in a language, and with moral and philosophical concepts, evolved by an alien social order.

The political implications of the Trusteeship nevertheless forced the Australian Government to continue educational window dressing. An unhappy side effect was felt by intelligent young New Guineans selected more or less arbitrarily in Government and mission schools to undergo a training which well nigh foredoomed them to accept hopelessly heavy responsibilities among their own communities in the future. The most unfortunate were the children who won scholarships to Australian secondary schools where they became conditioned over a number of years to white economic and social standards, only to be forced in the end to return to a primitive society from which they were by then intellectually and emotionally divorced.

In simple human terms, the creation of an educated élite by these means is a ruthless business. Whether the members of such an élite will in their maturity entertain sentiments of gratitude to Australia for the type of education given them is a moot point indeed. It is not without significance that many contemporary African and Asian leaders still most bitterly hostile to the dispossessed colonial Powers are themselves the product of European education systems. They may be an élite but they have not been able to perform miracles and bring political stability or economic prosperity to their backward countries. Current history suggests that these countries will enjoy political stability and economic prosperity only

when their internal social order has been changed by forces
of enlightenment of which literacy and academic performance are only the servants.

To sum up, it can be said that by the end of 1964 the 'crash'
policy in New Guinea had not produced enough educated
natives to staff even the lower echelons of the public service
or meet the demands of expatriate commerce and industry
for clerical and office workers. It was not remotely within
sight of producing enough candidates for professional training to maintain—let alone develop—the social services then
being provided in New Guinea by Australian personnel.

At non-academic level, the picture was a little more encouraging. As we have seen, primary exploration was complete by
the end of 1963, although pacification was not. But from the
mid-1950s onward, consolidation of Administration influence
in controlled districts went on apace. Savage society had been
effectively constrained by new disciplines, and progress had
been made towards teaching at least some of the people new
skills and providing them with new social motivations. Subsistence horticulture benefited by the introduction of new
food plants, and in some places by the adoption of new
methods of cultivation and the introduction of fresh strains
of domesticated animals.

In the main the Administration concentrated upon persuading the people to make the first, long step from the archaic
economy of subsistence and barter to a smallholder cash-crop
economy. In a number of areas, notably the eastern highlands
and the Gazelle Peninsula, the people responded. Experimental plantings of cocoa and coffee before the war had been
successful and in the reconstruction period a degree of
priority in effort was accorded the beverage crop industries.
The pilot cocoa plantations established on New Britain, New
Ireland and Bougainville, and in the Morobe and Madang
districts of the mainland, were rehabilitated and the Administration vigorously encouraged further plantings, particularly by native landowners who were given every possible
help with cultivation, processing and marketing.

By 1963, exports of cocoa from the Territory totalled about
12,000 tons, valued at more than £2,000,000, and production

was expected to increase substantially if world prices held up. By this time, about one-quarter of the cocoa was produced by indigenous planters, especially the Tolai people, socially the most advanced group in the Bismarck Archipelago. Native cocoa planters on the Gazelle Peninsula became financially prosperous even by European standards and, under the stimulus of their example, their fellow tribesmen ventured to branch out into other profitable commercial enterprises. The Tolais were the first of the New Guinea tribal groups to comprehend and accept—although with reservations—European economic motivations.

Another success in the economic form of education was scored in the highlands where as early as 1950 experimental plantings of coffee had begun. Soon after the war, the Administration made limited areas of leasehold land available to European planters in the Goroka and Wahgi valleys, where they concentrated on growing high-grade *arabica* types. Despite the dependence of these pioneers upon air transport, both to obtain equipment and supplies and to send their crops to the coast, they made their enterprise pay. Then the Administration, and many of the settlers themselves, helped native smallholders to set up plantations. About 60 per cent of New Guinea's coffee crop in 1963 (4,137 tons valued at £1,700,000 in the year ended 30 June) came from native holdings. About two-thirds of production was marketed in Australia under tariff inducements. A Coffee Marketing Board was formed to control the industry's standards and to promote overseas outlets for the crop.

In both cocoa and coffee districts, Australians provided the commercial initiative and the technical help and supervision necessary to put and keep New Guinean planters in business. Success in these industries fostered the idea that an effective economic partnership between the races might be established. This idea was more fully realized in the highlands than elsewhere. White settlers who went to the pleasant climate of the highlands were of a new generation—a generation entirely unlike the Pacific planters and traders of the late nineteenth and early twentieth centuries. They were willing to accord the indigenous people a courtesy, tolerance and understanding unknown in pre-war race relationships. On their part the highlanders were more industrious, co-operative, adaptable and—with reason—considerably less resentful of intruders than the lowlanders had been in the early days. Enlightened post-war administration succeeded admirably in minimizing the trauma of contact. What educative processes could be contrived for speeding social evolution were not retarded at the outset by racial resentments and distrust.

In other parts of the Territory, the partnership approach to economic education was not so promising. The copra industry, financial mainstay before and after the gold mining boom, made little progress. Although the Administration had from the beginning tried to encourage and even force New Guineans to plant coconuts, in 1962-3 only about 26 per cent of coconut products derived from native holdings. The rest, valued at about £7,500,000, came from 261,000 acres under expatriate ownership or management.

Attempts to interest the hill tribes in growing rubber did not meet with much success. Most of the Territory's £1,000,000-a-year rubber production still came from estates run by expatriates. Several experiments with commercial rice production by native co-operatives were badly guided and failed. Although soils and climate were suitable, various factors, some of them political, thwarted projects to grow sisal hemp, kenaf, cotton, sugar and vanilla. Operation of commercial fishing and timber industries proved, for the time, to be wholly beyond the technical capacity of New Guineans. Thus exploitation of the Territory's most obvious natural resources would for long be dependent upon the problematical investment of foreign capital and know-how.

Efforts to persuade the tribesmen to raise cash vegetable crops—an even more important venture in education than in economics—succeeded very well in a few districts, and the successes will no doubt proliferate if given time. But it cannot truthfully be claimed that in the nineteen years following the war most New Guineans showed any great disposition to abandon their traditional methods of agriculture and enter eagerly—and responsibly—into the forms of partnership offered them by the whites. When pacification destroyed the ancient standards and ancient religious codes, the loss unhappily created no revolutionary economic philosophy. It created only the vague revolutionary longings expressed in Cargo Cult. A good deal of fuss was made about the few hundred tribesmen who became prosperous by planting cocoa and coffee, but they were by no means representative of the population. They were the exception rather than the rule, and even they would not long continue to operate successfully if white supervision were withdrawn.

The Administration nevertheless continued patiently with its work in agricultural education, and in 1963 announced that it hoped to have established by 1967 more than 100 agricultural extension centres and to provide training for 1,500 native farmers every year. The scheme would employ nearly 250 extension officers and 900 native assistants. It remains to be seen how much, how quickly and how permanently this ambitious and expensive project—which, at the time of writing, is up to schedule—will affect the pattern and efficiency of indigenous agriculture.

Closely associated with this endeavour to extend cash-cropping was the move to encourage the formation of native co-operatives: primary associations which arranged marketing, and secondary associations which sought among other things to amalgamate the purchasing power of the primary co-operative groups, to control the volume of production in accordance with market conditions, and to concentrate capital for the purchase of such assets as small ships, land transport and agricultural machinery. In 1955, the Administration provided for registered native co-operatives to negotiate loans of up to £5,000 for approved projects. By 1964, these co-operatives had at their command capital of more than £500,000 and their membership totalled more than 80,000. Here, without any doubt, was an educational scheme which must affect the lives and attitudes of a significant proportion of the people.

It is somewhat harder to assess the overall value and progress of trade training in the Territory. No one knows how many native carpenters, plumbers, bricklayers, mechanics or electricians became competent workmen as a result of the New Deal either in the technical schools or under the apprenticeship system introduced in the late 1950s.

By 1963, somewhat less than 1,000 pupils were attending technical schools, a number better able to supply the demand than might appear. Regular artisan employment was available only in timber mills, mines and large plantations, or in public works projects. New Guinea's grass-thatched villages offer no work for master builders and A grade motor mechanics—and the great majority of the people still live in grass-thatched villages. The New Guinea tradesman earned his wages not by serving the direct needs of his own people but the needs of those who had come to press him and his compatriots into the mould of an alien culture. The entire objective of Australian educational policy in New Guinea was, after all, to press the people into the mould of an alien culture, and to impose upon them an alien language, an alien morality and an alien social organization. Although it may be easy to condemn the objective, yet it must be acknowledged that the indigenous culture was an anachronism that the twentieth century could not tolerate. The Stone Age and the Atom Age had no chance of peaceful co-existence in an ever shrinking, ever more crowded and competitive world.

Inseparable from the efforts made by Australians to teach New Guinea primitives how to survive among more advanced peoples was the effort made to protect and improve native health.

Early colonists remarked the lassitude of the coastal New Guineans: their dislike for prolonged exertion, their lack of initiative, inability to concentrate, slowness to learn, and poverty in mental and physical stamina. Observers too intelligent to accept the pat Victorian explanation that these deficiencies were inherent in 'lesser breeds' were inclined to attribute them to a humid, equable tropical climate which failed to provide physical stimulation and challenge. Very few were perceptive enough to realize that the low vitality of the people was due neither to temperament nor to climate but to ill health—ill health caused by unsatisfactory diet and by endemic malaria, intestinal parasites, dysentery, skin infections and other diseases which diminished their physical efficiency.

Only lately have medical scientists been able to arrive at

assessment of the effect of diet deficiency and endemic disease on the capacity and performance of New Guineans. In 1958, Dr J. T. Gunther, then Director of Health in the Territory and later Assistant Administrator, concisely defined the native health problem in these words to the Australian Institute of Political Science:

> Today our Papuan or New Guinean . . . is a small man. His expectation of life is 34 years, though from the age of five years it increases to nearly 43. At 21-30 years the male averages 121 lbs in weight and the female 105 lbs. The male is 62.7 ins tall and the female just 60 ins. There are undoubtedly significant variations of these figures, but to me they indicate that the population is not healthy: the expectation of life is half what it should be; the infant mortality twice to 10 times what it should be . . .
>
> The indigenous people of the Territory are only 80 per cent well. Disease, especially malaria and hookworm, allows them only 80 per cent of the blood they need and this anaemia must deaden the mental processes in similar ration. They sustain themselves with less than 80 per cent of their food requirements.

Yet it should be emphasized that Dr Gunther's dismal picture of public health in the islands is not, in its gross aspects, a result of white infiltration and the introduction of alien diseases. There is every reason to believe that the life expectancy of New Guineans has increased since the coming of Europeans and that the debilitating effects of poor nutrition and endemic disease have been somewhat reduced.

In Polynesia, in Micronesia, and in Melanesian islands such as New Ireland and New Caledonia, diseases introduced by Europeans caused tragic depopulation in the nineteenth and early twentieth centuries. Some districts of mainland New Guinea suffered similarly. By and large, however, the work of medical missionaries and the relatively small Government health services more than compensated, if only by reducing infant mortality, for the lives lost through introduced epidemics, tuberculosis and venereal disease.

Before the Second World War, medical services in the Territory, whether supported by missions or the Administration, existed more to protect the health of recruited labourers or communities in close proximity to large mission stations than to serve the population as a whole. Very little was done —or could be done—to attack malaria, the main killer of young children. Dr Gunther wrote: *Control malaria and you will double the expectation of life . . . and double the population in 17 years.*

Drugs, insecticides and biological techniques developed during the war made malaria control possible in theory, but in practice it remained a remote goal in terrain where the cost of a sufficiently broad programme of mosquito eradication was completely beyond the Administration's purse.

However, from about 1959 onwards, massive spraying in selected areas offered a degree of protection for more than 200,000 people. In 1963, medical authorities announced that complete control of malaria in the island of Bougainville was at least within sight, and the following year claimed a dramatic reduction in the incidence of infection among the Sepik River tribes. But no one had the temerity to estimate how long a similar job would take in the Gulf of Papua or the delta of the Fly. The best that could be said was that the expansion of health services in rural areas and the increasing availability of drugs had markedly reduced malarial mortality among young children.

In other aspects of public health, the progress of the post-war programme was more satisfactory. Yaws, a disease which is seldom fatal but which strikes viciously at comfort and happiness, was practically eliminated by medical patrols giving mass inoculations even in remote and semi-controlled areas. Tuberculosis was a stubborn problem, but BCG vaccination on a scale comparable with anti-yaws inoculation held in check a scourge which might well have decimated the unsalted populations of the high valleys if no protection could have been given them. Modern drugs also greatly reduced the incidence of venereal diseases.

Medical services also included improvements to existing hospitals, the building of more hospitals and aid posts and the training of a large cadre of native medical assistants for duty in rural districts. Leper hospitals—called 'Hansenide colonies' in an age which sets store by euphemism—halted the spread of this dread but not highly contagious disease.

Typhoid, measles, whooping cough and epidemic bacillary dysentery were also kept in check, although acute respiratory infections, notably pneumonia, still exacted a heavy toll. The expanded health services provided under the New Deal cost as much as education and prolonged the life of hundreds of thousands of New Guineas, but they did not even approach a solution of the problem of how to improve quickly the general physique and energy reserves of the adult population. They preserved life without much increasing the capacity to enjoy it. This in itself begot the type of dilemma which is plaguing under-developed nations the world over.

To quote Gunther again:

> Where the medical services can get to the people there is a possible population increase of births over deaths of five per cent per annum . . . In at least one area [the Upper Chimbu where there are 600 people to the square mile] we are already beginning to see the ill effects of population pressure, and in other areas it is not a generation away . . . I have a feeling that this population increase is outstripping the tempo of development, valiant though our efforts are.

Put even more plainly, the development programme was now saving the lives of more New Guineas than it could educate usefully or feed adequately. The time must soon come when the burden of providing social services which New Guineas could not themselves support by their own productivity would become intolerable for Australia.

The all-important but unanswered question was: Would Australia be able to hang on long enough for indigenous productivity to increase to the level where it could support expanding education and health programmes. If increased productivity must await the end results of the current education and health programmes, then the answer was certainly 'No'. Valiant the programmes might be, but quantitatively and qualitatively they were inadequate to achieve the quick results—or even the appearance of quick results—which the political situation demanded.

10

Instant Democracy

IN any part of the world, a viable modern State cannot be shaped solely by administration of civilized law by honest trustees, by heavily subsidized health and education services, and by paternally initiated and guided projects in social development. For in this context as in many others, independence and self-support are interchangeable terms. After twenty years of intensive effort and experiment following the war, the Australian Government found itself once more, but with a new sense of urgency, facing up to the old, old problem— how to make New Guinea produce enough to support the kind of social order that the idealists believed desirable for it.

In 1953, Australian taxpayers contributed £4,600,000 towards the cost of developing the Territory. Eleven years later their contribution had risen to £28,000,000 a year. The Minister for Territories estimated that £50,000,000 might be needed by 1970. Expenditure on health and education alone had already trebled in the decade.

During the same period Australia itself had experienced unprecedented growth and prosperity, so that the people were not required to make onerous sacrifices to support the Government's New Guinea benefactions. But the time was not far off when the burden would become uncomfortable. The cost of laying the sub-foundations of a modern State in the Territory was by now increasing far more rapidly than the country's ability to produce revenue. Despite the introduction of income tax—which, of course, fell almost wholly on the expatriate population—and the decline in purchasing power of the Australian pound, internal revenue rose only from £2,500,000 to about £9,000,000 during the period in which the Commonwealth's grant was multiplied by five. Between 1958 and 1963, total trade grew from £32,500,000 to £41,400,000, but exports accounted for only about £17,000,000 of the increased figure.

The thriving prosperity of such centres as Port Moresby, Rabaul and Lae, with their small but well developed industries, depended not upon indigenous productivity but upon the size of the public service. By the end of 1964, Government servants numbered more than 6,000. These people and their dependants constituted the bulk of the European population. Of the rest, a considerable proportion earned their living from commercial and service enterprises that were chiefly sustained by public service spending.

Despite the much publicized success of cocoa and coffee plantations, other primary industries languished. Little diversification was achieved. Since the war, hope of discovering payable oilfields had attracted a speculative investment of about £30,000,000, mainly in Papua, but by late 1964 no strike had been made and the local economy had derived little benefit from this injection of capital. Mining generally declined after the Morobe goldfields were worked out. By no stretch of the imagination could the economy of New Guinea be regarded as healthy, or even growing at a rate to warrant reasonable expectation of self-sufficiency being achieved within the foreseeable future.

The causes were evident. The natural resources of the country were apparently considerable, but no systematic and comprehensive survey of them had been made. In any case, ownership and ultimate control of the resources were vested, under the terms of the United Nations Trusteeship and by repeated policy declarations of the Government, in the natives; and the natives lacked—and would for many years continue to lack—the enterprise and skill to exploit them on their own account. They could only be exploited by expatriate capital and under expatriate technical and commercial guidance.

But New Guinea did not attract—and indeed had never attracted—private investment of the volume necessary to trigger economic take-off. In the old days, as we have seen, the main inhibiting factors were the policy against land alienation and the high cost of inefficient labour—factors which the Government deliberately perpetuated in its native protection policy.

Modern methods of mechanization later reduced to an extent the costs of labour in some segments of primary industry. However, substantial private investment even in these fields—notably mining, timber, sugar, tea and fibre crops—remained unattractive for the simple reason that the Territory's political future became increasingly uncertain as the anti-colonialist elements in South-East Asia became more vociferous and influential.

Post-war Australian policy had undoubtedly been motivated by a desire to establish among Asian nations a reputation for responsible liberalism and to dissociate the Australian image from that of oppressive nineteenth-century colonialism. It had seemed that this might be achieved by helping a dependent, coloured people to flourishing independence, but as the policy was put into practice it gradually revealed that New Guinea could not be ready for true partnership with modern States for a very long time. Notwithstanding, Afro-Asian and other elements in the councils of the United Nations demanded that Australia should set a target date for according the Territory political self-determination. This the Australian Government repeatedly refused to do, on the sensible grounds that it could make no accurate forecast of when the people would be capable of achieving homogeneity and managing their own affairs. The basic economic problem had still to be solved, and education had not yet begun to take effect in the lives of New Guineans.

The Australian attitude was reasonable, but reason quite obviously had but a small voice in the frenetic clamour of the world's backward peoples for a heady draught of political liberty at whatever cost. Even the tragedy of the Congo did not moderate the cries of the African and Asian nationalists for 'Freedom now—and for all!'

As the last vestiges of the old colonial patterns in Asia and Africa were erased—often with the unhappiest results for all but the indigenous oligarchy which inherited privileges and responsibilities for which it was unfitted—Australia's position in New Guinea became more difficult.

What to do? Should Australia with its limited resources press on with a programme that might take more than a century to reach worthwhile results? Or should it build a political façade, behind which it could bow out some time thereafter with hypocritical grace in the face of 'popular demand' and 'world opinion'—leaving New Guineans either to revert to savagery or look elsewhere for help and leadership?

If the Australians decided to stick to their original objective of balanced development, even though attainment of large-scale results seemed to have receded in point of time, they invited the abuse of every Asian demagogue preaching holy war against the remnants of European influence in the East to distract attention from his own ineptitude. Further, they invited the disapprobation of the United Nations—an organization to whose reactions small nations remained sensitive even though it was now far more occupied with cleaning up or containing the bloody chaos let loose by the premature 'liberation' of colonial territories than with negotiating the fair settlement of international disputes.

If, on the other hand, the Australian Government decided to get out of New Guinea as quickly as the semblance of respectability would allow, it faced a multitude of embarrassments, including the possibility that withdrawal would be followed by internal disorder, intervention by an Asian Power and eventual expropriation of commercial interests which—if not of much overall importance to the Commonwealth economy—were long established and therefore of sentimental significance in domestic politics.

By 1962, the preponderance of opinion among professional political scientists was that Australia would be forced to choose the second course—to give New Guineans independence before they were ready for it and deal with the consequences as they came.

The basis of this opinion was that the task of educating the people, transforming tribalism into nationalism, and creating an economy adequate to support nationalism, had already been proved to be beyond Australian resources. There remained no valid military or economic reason for persisting with the attempt, and even those who advocated persistence on moral grounds were forced to admit that the Hasluck policy now appeared as impractical.

Military strategists pointed out that control of the eastern half of the island was no longer such a factor in the defence of Australia as it had been before the development of nuclear armaments—and, indeed, commitment to defend New Guinea might prove a costly embarrassment when the forces available even for continental defence were inadequate. Economists said boldly that the chances of the Territory enticing private capital investment on a scale large enough to ease the financial burden on the Federal Treasury were highly remote. Sociologists re-emphasized that although savagery might be repressed with dramatic speed in such a country, the civilization of its people could proceed only with intolerably expensive and perilous slowness.

For about fifteen years, those who had made and administered policy in New Guinea had pursued an ultimate objective which experience had shown to be unattainable. Now their problem was to find some politically acceptable means of withdrawal—and preferably a means which would not destroy the achievements which had benefited the native peoples. Oddly enough, a lead came from an unexpected source—an agency of the United Nations.

Until 1962, the triennial Visiting Missions which checked up on the Trusteeship had rather uncomprehendingly observed and vaguely approved the Australian policy. Members representing nations that had won independence since the war were always the first to express their surprise and consternation at the backwardness of the local people and their apathy in political matters.

In 1962, however, the routine inspection party was headed by a perceptive and experienced British colonial administrator, Sir Hugh Foot. For the first time, the report to the Trusteeship Council was sharply—and authoritatively—critical of Australian paternalism. It advised in effect that Australia should immediately abandon the Hasluck ideal of creating a democracy based on literacy and general enlightenment, and get on with the business of selecting and training an indigenous élite to which the responsibilities of leadership

Friends, New Guineans, countrymen! The candidate for Nop Nop addresses the electors.

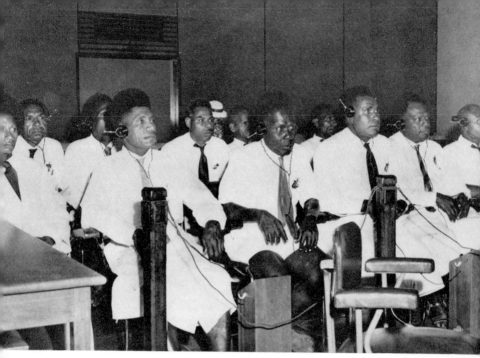

ABOVE: *The Legislature listens to translations of debate in many tongues.*

BELOW: *The village treasurer takes stock of the community's assets in shell money (tambu).*

could be handed on as quickly as possible. It suggested that the apparent political apathy of New Guineans would be best overcome not by persuasive education but by progressively handing over to them the responsibility of managing—or mismanaging—their own affairs.

Less sensational but hardly less significant was the advice that the Australian Government should cease its courtship of speculative capitalists who might be tempted to investigate and invest in New Guinea if they believed in vague assurances of the country's future stability. Instead it should get down to drawing up a realistic prospectus, prepared on the basis of a World Bank survey of the Territory's resources. When the resources and their accessibility were expertly evaluated, both public and private investors would be in a position to balance the chances of taking profit against the risks of expropriation if New Guineans at some time in the future should renounce political allegiance to their Australian protectors.

The Foot report shocked the people who on idealistic grounds still supported the Hasluck policy of hastening slowly and building as soundly as external pressures and domestic funds would allow, but it obviously did not shock the political analysts who had already condemned as impracticable the ideal of creating by education and guidance an egalitarian partnership between rich white Australians and poor brown New Guineans.

The Legislative Council had already appointed a Select Committee on Political Development to investigate means by which more rapid progress towards representative government might be made, and when the Trusteeship Council endorsed the Foot report the Government moved with celerity to implement its major recommendations.

At this point, it is profitable to summarize the action taken by the Australian Government to promote, in the contemporary sense, political as distinct from general and technical education among the New Guinea tribes.

Education of more advanced groups in the procedures of democratic government had begun soon after the administrative union in 1949. It started, as we have seen, with the establishment of the village councils, which later became

N

known as local government councils. These bodies, of course, exercised their limited powers under strict supervision because the purpose of setting them up in the first place was to proselytize a European system of government rather than to promote evolution of an indigenous system. The fate of Paliau and his movement had clearly shown that.

In 1951, five councils were legally constituted in the Territory—one in Papua and the others in New Guinea—comprising 89 informally elected members representing about 18,000 people. In 1961, 43 councils were established with about 1,200 members representing 309,000 people. By 1963, the great leap forward had been made—73 councils represented nearly 700,000 people.

In the beginning many natives were chary of giving the council movement their unqualified support. In some sophisticated areas, notably the Gazelle Peninsula, the real leaders of the people stubbornly opposed their establishment. They realized that councils must operate under white scrutiny, and shrewdly reckoned that the kind of communal integrity they preferred—an integrity rooted in tribal custom and tradition —would be more easily preserved if important decisions remained the province of the *kiwungs*, or conclave of elders, who had carried out this role since time immemorial. The Administration had to exert a great deal of persuasion, and in some cases open pressure, before tribesmen would agree to form a village council. Often they blandly offered the excuse that they were not yet educated enough to run their own affairs. The *kiap* knew how—so let him do it!

In other districts, like the Aitape coast, the natives resisted the formation of councils because they involved a forced cooperation between tribal groups among which old enmities still smouldered hotly.

Although the Administration in most cases eventually overcame resistance and the new system appeared on the surface to be making progress, the *kiwung* in its various forms survived. It continued to influence tribal attitudes much more than the Administration men cared to admit.

The hasty superimposition of alien political institutions on what endured of the old order could hardly have been expected to bridge in the span of a decade or so the gap between

the races. Yet the Government proceeded with political education at a rate which increasingly outstripped its capacity to
work genuine changes in social attitudes.

At the territorial as distinct from the local level, provision
was made in 1960 for the indigenous people to receive greater
representation on the Legislative Council. The Papua and
New Guinea Act was amended to provide for reconstruction.
The new Council (elected the following year) was to comprise thirty-seven instead of twenty-nine members—the
Administrator, fourteen official members, six members
elected by the indigenous population, and ten appointed non-
official members, of whom five were to be New Guineans.
The old Executive Council was abolished and replaced by an
Administrator's Council of three official and three other
members of the Legislative Council, two of whom must have
been elected.

Thus for the first time there was a non-official majority in
the central legislature and an elected constituent in the
executive—a considerable step towards creating the machinery of representative government, even though the power to
decide really important matters still remained in the hands
of the Commonwealth Government through the Department
of Territories.

It is noteworthy that the missions had no statutory seats
reserved for them on the Council, although the Minister
'asked' the Administrator to consider the nomination of two
persons representing their interests 'where there was a recog-
nizable case for voices that will be raised for sections of the
population whom missions can claim to know more closely
and understand more clearly than others do'.

The election of native members was contrived through the
village councils in those areas where councils had been established, and by proclamation of electoral groups in areas where
they had not been established. Each council or group was
allocated a number of votes in the electoral college roughly
proportionate to the size of the population they represented.
Any native who could muster six sponsors could nominate as
a candidate. The village council or electoral group delegates
then made their choice among nominees in each electorate,

by secret ballot at a meeting presided over by the Returning Officer.

At the elections for the reformed Legislative Council held in March, 1961, 108 indigenous candidates presented themselves for the six seats. Those elected nominally represented about 500,000 people.

During the life of this Council the native members comported themselves with considerable dignity but great caution. With one exception—John Guise, a privately educated man of mixed blood who expressed himself fluently in English—their contributions to debate were stereotyped and seemed often merely to reflect or elaborate the opinions of European members rather than to offer a genuinely indigenous viewpoint on contentious issues. On various occasions they were at pains to emphasize the gratitude of their people for continued Australian leadership and their belief that self-government would have to await the results of a long period of education and preparation, and to make mild criticism of those elements in the Trusteeship Council who advocated haste and pressed for the announcement of target dates for independence.

For each sitting of the new Council, the Administration brought fifteen other native leaders to Port Moresby as observers and gave them courses of instruction in political theory and procedure. In both 1962 and 1963, parties of selected natives were sent to Australia to observe and receive instruction in the workings of government there.

While the pace of specific political education of this kind was being stepped up, parallel reforms in the structure of the administrative system were also put in train. In 1960, Professor D. P. Derham, Professor of Jurisprudence at the University of Melbourne, made a survey of the Territory's judicial system at the invitation of the Government. The Territory's Annual Report for that year said:

> In instituting this inquiry, the Administering Authority was moved by the following considerations—that a system of justice is one of the essential pre-requisites of self-government; that such a system needs high standards in the Bench, the accessibility of Courts to the people, the confidence of the people in the Courts, and the habit of relying on the Courts to protect

the personal rights and property of the individual and to re-
dress any wrong or injury suffered by the individual; and the
need in this as in other fields to prepare the indigenous people
for full participation in the work of their own institutions.

After the survey, Professor Derham's report recommended
substantial changes. The Territory, he pointed out, was going
through a period of transition from pure executive government of a paternal kind to a form more in accord with parliamentary and constitutional government of the Western kind.
It was therefore necessary to begin a methodical separation of
the executive from the judiciary. While he did not recom-
mend alteration of judicial procedures in remote areas of first
contact, where 'government by patrol' might have to continue
for some years, he urged that in more advanced localities the
district courts should be increasingly staffed by full-time,
qualified stipendiary magistrates instead of Native Affairs
officers performing judicial duties part-time. Indigenous
people should be trained as magistrates, clerks of court and
interpreters, and customary native courts should be increasingly integrated with the judicial system as a whole.

The Derham report accelerated reorganization in this field
administration. Prisons had already been removed from
police control, and now the police were formed into a separate department of the public service. An ambitious and
expensive programme of building courthouses throughout
the Territory began, with the motive of presenting to the
people a *visible* separation of the executive from the judiciary. Rules were enumerated for defining native custom precisely in court cases where custom was a factor in arriving at
just decisions.

The Administration announced a training programme to
prepare natives for participation in the work of the courts.
It also announced its decision to abolish the old Courts for
Native Affairs and to replace them with local courts, operating under simplified procedures and with low limits of jurisprudence, in which selected New Guineans would sit as
justices with a magistrate but without power of decision. It
was planned eventually to amalgamate these local courts with
district courts.

The recommendations of the Derham report sharply

pointed up how slow progress towards a self-supporting civilization had been to date, and how much the people had yet to learn before they could sustain autonomous democracy.

Nevertheless, the backers of political education raced ahead with setting up machinery through which untutored natives might express, in the democratic convention at least, their ideas about what civilized laws should be applied. The hopeful assumption was that backward people did not need nearly so much training to make good, new laws as they needed to administer good, old ones!

The publication of the Foot report appeared to justify even greater haste in forced political development—or, if it did not justify it in the strictly moral sense, at least it gave Australian politicians an excuse for yielding to the pressures of expediency. With relatively minor modifications, the recommendations of the Foot report were implemented. In May, 1963, the Australian Parliament again amended the Papua and New Guinea Act to provide for replacement of the Legislative Council by a House of Assembly consisting of ten official members, forty-four members elected from a common roll in single-member constituencies on the basis of adult suffrage, and ten non-indigenous members elected on the same basis. The strength of the Administrator's Council was increased from seven to eleven members, seven of whom had to be appointed from the House of Assembly.

The stated intention in creating this instant parliament was to make the natives put forward into the legislature those whom they regarded as their natural leaders. But how could forty-four men fairly represent the will or opinion of perhaps 1,000 tribes still speaking many hundreds of languages and using no common one? The defect was clearly seen by the people who concocted the formula, and they admitted that the system would in effect disfranchise many of the numerically weaker groups. Tens of thousands of New Guineans must accept representation by men whom they did not know —except possibly as members of hostile tribes—and with whom they had no direct means of exchanging information and ideas. The imperfections of such an institution were legion. When such a House of Assembly arrived at majority decisions on locally contentious matters, discontent and resentment would inevitably arise among a considerable aggregate of minority interests which had been deprived of a voice even in debate. And in a House of Assembly so elected, multiple language interpretation would be necessary if all members were to comprehend and participate in proceedings and debate. Moreover, the intellectual quality, education and sophistication of members would vary even more embarrassingly than it did in the Australian House of Representatives!

The common roll on which the election was to be conducted was synonymous with the official census lists compiled over the years by Administration patrols. Even tribesmen who a few months before the election might have been raiding for heads or eating the flesh of enemies killed in war—for there were still many of these people in the newly opened up areas of the west—were legally entitled to nominate as candidates and to vote in the election. They might have no knowledge at all of any world beyond the horizon, nor have seen a wheeled vehicle, a printed book or any metal tool more refined than an axe or a knife, but they were entitled and, indeed, cajoled to express through the ballot box an opinion about who should govern them now that they could no longer be permitted to govern themselves according to the tenets of the Stone Age.

It is hard to believe that either Sir Hugh Foot or any of the other authors of the political reforms which culminated in the establishment of the House of Assembly believed it to be the foundation on which a form of responsible democratic government could be built in the future. It is equally hard to believe that they did not clearly envisage it as the means by which Australia might in the near future be able to disengage from a thankless and profitless task.

But the Commonwealth Government did not publicly acknowledge the radical changes it made in the objectives of its New Guinea policy from about 1961 onwards. It tended rather to conceal them. Early in 1963, the writer published in Australian newspapers the opinion that forthcoming amendments of the Papua and New Guinea Act indicated that the Commonwealth would be prepared to give New Guineans political autonomy by 1972. The reaction of the

Menzies Government was immediate and angry. It had to be, because the Australian electorate was not yet emotionally prepared for so precipitate a withdrawal from New Guinea. For fifteen years it had been persuaded to accept the increasing burden of administration and development costs on the grounds that control of the Territory was strategically vital and that, in any case, Australia had an important moral commitment to the natives. At times, inefficiency in the management of New Guinea affairs had provoked sharp public and Parliamentary criticism, but on the whole the Government's record in the country had been regarded as praiseworthy.

Territories' Minister Hasluck and the Prime Minister therefore found it expedient to deny categorically that the Government foresaw the possibility of giving the Territory independence by 1972, and that it was deliberately preparing the way for that event. Australia, said Hasluck, would stay in New Guinea as long as the indigenous people needed and wanted Australian help. He claimed that speculation about so early a withdrawal was irresponsible and mischievous, and several times in ensuing months he repeated that Australia would not get out of New Guinea until asked to do so by the New Guineans themselves. Australia would if necessary, he said, resist the pressure of world opinion in this matter.

This re-statement of the Australian intention appeared on the face of it to be unequivocal, but it was in fact the reverse because it implied that the native people would want Australian help and leadership as long as they needed it. In the light of events in other colonial territories within recent years, this was an arrant sophistry of which Hasluck, as a competent historian in his own right, must have been fully aware. No knowledgeable observer of the situation could avoid the conclusion that within a few years an articulate and preponderant section of native representatives in a House of Assembly elected by universal suffrage would be asking for political freedom—irrespective of their ability to sustain or benefit from it. There was no valid reason to believe that the tribes of New Guinea would favour continuation of government by aliens much longer than the tribes of East Africa had done.

Although Hasluck's statements fell far short of candour to

the electorate, they were politically astute. They gave room for future manoeuvre—at once making reply to United Nations critics who complained of Australian 'tardiness and evasion' about nominating a target date for independence and also soothing domestic fears that the Government intended a disengagement so hasty that it might be the prelude to a Pacific Congo.

When the Menzies Government was again returned to power in the Australian Federal election of December, 1963, Hasluck—who had until so recently tried consistently to maintain a rational balance between the political, social, educational and economic elements in the planned development of New Guinea—did not resume his old portfolio. He was promoted in Cabinet and became Minister for External Affairs, a well deserved acknowledgement of his personal capacities despite his long championship of a morally admirable but impractical New Guinea policy. A comparatively obscure Queenslander, sixty-one-year-old C. E. Barnes, who had never shown in his contribution to Parliamentary debates any particular interest in New Guinea, was put in charge of its affairs. The die, most obviously, was cast.

The election of the new House of Assembly took place in March and April, 1964, and extended over several weeks because there were not enough electoral officers to supervise simultaneous voting. It was a bizarre and colourful proceeding which received a good deal of publicity calculated to imply that Australia was making a courageous experiment in democratic education.

Before the poll was taken, patrols visited all areas where a census had previously been taken and explained, as well as they could, why and how the Administration was asking the people to vote and how candidates could be nominated. Electoral patrols later conducted the ballot. With so many illiterates participating, it could not be secret but it was reasonably private between voter and electoral officer.

The idea of adventurous young patrol officers struggling through steaming jungles and swamps, fording mountain torrents and traversing precipitous razorbacks to carry the inspiring message of democracy to communities of Stone Age savages, briefly captured the imagination if not of the world then at least of Australian newspaper readers. The whole enterprise appeared dramatically idealistic—indeed even quixotic at times—for as it progressed reports from some of the more remote areas shocked even those who were ingenuous enough to hope that the conception of a new parliamentary democracy was taking place. In several recently controlled districts of the interior, villagers panicked and boycotted the poll because they believed that it presaged the imminent withdrawal of Government protection and a return to the terrors of inter-tribal raiding. On New Hanover, off the tip of New Ireland in the Bismarck Archipelago, the people remembered the incredible surplus wealth of the Americans and their reckless generosity in wartime. So the New Hanoverians withheld their local government tax money and established a fund of £1,000 to 'buy' President Johnson of the United States to come and rule over them! They were most emphatically opposed to electing anybody to represent them in the 'English' Government at Port Moresby.*

In districts prone to Cult, some candidates sought support by making wild millenarian promises and prophecies. Officers of the Administration were obliged to warn these naturally gifted politicians that democracy in New Guinea had still some distance to go before such tactics could be tolerated. They then presumably retired to exercise their talents as spellbinders in the dark meeting places of the *kiwungs* instead of on the floor of the House.

It can hardly be doubted that the vast majority of New Guineans who voted in this election were ignorant of the important issues involved. Candidates were often nominated and supported at the ballot because they were known to be *persona grata* with the Administration, not because they were men able to represent the true desires and aspirations of their tribes. It is a peculiarity of New Guinean psychology, remarked on by many Europeans who have occupied posi-

* The Johnson Cult was still giving the Administration trouble as late as June 1965. Numerous arrests for tax evasion had been made, convictions recorded, and riotous assemblies dispersed by the police.

tions of authority there, that a native questioned on serious matters by a superior tends to make the replies he believes the questioner wants to hear, regardless of the facts. This attitude cannot have failed to have had effect on the constitution of the first House of Assembly, in the same way as it has already had an effect on the constitution of local government councils. The men who are truly representative of tribal thinking and who are capable of swaying the emotions of the people are not yet to be found in Port Moresby's rather pathetic Parliament of a Thousand Tribes, learning the procedures of debate. They are still deep in the jungle and they still believe in the power of witchcraft, the morality of payback and the malign intent of traditional enemies.

Since this is the inescapable truth, one cannot attach too much importance to the election of six European candidates who contested open seats against native nominees in the 1964 election; or to measured statements by a few veteran recipients of white approval and patronage—forerunners of the synthetic élite—to the effect that New Guineans realize they will need Australian guidance and help for many years. It may be true that intelligent natives elected to the House genuinely recognize the *need*, but what the people *want* may be a very different matter.

Yet, even if the first House is neither truly representative nor democratic, it is nevertheless the first form of an institution through which the political aspirations of the minority of sophisticated New Guineans and of the powerful tribal groups such as the Sepiks, Tolais and Chimbus, will eventually find expression. These elements—the sophisticates and the candidates speaking for groups which feel themselves strong enough to dominate the rest—will surely be the first to ask for independence. As we do not know exactly when and in what circumstances the demand will be made, we cannot foresee precisely what effect severance from Australia will have when it comes, particularly as the situation is complicated by the emergence of the Republic of Indonesia as a major Power in South-East Asia.

In 1963, the Indonesians won control of the western half of New Guinea from the Dutch. Up to the time of writing, their attitude towards Australian New Guinea and its peoples has remained obscure, but their presence is a potent element in the political chemistry of the region and it is necessary to trace how it came about before moving from the field of historical analysis into the realm of prediction.

Except for the brief period of occupation by the Japanese armed forces during the Second World War, Asians have had only negligible influence on the life of the New Guinea tribes. The pressures for change were exerted solely by the European colonists of the Pacific. But with the arrival of Indonesian colonists in West New Guinea in 1963, it seemed certain that Asian expansionism would henceforward be increasingly felt throughout the whole region.

11

Birth of a Sick Giant

STUDY of the political and social development of New Guinea would be incomplete, and any prediction of its future unsoundly based, without consideration of the circumstances in which the Republic of Indonesia won sovereignty over the western half of the island after a bitter dispute with Holland lasting more than fourteen years.

The Republic is a political union of South-East Asian peoples first brought together within the administrative structure of the Netherlands East Indies Empire, an empire which collapsed when the Japanese occupied its territories in 1942 and which was never effectively reconstituted.

Despite the claims of present-day Indonesian leaders to an ethnic and cultural entity, the Union owes its existence far more to the hegemony created by Dutch rule over 350 years than to consanguinity or other affinities between the peoples which comprise it. Their degree of development varies greatly: from the sophisticated Javanese who were civilized when the Dutch conquered them in the seventeenth century, to the primitive tribesmen of Timor, the Moluccas and Borneo, who are today in their own right only a little more advanced culturally than those of New Guinea.

The disparate peoples now known as Indonesians won their independence from the Dutch in 1949 after four years of struggle; but ownership of West New Guinea remained in dispute until 1963.

To understand why the rancorous quarrel developed about who should have the thankless task of ruling over 160,000 square miles of forbidding jungles, swamps and mountains, it is necessary both to review Dutch rule in the East Indies

and to examine briefly how the Indonesian Republic came
to be established.

As we have seen, the Dutch claim to control the territories
of the Sultan of Tidore dated from 1828, although they did
not set up administration posts at Manokwari and Fak Fak
until 1898. Thereafter, development of the region was almost
imperceptible until just before the Second World War. In
1939, there were only ten permanently staffed Government
stations in the Netherlands New Guinea Residency and fewer
than 25 per cent of the estimated population of 700,000
people were, by Australian standards, under control.

The east and west halves of the island might have been in
different hemispheres for all the communication there was
between them in peacetime. During the war, military commanders perforce regarded the country as a geographical
whole, but soon afterwards the separation reasserted itself.

From the nineteenth century, Australians looked on New
Guinea as a part of Australasia, and when they assumed control in the east they attempted to integrate all aspects of
development on that basis. The Dutch, for their part, regarded the island as an extension of South-East Asia. For
about seventy years, the two territories were administered on
entirely dissimilar lines and with dissimilar objectives.

Paternalism certainly had no place in the political philosophy of Dutch colonialists, particularly in the New Guinea
Residency where the incompetents or unreliables of the
colonial service were banished to expiate their sins. The
missionaries who toiled heroically among the head-hunters of
the coast may have been concerned with the bodies and souls
of the West New Guinea heathen, but The Hague most certainly was not. Such economic development as there was,
occurred spontaneously. Military expeditions did most of the
basic exploration of the lowlands in the early days, and the
only inland government station of any consequence was at
Tanah-Merah, on the middle reaches of the Digoel River,
where for many years a penal colony accommodated in maximum security the most troublesome Javanese and Sumatran
political prisoners convicted for agitation against Dutch rule.

At various times, small-scale settlement schemes were proposed. In the 1920s there was talk in Holland about establish-

ing agricultural colonies of Eurasians near Hollandia and on Geelvink Bay. In the depression years of 1930-1, the proposals were extended to include unemployed from Holland, and some of these unfortunates did indeed migrate. But the country was too hard for them and the Government not interested enough to give them the financial and technical help they needed to make themselves self-supporting. Within a few years, only the toughest and most stubborn remained.

Much earlier, minor migration of Javanese had been encouraged. About 2,000 New Guinea-born Javanese were successfully cultivating paddy rice near Merauke on the south coast both before and after the war.

The pre-war expatriate economy depended mainly on copra production of 3,000 or 4,000 tons a year, on copal gum crops from wild *Agathis* trees in the Vogelkop forests, and on crocodile shooting and trochus fishing.

Before 1949, in spite of the Sorong oil discovery, West New Guinea appeared to the Dutch as a singularly worthless piece of real estate compared with the rich outer islands to the west where great industrial and commercial development was still possible. But when control of these assets was taken from Holland by the Indonesian revolution, the Cinderella colony soon appeared in a different perspective.

Because it became a political and ideological battleground between an emergent Asian Power and a declining European Power, West New Guinea assumed an importance in world affairs quite disproportionate to its size, position and potential.

On 15 August, 1945, two veteran Indonesian revolutionaries, Soekarno and Hatta, who had before the war led independence movements in the Indies and had with Japanese help during the latter stages of the occupation operated a crude form of national government in Java and Sumatra, proclaimed the Republic of Indonesia and renounced allegiance to the Dutch Crown.

Holland had suffered severely in the European war and was in no condition immediately to assert authority by force of arms in her rebellious Asian colonies. Neither could she obtain help from any of the victorious Allies. The attitude

of Soviet Russia to old-style imperialism had long been
obvious; the United States were preparing to give independence to the Philippines, the only American colony in the
East; and the British were already committed to the decolonization of India, Ceylon, Burma and, eventually, Malaya.

From the beginning it was perfectly clear that the *status
quo* could never be restored in the Netherlands Indies, and
that Holland must sooner or later concede some form of
political autonomy to the entire region. The Dutch, however,
were naturally determined to save whatever they could of
their enormous property assets in the old empire, and they
manoeuvred adroitly to keep separate the revolutionary
movements in the Outer Islands and Borneo from that of
Hatta and Soekarno—a tactic of 'divide and bargain' from
which they had every expectation of deriving satisfactory
salvage.

A period of chaotic disorder followed the proclamation of
the Republic. The situation was worst in Java. British troops
landed at Batavia late in September to police the disarming
and repatriation of the large Japanese garrison forces remaining, and to restore order as far as possible until the future
political status of the island could be determined. Correctly
but perhaps unfortunately, the British brought with them a
Dutch Lieutenant Governor-General, Dr H. J. van Mook,
and recognized him as the representative of the Dutch Crown
in which legal if not actual authority still resided.

In November, a serious clash occurred between the British
troops and the Republican forces at Sourabaya—an event
which triggered off the long and confused series of minor but
often savage military engagements that served only to obfus-
cate the true course of the revolution. This was in fact determined far more by intrigue and counter-intrigue than by
armed conflict.

In time the Dutch were able to summon up enough military strength to control the Outer Islands and Borneo, but
they made little headway on Java-Madura and Sumatra, the
heartland of the revolutionary movement.

In 1946, after a succession of conferences with the Republican leaders representing all the various provinces of the old
empire, the Dutch bowed to the inevitable and negotiated

the Linggadjati (Cheribon) Agreement. This agreement recognized the authority of the Republican Government over the islands of Java-Madura and Sumatra, and it provided for the creation by January, 1949, of the United States of Indonesia. The States of the Union were to comprise the Republic of Indonesia (Java-Madura-Sumatra), Borneo and Great East Indonesia (the Lesser Sunda Islands, Timor, Celebes, the Moluccas, etc.) All States were to be associated with Holland, much in the manner of the British Commonwealth nations with the United Kingdom, and each was to retain the right of secession from the Union if its people indicated that desire 'by democratic procedure'.

The Linggadjati Agreement stated that the Union's sovereignty should extend over the entire territory of the former Netherlands East Indies—a contradiction of one important point made by van Mook at the conferences which led to its signing. Van Mook had pleaded successfully against the inclusion of West New Guinea in East Indonesia, on the ground that the territory and its people were so undeveloped that they needed special consideration and would, in any case, impose insupportable administrative burdens on the new States.

The Linggadjati Agreement broke down almost as soon as it was signed. Secessionist movements sprang up in various parts of the Indies because the people of the Outer Islands and powerful minorities in West Java, although they wanted freedom from the Dutch, disliked and distrusted the clique now leading the revolution from headquarters in Jokjakarta.

The newly recognized Jokjakarta Government, interpreting the Agreement in its own way, now demanded virtual control of the interim central administration that was to be set up pending legal establishment of the United States of Indonesia. The Dutch resisted the demand and instituted a blockade to prevent the Republic entering into foreign trade. As disorder was mounting, the Dutch also suggested formation of a temporary Federal Government on equitable terms, its decisions to be enforced by a joint police force.

The Republicans asserted that they could maintain order in their own territories and rejected the suggestion. The Dutch then outlawed the Republicans and were within an ace

o

of crushing them by military force when the Security Council of the United Nations intervened. It appointed a Good Offices Committee, and under strong international pressure the Dutch were forced to agree to a cease-fire and withdrawal of troops.

The Good Offices Committee persuaded both parties to sign the Renville Agreement in January, 1948. This provided for the establishment of a Convention to draw up a constitution for the proposed United States of Indonesia. The Dutch were in the meantime to retain sovereignty but agree to transfer their powers to a provisional Federal Government in which all States were to be fairly represented.

Again the Republican Government attempted to interpret terms to suit itself. The Dutch lost patience and, capitalizing on anti-Jokjakarta sentiment in the Outer Islands, took steps to create a United States of Indonesia *without* the Republic although with the means by which it could join the Union later if it so wished.

Now, to complicate matters, a Communist revolt broke out in Republican territory. The Dutch used their military forces once more in what they called a 'police action', captured Jokjakarta and interned the Republican leaders.

Again the United Nations intervened to cancel the Dutch victory. At whatever cost (short of admitting the Communists), the Indies must be de-colonized! The Good Offices Committee was disbanded and a Commission for Indonesia established. It insisted that the Renville Agreement must be adhered to and the Republican leaders released. Holland had no choice but to agree to treat again with the men who consistently ignored or perverted the meaning of agreements they had just signed.

Unfortunately, the Renville Agreement did nothing to clear up the ambiguity about the status of West New Guinea.

By the time the Round Table Conference was convened at The Hague in 1949 to define the detailed structure of the United States of Indonesia, the Dutch had made up their minds not to cede sovereignty of the New Guinea Residency if they could possibly avoid it. The Republicans, who had gained so much in four years of frantic plotting and counter-plotting, were not disposed to haggle over a trifle which they were sure they could pick up later if they wished. They accepted a 'postponement clause' suggested by an Australian member of the United Nations Commission, Mr T. K. Critchley. This provided that West New Guinea should remain in *status quo* under the stipulation that its future should be the subject of negotiation between Holland and Indonesia within a year.

What moved the Dutch to cling so tenaciously to this last poor fragment of an empire?

In the first place, there were domestic political considerations. The loss of their East Indian Empire had been no voluntary abdication. Defeat after defeat in the campaign of international intrigue which preceded the transfer of sovereignty stung the pride of the Dutch people. With a good deal of justification, they felt that they had lost their empire less to the prowess of the Indonesian revolutionaries than to the determination of the great Western Powers to force them into a type of de-colonization for which the Indies were unprepared.

Retention of West New Guinea in face of Indonesian demands was a small but critical face-saver which probably allowed the Act transferring the rest of the Indies to the Republic to pass the Dutch Parliament with the necessary two-thirds majority.

There were other considerations. Van Mook's argument that the country and its people were so primitive that they needed special provision and would have imposed an intolerable burden on the resources of the State of East Indonesia if incorporated in it, had factual merit. The Dutch further argued that there were no cultural and ethnical links between the peoples of New Guinea and the peoples of Indonesia, and that if the principle of self-determination were to be followed the New Guineans should be given a chance to choose who should rule them.

But, as always in such situations, ethics were a far less powerful force than expediency. The bitter hostilities engendered by four years of revolution had presented the Dutch with a tragic refugee problem. What were they going to do with more than 100,000 Eurasians who had supported them—and with loyalist elements in the colonial army who were marked men because they had fought and humiliatingly defeated Republican troops in the two police actions? Holland, already over-populated, could admit only a limited number of these people. Might not New Guinea, with good luck and better management, provide a new homeland for them?

Last but not least, the firm establishment of sovereignty and successful exploitation of New Guinea's natural resources would give Holland a wedge of permanent influence in the area and could greatly increase her future bargaining power in industrial and commercial adjustments with the new Republic.

As soon as the Charter of Transfer had been ratified, Holland energetically set about reorganizing the administration of the New Guinea Residency. The Hague decreed it a separate territory and divided it into four districts, each under control of a Resident. This the Indonesians denounced as a breach of faith—a change of status before the future of the Residency had been settled by negotiation.

Whatever might have been the merit of that complaint, Indonesia itself broke the Round Table agreement by altering the constitutional structure of the Republic from a federal to a unitary type—a move precipitated by separationist revolts in West Java instigated by an adventurer named Raymond Westerling.

Westerling had held the rank of captain in the Netherlands Army and had taken part in a number of police actions in the Outer Islands at the time the Dutch were re-establishing control there. He was a ruthless man of magnetic personality, and an efficient soldier at the company commander level. But he was a political illiterate, and suspected of having committed atrocities in the Celebes.

Nevertheless, Westerling managed to win support in West Java for a last-minute attempt to set up a federal system not dominated by Jokjakarta. He recruited and trained a small secret army dedicated to the destruction of Soekarno and Hatta.

In January, 1950, Westerling's 500 rebels surprised and defeated units of a crack Republican division and captured the city of Bandoeng. But the coup was short-lived. A plot to seize and kill key men in the Central Government and extend the revolt to Jakarta misfired. Westerling fled to Singapore when the Dutch Government—again under pressure from the United Nations—threatened to use the military forces still at its command in Java to crush his rising.

Westerling's rise and fall were meteoric, but the whole affair inflicted on Soekarno and his followers what they considered an intolerable humiliation. Their military inefficiency and their unpopularity even in Java were exposed to the world. They furiously accused the Dutch of having inspired and supported Westerling in his plot. Westerling did indeed have the support of many Dutchmen, but they were certainly not agents of their Government. The truth of the matter is that if the Dutch Government had not warned Westerling that it would be compelled to help the Republic crush his revolt, he would have succeeded in at least wrecking Soekarno's political organization.

After the Westerling affair, there was little hope of the Round Table agreements being honoured. Soekarno realized that his only chance of remaining in power lay in fanning the embers of anti-Dutch, anti-foreign sentiment. He denounced the Federal Constitution in August, 1950, and proclaimed that the authority of the Republic extended over the whole area previously administered by the Dutch. As a result, he had to deal with more ill-conceived and poorly-led secessionist revolts in the Celebes and the Moluccas. Again he declared that these had been instigated by the Dutch.

In such climate, compromise on West New Guinea was impossible. In the twelve months following the Round Table meeting, two abortive Ministerial conferences had failed to agree. Thereafter there was no spontaneous effort by either party to settle their dispute in bi-partite negotiation.

Throughout this long quarrel, the attitudes and actions of Australian politicians were inevitably under scrutiny. Indeed the ability of Australia to hold a sphere of influence beyond its northern shores as a buffer against the turbulence of emerging Asian autonomies may perhaps be gauged by the way in which Australian leaders reacted during this period.

The Dutch resolution not to cede West New Guinea was without doubt fortified by the Australian viewpoint after

1950. The Labor Government which had committed the Commonwealth to the New Deal in eastern New Guinea had consistently supported the Indonesian revolutionary cause in the United Nations; but by the time the conservative Menzies Government came into power, the practical implications of the revolution were more apparent. The corruption, instability and administrative inefficiency of the Republican Government were now alarmingly clear, and by no manner of means could it be argued that giving these people sovereignty over 700,000 primitive New Guineans would be in the interests of the tribesmen. Furthermore, the growing strength of the Communist Party in the new Republic suggested that the creation of a land frontier with Indonesia might at some future date give rise to embarrassing difficulties for the Australians, who had long been growing uncomfortably aware of their dependence upon the United States of America for effective defence against any major Asian aggression.

In August, 1950, the Menzies Government indicated that it did not consider Indonesia had any valid claim to West New Guinea. The Minister for External Affairs, Mr P. C. Spender, made a statement to this effect during a visit to Holland. The Dutch, unwarrantably encouraged by the *volte face* from the Labor attitude, proceeded to develop their New Guinea policy on the assumption that they could continue to count on Australian support if they matched the Australians in benevolence towards the indigenes.

In many ways the Dutch did match the Australians in benevolence, although as a people long instructed if only recently informed about the pitfalls of colonial administration they did not make the mistake of awaiting the day of complete pacification and basic mass education before trying to form an indigenous élite to which they could hand over the reins of regional government should it become necessary to install a puppet regime disguised as autonomy.

As in the case of Australian New Guinea, West New Guinea's planned development cost more and more as the years went by, and the prospect of the territory achieving economic viability receded. The oil strikes in the Vogelkop

proved of less quickly realizable value than had been antici-
pated. The wartime discovery of large nickel ore deposits in
the Cyclops Mountains near Hollandia did not attract the big
investment of private capital necessary to exploit them. Agriculturally, the western half of the island was a more difficult
proposition than the eastern half. Schemes to settle Eurasian
refugees on the land failed largely because immigration
priority was given to worthy but mainly aged and bewildered
white-collar workers who were as little fitted to wrest a subsistence from a raw clearing in the jungle as their counter-
parts in the suburbs of Amsterdam or Rotterdam would have
been.

The struggle of the Dutch to develop West New Guinea's
economy during the 1950s was even less successful than that
of the Australians in the east, not because they were inept but
because the resources of the country were far harder to tap.

The value of mineral, forest, agricultural and marine production remained proportionately far below that of the Australian territory, and the trade balance was even more unfavourable.

In 1959, the imports of Dutch New Guinea were valued at
£10,000,000 and exports at less than £3,000,000, a ratio not
significantly varied in the ensuing three years. But in the
west, as in the east, the appearance of prosperity in the main
settlements was due to the spending power of the expatriate
public service rather than to the productivity of local industry. In 1961, one disenchanted observer of two 'missionary'
projects to uplift the natives calculated that in Dutch New
Guinea most imports consisted of processed foodstuffs for the
expatriate population, and the value of imported alcoholic
beverages equalled that of transport equipment. Similarly, in
Australian territory, the value of imported liquor and tobacco
combined was approximately equal to that of fuel oil!

Attempts to diversify primary production in West New
Guinea were less successful than they were in Australian territory, and coconuts continued to be the mainstay. By 1961,
copra exports totalled about 5,000 tons a year, or about one-
fourteenth of the copra exports from Papua-New Guinea.
The second important export item was nutmeg, grown mostly
on the Onin Peninsula. Production more than doubled be-

tween 1950 and 1960, and yielded satisfactory profits owing to an enormous increase in price following the collapse of the Indonesian nutmeg industry. A beginning was also made with cocoa, coffee and rubber plantations, but by the time the Dutch were ousted in 1963 actual production was still minute.

No doubt the methodical and intense way in which the Dutch Agriculture Department tackled the formidable problems in tropical New Guinea would have shown profits in the end, but there was no time for the pay-off. Political change by far outstripped every other sort of change.

Between 1946 and 1950, a veteran New Guinea administrator, J. P. K. van Eechoud, who had set up the first Government post at the Wissel Lakes before the war, held the office of Resident Commissioner. A man who knew and liked New Guineans, his policy was to delegate responsibility and authority to natives wherever possible. He belonged to the school which believed that too-rapid development was less dangerous to their eventual welfare than too-slow. In 1944, he had trained a Papuan battalion for service against the Japanese, and had been impressed by his men's qualities as troops. In peacetime he appointed natives to the lower ranks of the Government patrol service—posts which had previously been held by Indonesians.

In 1950, however, after The Hague had made up its mind to hold on in New Guinea, van Eechoud was replaced by a Governor, S. L. van Waardenburg, who was preoccupied with refugee resettlement. The pace of administrative education for natives perforce slowed down. In 1953, Dr J. van Baal replaced van Waardenburg and inherited many of his problems, plus the worry of economic projects which were by now either stalled or going wrong.

Before van Baal had been long in office, the expectations and motives of the Government at The Hague clarified. Experience had already shown that the chances of the colony supporting itself within the foreseeable future were negligible. The social development of the native population as a whole would be even slower and more painful than it was in Australian New Guinea. The terrain was more difficult, and an enormous amount of exploration and pacification had yet to be done. The refugee settlement experiments had failed. Holland's reason for continuing in the country was now simply a matter of prestige—and the hope that the foothold in New Guinea would still prove politically valuable if the Indonesian Republic fell apart.

Ironically, the Dutch refusal to quit turned out to be a most powerful factor in sustaining Indonesia's overall political cohesion. Throughout the 1950s, the Republic's economic situation went from bad to worse, and regional rebellions continually threatened Soekarno's Government. He was able to hold the whole jerry-built structure together only by preaching with ever-increasing vehemence that the Dutch were still plotting to re-conquer Indonesia from the base of West Irian, as the Republic had renamed the territory of West New Guinea. The sacred duty to free West Irian became an excuse for growing domestic poverty and maladministration—a permanent diversion to make the Indonesian people forget their empty rice bowls and other grievances.

No doubt the Dutch realized that their refusal to yield was helping Soekarno rather than hindering him, but they were caught in the proverbial cleft stick. If they got out, they lost all foothold in South-East Asia and could expect no advantage from any change in government or in the constitutional structure of the Republic. If they stayed, there was always hope that the disruptive forces of administrative inefficiency and economic distress would outweigh the cohesive effects of the West Irian bogey which Soekarno's propaganda conjured up.

So the Dutch set about designing the democratic décor of a model colony being prepared for democratic self-determination. When plans to help the unfortunate refugees went awry, they concentrated attention on good works for the indigenes.

Between 1945 and 1957, the public health services made admirable progress and a workable scheme for training native medical assistants for field service was started. But the benefits were confined mainly to the coast. As yet no serious effort had been made to open up the highlands where more than half the population lived. It was not until 1958 that small administration teams moved into the Grand and Baliem valleys, an area not unlike the heavily populated Mount Hagen-Chimbu region of Australian New Guinea, and began pacifying the warlike tribes there. Even then, few resources were diverted inland. Dutch policy differed from the Australian. The objective of the Dutch was to concentrate on the coast and to consolidate its settlements before worrying about the highlands—just as they were interested in creating a native élite rather than equality of social development as a foundation on which to build the autonomous West New Guinea State.

From the outset, they put emphasis on post-primary and secondary education. By 1961, a small number of West New Guinean students was attending universities in Holland. Nothing specific was done to encourage or discourage native participation in commerce, but when all hope of keying the colony's economy to the skills of Eurasian migrants had to be abandoned, the Dutch moved into their own crash programme of native development, mainly in politics.

Since van Eechoud's day, unofficial village councils operated in more advanced areas such as the Vogelkop—much as they had done in Hubert Murray's Papua—but not until 1959 was a local government with real powers officially constituted. This happened on Biak when a regional council elected on manhood suffrage administered the affairs of about 30,000 people. The following year, a similar council was established on the island of Japen, and others thereafter functioned on the mainland.

A faster pace had been set in educating New Guineans for administrative work. In 1957, when Dr T. H. Bot was appointed Secretary of State for New Guinea, about 30 per cent of Government posts in the colony were held by New Guineans. This was an immeasurably higher proportion than in Australian New Guinea, where in spite of a progressive official policy any moronic European was still more trusted and better paid than a highly intelligent native performing comparable duties much more efficiently. By 1961, more than half the public service jobs in Dutch New Guinea had been taken over by indigenes. They were, of course, in the lower echelons; for the Dutch—like the British and unlike the Australians—required sound academic qualifications before appointing men to positions of real authority in their colonial service.

In the same year, the Dutch Parliament passed legislation providing for the election in 1961 of a New Guinea Council, a body ultimately intended to comprise forty-eight members elected on common roll franchise. On 5 April, the first session was inaugurated with twenty-eight members, of whom two were directly elected by ballot to represent the sophisticated Hollandia and Manokwari constituencies, fourteen were chosen by electoral colleges (fifty voters choosing one elector and these electors in turn choosing the Council member), ten were appointed by the Governor to represent primitive areas not able to vote, and two were official European nominees. Although the real power remained with the Governor and the Council of Heads of Departments (something like the Australian Territory's Executive Council), this was a step which went a good deal further towards providing representative government than any move the Australians had yet made. An indigenous majority existed in the first quasi-legislative body in West New Guinea—and the Dutch had taken the risk, tongue in cheek, of giving assurance that any native representative who favoured union with Indonesia would be heard and his arguments considered without prejudice to his position.

It is convenient at this point to pause to explain why the Dutch embarked upon almost reckless acceleration of political reform.

In 1952, the Dutch Parliament had amended the Constitution to incorporate West New Guinea in the Kingdom of the Netherlands, thus finally closing the door on further direct negotiation with Indonesia on the status of the territory.

Indonesia then carried the dispute to the United Nations, arguing her claims on legal grounds but nevertheless making it clear that legalism was subservient to political compulsion. The Dutch must at all costs be dislodged from their last relic of empire. Anything less represented an affront to Indonesia's pride and a threat to Indonesia's security. The matter was debated in the General Assembly three times between 1954 and 1957. On each occasion, the Indonesians failed to obtain the two-thirds majority necessary to give United Nations backing to their claim. And on each occasion, the Australian representative supported Holland in the contention that the Indonesian claim had not ethnical, legal or moral validity.

It was easy to justify this attitude on moral grounds. Why should the Indonesian Government, pitifully incapable of discharging its responsibilities to the multi-racial elements within the existing Republic, be given control additionally of 700,000 hapless primitives?

The ethnical and legal grounds on which the Indonesians based their case were at least more debatable, but they are hardly worth enumeration because morality, legality and ethnic considerations did not play any part in the ultimate solution of the problem. Indonesia refused an offer to have the case tried by the International Court, so that in the long run power politics alone decided the issue.

Australia was alarmed by the prospect of Indonesia gaining a footing on what it regarded, in an archaic military concept, as a springboard for any Asian invasion of the continent. The Menzies Government therefore continued to make encouraging noises to the Dutch without, apparently, any intention of supporting them if it came to the sticking point.

After failure in 1957 to obtain United Nations backing, Indonesia expropriated and nationalized whatever industrial and commercial properties the Dutch retained in the Republic. Still The Hague refused to budge. The only means now left to the Indonesians of pressing their claim was outright military action. Soekarno would probably have taken such a course there and then, but he now found himself with a right-wing revolt on his hands in Sumatra and later in the Celebes. The risings were caused by long-standing local dissatisfaction with the centralization of power in Jakarta and by inclusion of the Communist Party in the Councils of the Central Government, which had become a mere front for the dictatorship that Soekarno euphemistically called 'guided democracy'.

It took nearly three years to quell the Sumatra rebellion— again by methods of intrigue and counter-intrigue rather than by military action. But when it was quelled, Soekarno again needed to use the red herring of West Irian.

By this time, the Indonesians were putting mild pressure on Canberra, for they had become fully aware of the Australian anxiety to project a favourable image in Asia at almost any cost short of modifying their 'White Australia' policy excluding coloured immigrants. Indonesian politicians had repeatedly pledged that they would never go beyond peaceful means of finding a solution to the West Irian problem, but at the same time the Republican Government began a military build-up with Soviet help.

In 1957, the Australian Cabinet had agreed that Holland and the Commonwealth should co-operate in the administration of their New Guinea territories, but had reached no agreement on co-operation in political development. Furthermore, the Australians had rejected tentative suggestions that the two metropolitan powers should work towards a perfectly logical long-term aim—political union of the whole of the island.

The Dutch should surely by now have read the writing on the wall. Its message was even more clear in 1959 when the Minister for External Affairs, Mr R. G. Casey (later Lord Casey of Berwick) said that, although Australia still supported the Dutch attitude, it would not oppose any agreement to change the status of West New Guinea that was 'reached between the two parties by peaceful processes and in accordance with internationally accepted principles'.

In 1960, as soon as the last of the Sumatra trouble had been cleared up, Indonesia severed diplomatic relations with Holland and placed a large arms order with Russia. The following year, the Chief of Staff of the Indonesian Army, General Nasution, visited Australia and gave fresh assurances that the Republic would not resort to armed force. In March of the same year, however, the United States gave a small but pointed indication of its attitude by declining an invitation to be represented at the opening of the New Guinea Council.

This was the beginning of the end. The Americans—whose diplomacy in South-East Asia had failed to stem the rising tide of Communist influence because of a stubborn propensity for propping up corrupt, inefficient and reactionary regimes—had decided that it was necessary to appease Soekarno once more. If they did not do so, they felt, he might in desperation be forced to abandon the neutralist attitude which had hitherto given him such immense bargaining power and go openly into the arms of the Russians. Preparations were now undoubtedly being made to sell out Holland on the same 'internationally accepted principles' which had substituted a Javanese dictatorship in the Indies for Dutch colonialism.

The Indonesians began to concentrate troops and naval forces in areas adjacent to West New Guinea. Holland made a last attempt to avert the final humiliation. Its Foreign Minister, Dr J. Luns, told the United Nations General Assembly that his Government would be willing to transfer powers in West New Guinea to an agency of the United Nations which was willing to take over the preparation of the people for self-determination.

Indonesia opposed the offer with the old argument that West Irian was legally part of a Republic which had already fought for self-determination and won it. A group of African nations put forward a compromise plan, but their suggestion that a Commission examine the possibility of interim international control while negotiations were resumed between the disputants was defeated in the General Assembly. Holland then withdrew the Luns plan, and prepared for the inevitable.

Late in 1961, Soekarno abandoned all pretence of finding a peaceful solution. He warned the Republic to prepare for general mobilization and began moving front-line aircraft to forward bases.

At this stage, Australia's new Minister for Foreign Affairs, Sir Garfield Barwick (who had now succeeded Casey after his retirement from politics and elevation to the Peerage) clearly hinted that his Government had no intention of supporting Holland with anything more substantial than words. He issued an official statement early in the new year. Boiled down, this merely said that 'Australia did not underestimate the value of Indonesian friendship' and referred to a continuation of peaceful relations between Indonesia and the Netherlands. Ten days later, Prime Minister Menzies stated bluntly that Australia would not help the Dutch without assurance of support from the United States and Great Britain. The Australian Government, still believing itself to be substantially dependent on the United States for defence, apparently decided it was safer to invite Indonesian contempt than to provoke Indonesian hostility by offering the Dutch military aid.

The truth of the matter was that Indonesia was in no condition to launch a full-scale military invasion of West New Guinea without further Russian backing; but she was in a position to launch and sustain a war of petty infiltration which would have cost the Dutch more to contain than the colony obviously was now worth. It remained only to find a formula for disengagement in which some shreds of Dutch dignity could be preserved.

But the formula was not easily forthcoming. Soekarno, determined to give a colour of martial purpose and valour to the victory he had won by diplomatic manoeuvre, ordered naval patrols to enter West New Guinea waters. Dutch frigates spotted the force, sank one patrol boat and captured the second-in-command of the Indonesian Navy, Commodore J. Sudarso.

On 24 January, 1962, Soekarno ordered general mobilization, but he still did not launch an all-out attack. There was no need to risk the humiliation of being roundly beaten by the Dutch when the game was already won.

On 25 February, the United States Attorney General, Mr Robert Kennedy, on a visit to The Hague told the Dutch that his Government would not promise to support them if the Indonesians invaded.

Early in March, Soekarno announced that negotiations with the Dutch were imminent. (He had previously stated that negotiation would only be undertaken if Indonesia could be assured beforehand of their outcome.)

Ambassador Ellsworth Bunker, a veteran of American diplomacy in Asia, was chairman of the formal exploratory talks, which were held under United Nations auspices. Even while they were proceeding, Indonesian infiltrators landed by sea on the island of Waigeo and on the south coast of the mainland and paratroopers were dropped at numerous points near the settlements. The Dutch garrisons with native help had little difficulty in rounding up and capturing most of the bewildered and militarily incompetent invaders.

In August, 1962, after months of bickering and dickering, Bunker's prefabricated diplomacy won the day. The Kingdom of the Netherlands and the Republic of Indonesia signed an agreement under which administrative responsibility in West New Guinea was transferred to a United Nations Temporary Executive Authority. At the discretion of the Administrator of this Authority, the functions of government could be handed over to the Republic at any time after 1 May, 1963. The agreement also provided that the New Guineans should be given an opportunity to say, by general plebiscite not later than 31 December, 1969, whether they wished to remain under the control of the Indonesian Republic. Soekarno had been prepared to make this gesture as a sop to the sensibilities of those who still believed in the principle of self-determination, for he well knew that he could renounce it just as easily as he had renounced many of the other undertakings he had given to win a political point.

Despite blatant Indonesian agitation to obtain authority over the territory even earlier than had been agreed, UNTEA remained in West New Guinea until 1 May. The administrative team of seventy-eight officials representing twenty-seven countries succeeded admirably in its task of preserving order while the Dutch got out and the Indonesians came in. If the United Nations men did not manage altogether to soothe the trepidation of natives who had been subjected to intense anti-Indonesian propaganda by the Dutch, they at least sublimated it.

The Indonesian flag was raised at Hollandia on 1 May without incident, and members of a puppet People's Regional Council of West Irian took the oath of allegiance to the Republic. The Council comprised thirty-eight nominated members, of whom five were appointed to the Indonesian Parliament and six to the Peoples' Consultative Congress, a presidential advisory body.

West Irian had been 'liberated'. It was time for Soekarno to find another diversionary adventure in xenophobia. He was to find it in Malaysia, but how that came about is beyond the scope of this book.

When Indonesia had swallowed up Dutch New Guinea, people who believed in the ability of Western civilization to build a bridge between the Stone Age and modern times and to lead 3,000,000 New Guineans across it, were critical of Holland's failure to begin an intensive social development programme in the territory until the mid-1950s. But if a ruthlessly realistic examination of the situation were made, could it be said that the people of eastern New Guinea would in the long run be better off because the Australians had begun their New Deal about ten years earlier? Or could it be claimed with any confidence that the future of eastern New Guineans was brighter and more assured than the future of the tribes over the border?

The Australians had been more diligent in suppressing savagery, in increasing the population and in offering economic motives for change. On the other hand, the Dutch had produced by rough-and-ready and often hastily improvised methods at least a few New Guineans with relative competence in politics who were genuine and effective proselytes of nationalism.

In either case, the achievement was miniscule in the historical if not the moral sense. As a result of Holland's traditional involvement in Asian politics, the Dutch had been forced to abandon their experiment in cultivating civilization in the New Guinea hothouse.

The Australians had pretended for a long time that they were not involved in Asian politics—except possibly to pass themselves off as hearty, good fellows in search of Asian friends—and as a result they found themselves stuck with a similar experiment which was rapidly becoming too expensive and perilous to continue.

What would happen if Soekarno, or some other Asian demagogue in need of a diversionary crusade against the hated whites, were to threaten the de-colonization of Australian New Guinea by force?

Prime Minister Menzies, boldly categorical when Indonesian pressure had been switched from the Dutch in New Guinea to the newly independent federation of Malaysia, assured the concerned Australian electorate that his Government would defend Papua-New Guinea against attack as if

P

it were the Australian mainland. But what if the United States would not or could not underwrite that defence? Might not Sir Robert Menzies or his successor have to bow to 'the hard facts of international life', in exactly the same way as the Dutch had had to bow to them when the Prime Minister coined that phrase to excuse his withdrawal of the Australian support he had pledged to Holland all through the 1950s?

These questions occupied the minds of all who attempted to analyse or predict political trends in the Western Pacific after Soekarno had destroyed the last vestiges of Dutch influence in South-East Asia and turned his attention to destroying the residue of British influence in Malaysia.

In 1964, Indonesian opposition to Malaysia amounted to undeclared war. Guerrillas, saboteurs and political agitators crossed the frontier in Borneo and paratroops and seaborne forces landed on the Malay peninsula itself. In the effort to destroy the Malaysian federation and swallow its parts piecemeal, Soekarno was repeating the tactics he had used to clinch his victory in West Irian.

By this time, the Americans—heavily committed to the containment of Communism in Indo-China—had come to realize that appeasement would not necessarily prevent or much delay the growth of Communist influence within the chaotically disordered but still belligerent Indonesian Republic far to the rear. They were not prepared to write off the West's political and economic assets in Malaysia nearly as readily as they had been willing to write off the valueless swamps, jungles and mountains of West Irian. Their hope was shaken that Soekarno would hang himself if given enough time to make the rope, and be replaced by a moderate government. By the middle of 1964, the United States Government had indicated its unqualified disapproval of Indonesia's 'confrontation' of its neighbour. As signatory to the ANZUS pact, it supported the earlier Menzies declaration that Australian New Guinea would be defended as vigorously as if it were part of Australia; and when Malaysia brought the Indonesian invasions to the attention of the Security Council of the United Nations, it supported a motion condemning and deploring these acts of aggression. The Russians vetoed the passage of the motion, but as Soekarno did not attract backing from other members of the Afro-Asian bloc his cause suffered a sobering diplomatic defeat in the debate.

The United Kingdom, as sponsor of Malaysia, allotted additional troops, ships and aircraft to help defend its territories, and Australia and New Zealand made token contributions to these forces.

For the time being, fear was allayed that Indonesian infiltrators would move into eastern New Guinea and begin a campaign of 'liberation' there. But the basic situation remained unchanged. In its extraordinary political creation— the Papua-New Guinea House of Assembly—Australia had provided the means by which indigenous politicians could ask for independence whenever they were moved to do so, and with at least a semblance of expressing the sentiments of the tribes which they were elected to represent.

The questions which remained unanswered at the end of 1964 were these: How soon would the demand for independence come? And when it came, how quickly would Australia be prepared to accede to it?

12

The Enduring Difference

EARLY in December, 1964, the first authoritative estimate of the amount of money needed to found a self-supporting economy in New Guinea—an economy capable of generating public revenue to pay for administration, public services and development in the governmental sector—was officially disclosed by the new Australian Minister for Territories, Mr Barnes.

One of the recommendations of the Foot report had been that the International Bank for Reconstruction and Development should be invited to survey the economic potential of the Territory and make recommendations to assist the Government in planning a programme which would make possible the evolution of a self-supporting national community.

The invitation was issued and a World Bank mission conducted the survey in 1963. Its 430-page report, released about a year after field investigations were complete, was a thorough analysis of the Territory's unsatisfactory economic position. It suggested that this might be improved by the adoption of a Five-Year Plan under which the Administration would raise its spending to an average of £50.2 million a year, of which 27.5 per cent would derive from local revenue. Thus Australians would have to find in grants or loans £36.4 million a year, compared with £28 million in 1964-5.

There was no suggestion in the report, however, that such an increase in public spending would prove a panacea. The Bank's investigators pointed out that, given public spending on this scale, 'substantial economic growth is possible over the next five to ten years but economic viability in any meaningful sense will take several decades'.

216

With education and training [their report continued], the indigenous people can take an increasing role in the economy and government, and the natural resources of the Territory are considerable. However, the moulding of the human and natural resources into a modern economy will take great effort, time and money. Financial support from Australia—which now covers two-thirds of the Territory's expenditures—will need to be continued and even increased.

The Bank recommended an effort to double the acreage of major crops within ten years, to increase cattle herds ten-fold, and to increase timber production nearly fourfold within five years.

Clearly expansion of such magnitude would require substantial investment of private as well as Government money —and here the Bank's experts were frank. They wrote:

> The confidence of the European has been shaken by political developments in countries in the surrounding area, by uncertainties about the political future of the Territory, and about their own role in it. . . . One of the immediate difficulties facing the Territory in achieving the level of investment required to sustain a modern economy is an outflow of capital estimated at £3 million to £5 million a year.

If the Australian Government could stabilize confidence, they continued, European investors (largely Australian) should be prepared to reinvest locally a substantial proportion of their profits, but even if this were achieved, much more than a ploughing back of profits would be necessary to create a viable productive base. Substantial fresh private investment would be necessary to expand proven or promising industries and this might be stimulated by a revision of tariff policies and a provision of tax incentives.

Early in May, 1965, the Minister for Territories made an official statement in Canberra to the effect that the Commonwealth Government endorsed the objectives of the report and accepted its specific programmes on increased agricultural production as a working basis for planning in the Territory. The Government recognized, he said, that a realistic developmental programme would involve increased Commonwealth financial assistance and that total public expenditure could

reach £300 million over the next five years, including alloca-
tions for defence and civil aviation.

The Minister did not, however, commit the Government
to any specific development projects. He merely indicated
acceptance of the principles stated in the report, concurred
with its view that expansion in secondary, technical and
higher education must have high priority, and commented
that the rate of expansion of such activities as curative health
services, primary education, public utilities and general Government services should be related to the Territory's capacity
to contribute towards them.

The Australian Financial Review's account of the Minister's statement was perceptively headlined: "New Guinea
Program Still Obscure". But there was nothing obscure about
his estimate that implementation of the plans the Government had formulated would require the recruitment of an
additional 2,000 public servants from outside the Territory,
including about 500 qualified agricultural, livestock and
forestry officers, and 500 teachers for Administration secondary schools. How these experts were to be found in Australia,
where the shortage of teachers and technicians was then critical, was not revealed.

Nor was there anything obscure about Mr Barnes's remark
at a press conference following the release of his statement.
He was reported to have said that *the Government did not
believe that self-determination should wait until the Territory had a fully viable economy.* The hollow mockery of independence without viability, which Paul Hasluck rejected
only eighteen months previously, was now apparently to be
countenanced.

In assessing the real meaning of the World Bank report,
it should be kept clearly in mind that the mission was
emphatic that Commonwealth financial aid to the Territory
would not in itself cure the region's economic troubles.
Private investment was equally important, and private investment would be attracted 'only if political uncertainties could
be resolved'. Unhappily, events during the first year of life
for the Papua-New Guinea House of Assembly tended to increase rather than decrease those uncertainties.

From the viewpoint of the Western democracies, the political situation in South-East Asia had deteriorated rapidly. Indonesia, with moral and material support from both Russia and China, intensified hostilities against Malaysia. President Soekarno, realizing that he could expect no further economic aid from the West, withdrew from the United Nations and moved openly towards the Asian Communist camp.

Relations between Jakarta and Canberra worsened. A small force of Australian combat troops was despatched to the Sarawak frontier to help defend it against Indonesian guerrillas, so that for the first time Australian and Indonesian soldiers now faced one another as 'shooting' enemies.

At the same time the United States, which had for ten years been supporting a series of corrupt, inefficient and unpopular (but anti-Communist) governments in South Vietnam, suffered serious reverses. The Viet Cong insurgents, increasingly supported by men and material supplies from Communist North Vietnam, brought the Saigon Government's American-trained and American-equipped armies to the brink of demoralization and collapse. In a desperate effort to defend what little remained of their prestige and influence on the South-East Asian mainland, the United States began aerial bombardment of military bases and communications centres in North Vietnam, and committed regiments of Marines to ground operations against the Viet Cong.

The alarming turmoil in the populous world just to the north of the empty Australian continent forced the Menzies Government into another agonizing reappraisal of its defence situation. Although some consolation might be found in the fact that no potential Asian aggressor as yet possessed the naval power to launch a serious invasion of the Australian mainland, it was amply clear that the Commonwealth lacked the military resources to command from any hostile Asian nation the slightest respect for its views or interests.

Once more Australia's political leaders were forced to acknowledge that the integrity of their prosperous but sprawling and immature nation could be defended only with the aid of powerful friends.

The Menzies administration came to the decision that it must at last change its policy of courting Asian goodwill at almost any cost and throw in its lot with the unpopular

Americans. It dispatched a battalion of Australian combat troops to serve with the United States forces in South Vietnam, although it must have been fully aware that this action would provoke a contemptuous and hostile reaction from uncommitted Afro-Asian Powers, contribute little to the assault on the Vietnamese insurgents, and in all probability nullify whatever favourable impression had been created by years of benevolence in New Guinea and by enthusiastic contributions to the Colombo Plan for economic and technical aid in South-East Asia.

Little indeed appeared on the international scene during 1964 and the first half of 1965 which would tempt private investors to commit themselves to long-term projects in New Guinea.

Nor was the New Guinea domestic political situation much more reassuring.

In May, 1965, delegations of Japanese and Australian businessmen discussed in Tokyo the possibility of Japanese capitalists participating in the exploitation of New Guinea's natural resources—mainly in timber and fisheries. The Japanese suggested that they might be more attracted to the field if, in view of the notorious inefficiency of indigenous labour, Australian immigration laws were modified to permit their own nationals to be temporarily employed in the Territory as key technicians and skilled workers. The Minister for Territories, on a brief visit to Papua-New Guinea, told newspaper reporters that he thought consideration should be given to such a revision, without which the Japanese might be reluctant to commit their money. The matter was, however, discussed in the Australian House of Representatives on 18 May when the Prime Minister was reported to have directed the Minister for Territories on how to reply to an Opposition questioner. *The Age* in Melbourne next day quoted Sir Robert Menzies as saying to Mr Barnes: 'There is to be no immigration of Japanese—you had better make that clear.'

The crippling delicacy of the balance between political practicability and commercial commonsense was thus demonstrated once more. And even political practicability was becoming harder to measure by the old paternal standards.

Within months of its inauguration, the New Guinea House

of Assembly—illiterate, unrepresentative and bewildered though most of its members were—began to reflect the race tensions and dissatisfactions which had always existed but which had hitherto found no open avenue of expression.

As one of its first major 'legislative' acts, the House voted to dissociate the public service of Papua-New Guinea from the public service of Australia—although it realized that the dissociation would almost certainly be vetoed by the Commonwealth Government. Native members expressed bitter resentment of economic discrimination between the races when the Administration announced a differential salary scale for indigenous and expatriate civil servants. A young Papua public servant, Oala Oala Rarua, prominent in the establishment of the Territory's first labour organization, the Papua-New Guinea Workers' Federation, commented on the differential wages scale in an article for the quarterly magazine *New Guinea*. He wrote:

> The majority of Australians who come up to the Territory are the wrong types, who would find it hard to get the sort of money or job they are doing here if they remained in Australia. . . . They are reluctant to train Papuans and New Guineans to take over their jobs because they would lose everything if they did.

Differences of opinion on New Guinea policy also became apparent in Australia.

In mid-April, 1965, the deputy leader of the Federal Opposition, Mr Gough Whitlam, speaking at a seminar on the World Bank report organized by the Council of New Guinea Affairs, presumably reflected the views of an influential section of the Australian Labor Party when he said: 'Most countries would say it would be improper for Australia to rule New Guinea after 1970. I think it would not be to Australia's or New Guinea's advantage to prolong this (political control) beyond 1970.'

Mr Whitlam added that in his opinion the next House of Assembly, due to be elected in 1968, would secure self-government. This idea, he said, might upset some Australians in New Guinea who could feel that their good work in the Territory had been wasted.

In reply, Mr Ian Downs, a prominent white member of the House of Assembly, said that in his view independence for New Guinea by 1970 was not soon enough. Many whites in New Guinea would be appalled at the thought that it could not take place sooner.

When these statements were reported in Australian newspapers, the Minister for Territories told political correspondents that Australia would not hang back from granting independence to Papua-New Guinea when the people wanted it, but there was a widespread feeling among them that they were not yet ready for self-government. A few days later, M. Andre Naudy, leader of the 1965 United Nations Visiting Mission, also commented that there seemed to be fear of the future among local leaders and lack of confidence in their own ability to govern. Nevertheless, the House of Assembly in May, 1965, appointed a committee to begin the work of drafting a Papua-New Guinea Constitution.

What factor will carry most weight in determining the time when the restless Parliament of a Thousand Tribes will ask for real power? Will lack of self-confidence delay their demand, or will the native dislike of alien domination precipitate it?

Native dislike of alien domination is indisputable, even though it is difficult to generalize fairly about sentiments and attitudes in groups of people as varied in character and experience as the present-day New Guinea tribes. The belief, widely held in Australia, that most natives have come to regard white men as friends anxious to help and protect them, and lead them to a better life, is far from justified. It derives from propaganda that the Australian Government's policy in the country has been an almost unqualified success story. The truth is different. In fact, it is probably true to say that the more contact the tribes have with Europeans the more they tend to resent them.

In newly explored and pacified districts, the Administration officer—the *kiap*—is first accepted because he cannot be resisted. He is welcomed because he brings new magic, physical security the people have never known and emancipation from the gross fears and suffering with which primitive men in their natural state continually live. The confusions, doubts and inward conflict caused by a gradual destruction of the old social order come later.

In districts where the rule of civilized law has prevailed for several decades, the dominance of Europeans is resented; but it has been regarded until very recently as beyond challenge.

To some degree the resentment arises from bitter memories of the days when all 'masters' were arrogant and some brutal, and when all 'boys' were subject to humiliation and exploitation ranging from the gross to the petty. This belongs to the past, but the chief cause of resentment is the natives' realization of the inequality between the races which exists in the present.

Unhappily this inequality cannot be legislated out of existence, nor can it be removed by education of the individual alone. It will be resolved only by deep and unavoidably slow social change. It is an inequality in the material and spiritual condition of two societies, one of which is still virtually in the Stone Age and the other the heir to centuries of complex civilization. Only the vast disparity between the races in New Guinea has prevented conflicts such as the Maori, American Indian or African wars of the nineteenth century. The New Guinea tribes have not mounted serious resistance to white infiltration of their country simply because they have lacked the organizational and technical capacity to do so.

No one would wish to disparage the ingenuity and the humanitarian motivation of Hubert Murray's system of penetration and pacification by patrol, but it must be conceded that it would not have been practicable if the tribes had been able to combine against it or, indeed, if any individual tribe had been numerically strong enough to compensate for its inferiority in weapons. Similarly, many of the Cult outbreaks would surely have ended in bloody racial conflict if New Guineans had had the capacity to express in effective physical terms their emotional hostility to white domination.

Today however, for the political and moral reasons already discussed in this study, the Australian Government has committed itself to an intensive effort to reduce the inequality between the races—to teach the indigenous peoples new skills and the value of inter-tribal co-operation. It has made measurable progress with the task but it would, I believe, be over-optimistic to claim that it has at the same time effected much change in the basic emotional attitude of each race to the other.

Europeans living in New Guinea are, with few exceptions, just as firmly convinced of their innate race superiority as they ever were. They have merely moderated the blatancy with which they once expressed the conviction, and have generally accepted the ethic that the superior have an obligation to lift up the inferior. Again with few exceptions, they have no more understanding of the native mentality or morality than their predecessors. Irrespective of their productivity—which is, admittedly, usually if by no means invariably higher than that of natives—they expect and get economic preferment. They cannot and do not accept even educated natives as social equals. Intermarriage is discouraged and less common than it is in other parts of the Pacific, or in Asia and Africa. It might even be argued from the comparative rarity of miscegenation that the races are sexually antipathetic. While it is true that mutual respect, trust and friendship exist between individuals, the white minority and the brown majority live in emotionally uneasy symbiosis. Sophisticated New Guineans are aware of the European attitude and resent it without much intellectual appreciation of the cause. At least a proportion of white sophisticates are aware of the natives' attitude and realize the danger of the situation for both races when political education of the élite has created an instrument by which popular sentiment can be clearly and effectively expressed.

Legislators at all levels have tried hard by reducing legal discriminations to soften the natives' mute discontent with their inferior status. Public transport, places of entertainment, schools, sporting organizations and official functions have been 'desegregated'. In some cases, the zeal for egalitarianism has been carried to ludicrous and self-defeating lengths. In 1963, the Legislative Council repealed an Ordinance which had made it unlawful, from the earliest days of colonization, to supply intoxicating drink to natives. It was argued that the Ordinance was being evaded and that, in any case, it was an odious and deeply resented discrimination. The advo-

cates of repeal claimed that the change would most powerfully persuade New Guineans that the Administration was
sincere in offering them civil equality.

There can be no doubt that prohibition had been resented
by male natives living and working near large settlements;
but the majority of the population—the 'bush kanakas' whose
inarticulate existence so many resident bureaucrats and touring politicians ignore—were indifferent to repeal for the
sufficient reason that the cash earnings of any villager in a
year would hardly be enough to stand a single round of drinks
in the tribal clubhouse! The change therefore was an attempt
to appease a resentment cherished only among an urban
minority. Inevitably it backfired.

The first weeks of liquor reform at Port Moresby, Rabaul
and Lae—the settlements chiefly affected—provided the sad
spectacle of half-clothed, undernourished, illiterate and self-
conscious native labourers mobbing bars to spend their wages
or their small savings on a subdued but earnest drinking bout
from which only the Australian excise authorities and the
publicans derived any profit whatsoever.

Some hotel keepers mercifully tried to temper the impact
of the newly conferred freedom-to-get-drunk-and-incapable by
insisting that all their customers wear shoes. This was not an
unofficial means test or an insistence on decorum, but a
humane insurance against customers gashing their feet on
fragments of broken glasses and bottles strewn on floors covered with spittle and vomit. Probably the only satisfaction
which long-sighted legislators could have found in detached
observation of early reactions to liquor 'reform' was in the
commercial nous shown by a few shrewd native operators.
They invested in trade store shoes and rented them out at a
modest but profitable fee to compatriots who wanted to experience the ecstasy of getting drunk both publicly and
legally. Here surely was evidence that seeds of financial
acumen were hidden in the compost of a maddeningly unac-
quisitive, profligate people!

Soon, of course, the novelty wore off and the early excesses
diminished. But even the most moderate drinking of expensive, highly-taxed beer or spirits gravely affected the economic
position of urban families in which the breadwinner earned

no more than £3 or £4 a week. Wheaten bread is the staple food of urban New Guineans who are unable to cultivate gardens or fish and hunt, and in the months which followed the abolition of the liquor restrictions sales of bread by bakeries supplying the native market sharply declined. Native women were quick to complain to the Administration and to mission welfare organizations that their men were spending their money on drink and not giving them enough to buy food for themselves and their children. Administration spokesmen hardily replied that in a democracy the remedy lay with the women and not with the Government; Australian women often had to deal with similar problems. What they failed to point out was that the average Australian bread-winner earned about seven times a New Guinea urban worker's wages, and that the price of beer and spirits in New Guinea was considerably higher than it was in Australia.

The reform of the liquor law simply meant that natives were given the legal right to buy a drug which they could not afford but which white men were rich enough to use copiously. Far from diffusing the outlines of the 'colour bar', it brought into sharp focus its real substance—the social incompatibility and economic inequality of the races at their present stage of development. When natives were admitted to bars, the immediate reaction of Europeans was to retreat either to their clubs or to hotel lounges. In time, this segregated drinking became a little less pronounced as a mere matter of convenience; but segregated drinking is still a custom which the races themselves voluntarily observe, and it will continue the custom until hearts are as greatly changed as the statute books.

There are many people who sincerely believe that accelerated education and increased technical and economic aid will reduce native resentment and distrust of white management to such degree that a demand for political independence will be almost indefinitely delayed. They hold that the average New Guinean knows which side his bread is buttered on. Furthermore, tribal antipathies are being resolved so slowly that for several generations at least the impartial rule of Australians will seem to the aggregated minorities preferable to government by an artificially created élite dominated by representatives of larger and more advanced groups such as the Tolais or the Sepiks.

Those who take this viewpoint overestimate, I think, the power of education and the prevalence of commonsense among primitives. How heavily resentment of alien domination outweighs all material considerations, and how slowly formal education works in undermining it, was strikingly illustrated by the behaviour of Nauru Islanders in negotiations with the Australian Government in 1964.

Nauru is not part of the New Guinea archipelago. It lies on the equator several hundred miles to the east of the Territory's maritime boundary. It has always been administered separately, but it has in miniature posed somewhat similar problems in race relationship. Before the coming of white men in the middle of the nineteenth century, twelve tiny tribes or clans on the island were continually waging bloody feuds with one another and were regarded as fierce and skilful warriors by their more easy-going neighbours of the Gilbert and Ellice archipelagos. Early contact with whalers and traders produced the usual lamentable results, and in 1888 Germany annexed Nauru, suppressed the tribal fighting and arrested depopulation. In 1900, enormous deposits of phosphate were discovered on the island and were worked by the Anglo-German Pacific Phosphate Company until 1919 when German interests were expropriated and control was assumed by a Phosphates Commission appointed by the British, Australian and New Zealand Governments.

Under white rule, the material condition of Nauruans improved considerably, even though they did not play any part in the exploitation of the great wealth discovered on their territory. Despite every pressure short of conscription, few would agree to work in any capacity at the mines and most clung stubbornly to their traditional occupations of gardening and fishing—which were now, of course, made much less physically exacting by European tools and technique.

At the end of the Second World War, a concentrated effort was made to educate Nauruans and prepare them for partnership in the modern world. The Commission paid a lump sum of £45 per acre to owners for the use of phosphate-bearing land and devised a complicated system of royalties which provided all natives with a current income, a savings fund, and a fund for their rehabilitation or resettlement elsewhere when the phosphate deposits were exhausted. It should be noted that mining operations were confined almost completely to the infertile centre of the island which had never been used for horticulture, and did not much diminish the area available to the inhabitants for the cultivation of food crops. The fertile land was a narrow ring of alluvial soil between the coral skin of the atoll and its rocky, barren heart, and was not seriously encroached upon by mining operations.

The commonly held idea that the phosphate miners have been engaged in 'removing the island bodily' and leaving the unfortunate natives without any means of subsistence is entirely incorrect. If damage was done to Nauruans it was done by paying them a dole in compensation for exploiting resources which they themselves had not the knowledge, skill nor any particular desire to tap. Instead of having to work for a living, they came passively to depend upon Government housing, imported foodstuffs and other commodities purchased from royalties. Their ancient skills declined through lack of stimulus.

In hope of countering this dole mentality, a vigorous education programme began in 1923, and since 1947 education (in English) has been compulsory for all children between five and seventeen years of age. Scholarships at Australian secondary schools have been available to practically every Nauruan child capable of passing the entrance examinations. Perhaps half a century of stability and intense economic development would be necessary before such a concentrated educational effort could be mounted in New Guinea.

In 1964, after long preliminary discussions, a delegation of Nauruan chiefs came to Australia to consider resettlement of their people when the phosphate deposits were worked out. The Commonwealth Government offered the islanders Curtis Island, a tract of land off the Queensland coast—in potential much more agriculturally productive than Nauru —and every assistance in resettling any Nauruans who wished to emigrate there. They were to have control of their own local government affairs and enjoy the benefits of full Australian citizenship, a status not yet offered even the aboriginal people of the Commonwealth, much less the natives of New Guinea.

The Nauruans, however, rejected this offer outright although its terms were in reality generous and would have given them the opportunity of genuine integration with the Australian population.

The fact was that the Nauruans did not wish to integrate with Australians. They demanded instead complete autonomy in their new home—and, of course, an Australian guarantee that the autonomy would be protected. The Federal Government, understandably enough, refused to cede sovereignty of a part of Australia under such conditions, and the Nauruans then declared that they would prefer to remain in their ancestral home and take their chances of survival when the royalties ceased. They suggested that the Phosphates Commission should reclaim the areas 'destroyed', by back-loading soil to cover the excavations and increase the arable acreage on their island—an imaginative but economically and scientifically ridiculous proposition. They furthermore demanded political independence by 1967.

More than forty years of intensive protection and education under forced draught had not equipped Nauruans emotionally to accept the proffered partnership with Australians. They openly voiced the suspicion that they would be the victims of race discrimination if they migrated to Australia.

It remains to be seen if, when royalties payments actually stop and the islanders must again work and fight to survive, the disdainful pensioners of the Australian conscience will still put independence above all material considerations; but their rejection of the Commonwealth offer was clear indication that where partnership between unequal and dissimilar cultures is mooted, the intellect proposes but the heart disposes. The Nauruans had been given the most intensive education and the most generous economic help ever provided a subject people in the Pacific. Every effort was made to assist their integration with Western civilization. Yet emotional considerations prompted them to reject the chance of relatively painless absorption by the dominant culture, and choose instead the perils and hardships of unviable independence.

There is little to suggest that New Guineans would make a different choice if a similar opportunity could be offered them.

Provided outside pressures do not greatly hasten—or retard —the pace of political development during the late 1960s, it is reasonable to expect that a political party favouring early severance from Australia will have been formed and have won representation in the Port Moresby legislature by 1968. This party will give expression to sentiment which all honest observers must admit exists in the islands but which has hitherto been inarticulate. Such a party will probably originate and find its greatest support in regions where contact between the races has been prolonged, such as New Britain, the Rai Coast and the districts about Port Moresby. It will also attract an enthusiastic—even fanatical—following in economically backward areas like New Ireland, Buka Island and the Gulf of Papua where the decay of the old social order has created 'Cult mentality'.

Hesitancy about early independence will probably be most marked in the highlands, where the contrast between the status of the races has not yet become offensively obvious. The highlanders tend to despise the coastal people, and they are unlikely to support readily any proposal for the formation of a national government dominated by educated sophisticates recruited mainly in Port Moresby and Rabaul.

Lack of unanimity among New Guineans about precisely when autonomy should come might well pose for Australian statesmen the trickiest problem of the disengagement planned by the Menzies Government from 1960 onward and, as Mr Whitlam's statement in 1965 indicated, tacitly approved by the Labor opposition. Some native factions will seek time to increase their political influence by advancing the argument that most New Guinea tribes are neither socially nor technologically ready for self-government and that disorders will follow transference of authority. This argument will be hard to refute. Moreover, despite Mr Ian Downs's view, most Europeans with an economic stake in the country will powerfully support, in Parliamentary lobbies and elsewhere, the native groups which favour delay in severance, and the repercussions on domestic policies in Australia could be considerable.

Even if internal dissension on such crucial issues is not confused by foreign interference, the role of the Australian Government as midwife to the new Pacific democracy will be particularly onerous because it has so deliberately hastened parturition, although it has so strenuously denied the intention of doing so.

However, it is probably too much to hope that the tribes of New Guinea will be left alone to sink their differences, acquire some sense of national unity and negotiate the timing and the terms of their independence in uncomplicated bilateral discussion.

The expulsion of the Dutch from the western half of the island ended all hope of creating an independent Melanesian Federation extending from Manokwari to the New Hebrides, and the manner in which the Dutch departure was engineered gave warning that Indonesia might well have ambitions to extend her sphere of influence into the South-West Pacific —using again the pretext of helping subject peoples to throw off the 'yoke of white colonialism'. Thus the emergence of any indigenous group demanding immediate independence or political severance from Australia by a fixed date will almost certainly signal the beginning of attempts by Indonesian agents to intervene in the domestic politics of eastern New Guinea.

Until the middle of 1965, the effect on tribal sentiment of the Indonesian takeover in West Irian can only be described as minimal. When the United Nations troops withdrew in 1963, there was at first a vague fear in border districts that a new Asian invasion was imminent and that the Australians might once again be forced to leave. A few hundred refugees —mainly unemployed house servants, labourers or villagers who had co-operated too eagerly with the Dutch in rounding up paratroopers in 1962—crossed into Australian territory, bringing with them tales of atrocities and reprisals. News of this movement of population was minimized and soon afterwards an outbreak of cholera on the Mimika Coast justified the closing of the frontier. In due course, the scare died down.

Four hundred miles of sparsely inhabited jungles, swamps and high mountain ranges still constituted a formidable no-man's-land through which neither news nor rumour travelled fast. Within a few months, the fact that the tribes west of the border now had Asian masters instead of the Dutch was virtually forgotten by most New Guinea villagers.

But if the momentous events in Hollandia made little impact among the border tribes, the Australian Administration on the other hand was sensitive to its new vulnerability —painfully aware that at some time in the future it might have to cope with infiltration by political agitators. Work on a few military airfields was accelerated, the establishment of the Pacific Islands Regiment was increased, and priority given to developmental projects in the Sepik Valley which might be expected to emphasize the benevolence of the Administration towards the people.

But these measures did not constitute a serious endeavour to put the Territory's defences in order. They could hardly be expected to count for much at the future stage of political development when factions favouring immediate independence come into conflict with those who oppose it.

When this conflict occurs, the Indonesians will have at least an opportunity to influence native sentiment by supporting the cause of the 'liberationists'. Should these liberationists be strongly resisted by cautious and conservative elements, so much the greater will be Indonesia's opportunity to intervene, advantageously from her point of view, and claim credit for having helped in the expulsion of the 'white exploiters'.

It is difficult for any dispassionate analyst of the contemporary New Guinea scene to conclude that the majority of native peoples, once they have the means of expressing their emotional attitudes in political terms, will be content to delay a demand for self-government until the far-distant time when they have the cultural, technical and economic resources to set up in business as a modern, enlightened State in loose partnership with Australia. Even if the present educational programme were greatly accelerated and could attain its most sanguine objectives, half a century or more would be needed to synthesize the commercial and administrative classes without which no modern, enlightened State can function. In any case, Australia could not wait so long. Virtually alone in a decolonized world—or, to be more precise, a world in which the domination of the weak by the strong has assumed new forms—Australia has neither the resources, the will nor the need to maintain what is now rapidly becoming a strategically and economically profitless salient in South-East Asia. Political withdrawal from New Guinea will long precede attainment of the lofty objectives formulated by the visionaries who launched the vast missionary enterprise of the New Deal after the Second World War.

What will happen to the people of New Guinea when they have demanded and won independence from Australia while still nationally unviable?

There is perhaps a remote chance that they will become the beneficiaries of some international agency created to assist backward peoples—an agency willing and able to take up the task of education and protection where Australia relinquished it under economic and political pressure. The creation of such an agency with the unanimous backing of the Great Powers would solve many of the tragic problems which have risen from the precipitate decolonization of parts of Africa and Asia. But it seems hopelessly unrealistic to expect unanimity among the Great Powers, now seeking to build new empires by process of ideological domination just as ruthlessly as ever they sought to dominate the weak by military might.

It is far more likely that in due course the people of eastern New Guinea will attach themselves politically and culturally to their Indonesian neighbours. The point has already been made that no ethnic link exists between them and that they are temperamentally dissimilar; but it is equally significant that the dissimilarity between New Guineans and Indonesians is immeasurably less than it is between New Guineans and Australians. Expressed in crude terms, the truth is that New Guineans would find it much easier to become 'apprentice Indonesians' than 'apprentice Australians'.

The Indonesian Republic is multi-lingual, multi-racial and multi-cultural, but it is an effective political entity although it embraces so many inconsistencies and inequalities. It has already survived appalling vicissitudes and it will probably continue to survive.

It is, I believe, natural and perhaps inevitable for the people of New Guinea to gravitate towards Indonesia when political severance from Australia has been effected. Some form of partnership with an emergent Asian Power would be psychologically more acceptable to New Guineans than an indefinite term as protégés of a nation whose ethos is incomprehensible to them. Under stimulation of the need to develop the more sophisticated forms of social and economic organization which are prerequisite to civilization, they would find Asian models far easier to imitate than Australian. The cells of South-East Asian society are not so rigidly limited in function, not so dependent for survival upon the existence of a strong and competent central authority, and not so closely integrated with the specialization of productive skills.

When New Guinea is given independence, it will certainly not inherit an informed, responsible and experienced central legislature, nor a permanent administration which is efficient by European standards. In time, and with luck in escaping the danger of being swallowed up by expanding Asia, New Guinea society will evolve these institutions; but the changes, if they are ever made, will be made from the bottom up rather than the top down, and in some form of junior partnership with an Asian nation which has recently taken the same difficult step up the evolutionary ladder.

In 1965, when the implications of early political independence for New Guinea were for the first time clear to the Australian public, the idea was widely canvassed that autonomy need not necessarily mean the precipitate withdrawal of large-scale economic assistance. Would it not be possible, the optimists asked, to allow New Guineans to govern themselves but at the same time to continue aid long enough to allow them to get on their feet administratively and achieve economic take-off? Both nations might benefit from such an arrangement. Australians could hope for a friendly, stable, new nation on their northern frontier, and New Guineans would have the chance to draw real dividends from the large investments of money, skill and effort made on their behalf between 1949 and the date of independence.

In theory this solution would appear ideal, but there must be grave doubts about its political practicality. Under what circumstances would the Australian electorate be prepared to continue a multi-million pound subsidy of a nation which had clamorously demanded—and won—the privileges of adulthood without anything like the capacity to shoulder its responsibilities?

Conceivably substantial aid would be forthcoming from Australia if the act of separation could be accomplished without racial resentments being brought to the forefront; but racial resentments will inevitably be the mainspring of any demand for independence made in the House of Assembly.

It is also conceivable that substantial aid would be forthcoming if South-East Asia achieved political stability, and Indonesia, Australia and the international agencies now concerned with the Trusteeship could agree upon a common developmental policy for the whole of the region; but political stability and common agreement are not yet even remotely in sight.

A third possibility is that Australia, for strategic advantages at present hard to imagine, would accord New Guinea the political machinery of independence but seek to manipulate that machinery by economic pressure. But to allow the hollow mockery of which Mr Hasluck once spoke so feelingly would be an enormously dangerous manoeuvre for a weak nation wishing to remain on good terms with increasingly powerful Asian neighbours.

In all the circumstances, therefore, the relatively rapid withdrawal of large Australian subsidies after independence seems much more likely. Having chosen deliberately but emotionally to cast loose from Australia, the Parliament of a Thousand Tribes will have to face up to the consequences, which include eventual re-alignment with neighbouring Asian Powers.

A hastily independent New Guinea can certainly not stand alone. Without authoritative guidance from some source for perhaps fifty years, it will revert to the savage disunity which was its condition when constructive European influence

began to assert itself less than eighty years ago. The processes
of reversion cannot be gauged even by drawing a parallel
from the painful history of decolonization in Africa, where
at least rudimentary commercial and professional classes had
evolved before the new nationalism took hold. The Congolese
are sophisticates compared with the Tolais.

I am aware that these predictions about the future of New
Guinea will appear as disappointing, alarming or even offensive to many Australians who have been personally or vicariously involved in the New Guinea experiment. They may
seem to imply the failure of a project in which there have
been strong elements of humanitarian responsibility and
generosity, and on which large sums of money and much
heroic effort have been—and are still being—expended.

But the realities cannot be baulked.

If the project of the New Deal was really to attempt the
miracle of transmogrifying a rabble of Mesolithic men into
a modern nation by forcible pacification, conversion and
education, then failure will be inevitable because the objective was absurd.

If, on the other hand, the project has been practically conceived as a withdrawal from an ultimately untenable situation—a withdrawal conducted in an orderly, peaceful manner and at an orderly, peaceful pace so that as few people as
possible are hurt in the process—then success may yet be
attained.

Much will depend upon the sagacity and courage of the
Australian statesmen who will have to deal with the clamor-
ous confusion which must inevitably precede separation.
They will need to preserve a fair balance between aggrega-
tions of conflicting interests, and between what is desirable
morally and what is practicable politically.

Much also will depend upon the ability of the Australian
electorate to accept the realities of the situation in New
Guinea without emotional overtones, and to acknowledge the
fact that New Guineans are not children adopted out of
charity from whom loyalty and obedience may justly be demanded by generous foster parents. The probability that
New Guineans will be forced to seek closer ties with Asia

than those which could be fabricated to bind them to Australia during more than half a century of master-servant, teacher-pupil association must also be recognized without resentment or recrimination if anything of that highly volatile asset, goodwill between dissimilar peoples, is to be preserved.

The lesson Australians should have learnt from administration of the New Guinea colony could be of incalculable value to an Occidental nation living under the shadow of resurgent Asia. This lesson is that Nature herself has attributed to the races of men differences and inequalities which only the infinitely slow processes of evolution can eliminate. Civilization cannot be imposed upon backward peoples by conquest, nor taught them by missionaries, moralists or educationalists. But the growth of civilization in retarded societies can undoubtedly be stimulated when advanced nations have the wisdom to treat them with true tolerance and offer in their dealings with them no affront to human dignity.

Melbourne
May, 1965

Bibliography

No definitive history of Papua-New Guinea and adjacent areas has been published in English up to the middle of 1965, and few attempts have been made to examine as a whole the impact upon the tribes of European colonization and the recent Indonesian suzerainty in the west. The most comprehensive general and historical survey was Gavin Souter's *New Guinea: The Last Unknown,* which was published by Angus and Robertson, Sydney, in 1963.

There is, however, a copious literature of memoirs by travellers, explorers, government servants and missionaries dating back to the mid-nineteenth century, and a number of noted anthropologists have published regional studies of great interest. A few political and sociological commentaries have appeared irregularly and in various forms since the end of the Second World War. In my bibliography I have culled heavily from this vast bulk of material.

Serious researchers will find essential information in:

Annual Reports of the Lieutenant-Governor of Papua, 1906-7 to 1940-1. Government Printer, Melbourne and Canberra.

Reports to the Council of the League of Nations on the Administration of the Territory of New Guinea, 1914-21 to 1941. Government Printer, Melbourne and Canberra.

Annual Reports on Papua-New Guinea, 1946 to date. Government Printer, Canberra.

Reports of the United Nations Visiting Missions to the Trust Territory of New Guinea, 1950 to date. U.N. Trusteeship Council, New York.

Handbook of the Territory of Papua compiled by the Hon. Staniforth Smith, 1907-27. Government Printer, Melbourne.

Official Handbook of the Territory of New Guinea, 1937. Government Printer, Canberra.

Pacific Islands Year Book, 1932 to date (but not yearly). Pacific Publications, Sydney.

Handbook of Papua and New Guinea, three editions to 1961. Pacific Publications, Sydney.

Local perspective on the official record of events and trends can be best obtained by reference to:

Papuan Courier, weekly, 1930 to January, 1942.
Rabaul Times, weekly, April, 1925 to January, 1942.
Pacific Islands Monthly, August, 1930 to date.
South Pacific Post, September, 1950 to date.

Specialist and academic information and commentary will be found in:

South Pacific, journal of the Australian School of Pacific Administration, Sydney, 1946-55.
Oceania, which has printed many notable articles and papers on New Guinea over the years.

Systematic studies will be helped by:

Social Anthropology in Melanesia: *A Review of Research*, by Professor A. P. Elkin. Oxford University Press, Melbourne, 1953.
Annotative Bibliography of the South-West Pacific. Allied Geographical Section, 1944 (Vols I and II).
Pacific Island Bibliography, by Floyd Cammack and Shiro Saito. Scarecrow Press, New York, 1962.

In available books on Papua-New Guinea, the fields of scientist, administrator, missionary and traveller are interlocked, and the observations of each one contribute to a critical appreciation of the others' recorded experience. The following highly selective list may, however, help readers wishing to follow up their specific interests:

PRE-COLONIAL HISTORY

D'Albertis, L. M. *New Guinea: What I Did and What I Saw*. Sampson Low, London, 1880.
Armit, R. H. *The History of New Guinea and the Origin of the Negroid Race*. Trubner and Co., London, 1879.
Chalmers, J. *Work and Adventure in New Guinea*. Religious Tract Society, London, 1885.
Huxley, T. H. *Diary of the Voyage of HMS Rattlesnake*. Chatto and Windus, London, 1935.
Jukes, J. B. *Narrative of the Surveying Voyage of HMS Fly*. T. and W. Boone, London, 1847.
Lawson, J. A. *Wanderings in the Interior of New Guinea*. Chapman and Hall, London, 1875.
Moresby, J. *Discoveries and Surveys in New Guinea and the d'Entrecasteaux Islands: A Cruise of HMS Basilisk*. John Murray, London, 1876.
Romilly, H. H. *From My Verandah in New Guinea*. David Nutt, London, 1889.

EARLY COLONIZATION AND EXPLORATION

Bevan, T. *Toil, Travel and Discovery in British New Guinea*. Kegan Paul, London, 1890.

Fort, S. G. *Chance or Design*. Robert Hale, London, 1942. (Fort was secretary to Sir Peter Scratchley.)

Lyne, C. *An Account of the Establishment of the British Protectorate over the Southern Shores of New Guinea*. Sampson Low, London, 1885.

Lyng, J. *Our New Possession (late German New Guinea)*. Melbourne Publishing Co., Melbourne, 1919.

Meek, A. S. *A Naturalist in Cannibal Land*. Fisher Unwin, London, 1913.

Monckton, C. A. W. *Some Experiences of a Resident New Guinea Magistrate*. John Lane, London, 1921.

Murray, J. H. P. *Papua: or British New Guinea*. Fisher Unwin, London, 1912.

Royal Commission of Inquiry. *Method of Government of the Territory of Papua*. J. Kemp, Melbourne, 1907.

Thomson, J. P. *British New Guinea*. George Philip, London, 1892.

Woolaston, A. F. R. *Pygmies and Papuans*. Smith, Elder, London, 1912.

THE FIRST WORLD WAR

Foreign Office Handbook, No. 145. *German Possessions in the Pacific*. HM Stationery Office, London, 1919.

Lyng, J. As above.

Mackenzie, S. *Official History of Australia in the War of 1914-18*, Vol. X. Angus and Robertson, Sydney, 1927.

Rowley, C. D. *The Australians in German New Guinea, 1914-21*. Melbourne University Press, 1958.

PAPUA AND THE MANDATED TERRITORY, 1918-41

Blackwood, Beatrice. *Both Sides of the Buka Passage*. Clarendon Press, Oxford, 1935.

Booth, Doris. *Mountains, Gold and Cannibals*. Cornstalk, Sydney, 1929.

Champion, I. F. *Across New Guinea from the Fly to the Sepik*. Constable, London, 1932.

Clune, Frank. *Prowling Through Papua*. Angus and Robertson, Sydney, 1942.

Hides, J. G. *Papuan Wonderland*. Blackie, London, 1936.

Humphries, W. R. *Patrolling in Papua*. Fisher Unwin, London, 1923.

Hurley, Frank. *Pearls and Savages*. Putnam, New York, 1924.

Idriess, Ion. *Gold Dust and Ashes: The Romantic Story of the New Guinea Goldfields*. Angus and Robertson, Sydney, 1940.

Leahy, M. and Crane, M. *The Land that Time Forgot*. Hurst and Blackett, London, 1937.

Lett, Lewis. *Papuan Achievement*. Melbourne University Press, 1942.

———— *Sir Hubert Murray of Papua*. Collins, London, 1949.

Murray, J. H. P. *Recent Exploration in Papua*. Turner and Henderson, Sydney, 1923.

———— *Papua of Today*. P. S. King and Sons, London, 1925.

Reed, S. W. *The Making of Modern New Guinea*. American Philosophical Society, Philadelphia, 1943.

Rhys, L. *High Lights and Flights in New Guinea*. Hodder and Stoughton, London, 1942.

THE SECOND WORLD WAR

Dexter, David. *The New Guinea Offensives*: Australia in the War of 1939-45, Series I, Vol. 5. Australian War Memorial, Canberra.

Feldt, Eric. *The Coast Watchers*. Oxford University Press, Melbourne, 1946.

Johnston, George. *New Guinea Diary*. Angus and Robertson, Sydney, 1943.

Long, Gavin. *The Final Campaigns*: Australia in the War of 1939-45, Series I, Vol. 7. Australian War Memorial, Canberra.

McCarthy, Dudley. *South-West Pacific Area—First year*: Australia in the War of 1939-45, Series I, Vol. 5. Australian War Memorial, Canberra.

Odgers, George. *Air War Against Japan*: Australia in the War of 1939-45, Series III, Vol 2. Australian War Memorial, Canberra.

Paul, Raymond. *Retreat from Kokoda*. Heinemann, Melbourne, 1958.

Rhys, L. *Jungle Pimpernel: The Story of a District Officer in Central Netherlands New Guinea*. Hodder and Stoughton, London, 1947.

Scharmach, Bishop L. *This Crowd Beats Us All*. The Catholic Press Newspaper Co., Sydney, 1960.

Walker, Allan S. *The Island Campaigns* (medical) : Australia in the War of 1939-45, Series V, Vol. 3. Australian War Memorial, Canberra.

White, Osmar. *Green Armour*. W. W. Norton, New York, 1944.

PAPUA-NEW GUINEA, 1946 TO DATE

GENERAL

Dean, B. and Carell, V. *Softly, Wild Drums*. Ure Smith, Sydney, 1958.

McCarthy, Keith. *Patrol into Yesterday*. Angus and Robertson, Sydney, 1964.

Ruhen, Olaf. *Mountains in the Clouds*. Rigby, Adelaide, 1963.

Selby, David. *Itambu: Impressions of a Relieving Circuit Judge*. Currawong Press, Sydney, 1963.

Simpson, Colin. *Adam in Plumes*. Angus and Robertson, Sydney, 1954.

————— *Adam with Arrows*. Angus and Robertson, Sydney, 1956.

Williams, M. *Stone Age Island*. Collins, London, 1964.

POLITICAL AND SOCIOLOGICAL

Belshaw, C. S. *Changing Melanesia*. Oxford University Press, Melbourne, 1954.

Bettison, D. C., Fisk, E. K., West, F. J., and Crawford, J. C. *The Independence of Papua-New Guinea—What are the Pre-requisites?*

(Public lectures under the auspices of the Australian National University). Angus and Robertson, Sydney, 1962.

Cranswick, G. H. and Shevill, I. W. A. *A New Deal in Papua*. Cheshire, Melbourne, 1949.

Essai, B. *Papua and New Guinea*. Oxford University Press, Melbourne, 1961.

Hasluck, P. *Australian Policy in Papua and New Guinea* (Ministerial statement, 23 August, 1960). Government Printer, Canberra, 1960.

———— *The Economic Development of Papua and New Guinea* (Address to the Economic Society of Australia and New Zealand). Government Printer, Canberra, 1962.

———— *The Future in Papua and New Guinea* (Part of an address to the Public Service of Papua-New Guinea). Government Printer, Canberra, 1962.

Legge, J. D. *Australian Colonial Policy*. Angus and Robertson, Sydney, 1956.

Ryan, D'A., Healey, A. and Kerr, J. *New Guinea* (Lectures to the New South Wales Branch of the Australian Institute of International Affairs). Anglican Press, Sydney, 1962.

Various Authors. *New Guinea and Australia* (Papers read at the 24th Summer School of the Australian Institute of Political Science, January, 1958). Angus and Robertson, Sydney, 1958.

IRIAN (WEST NEW GUINEA), 1945 TO DATE

Bone, R. C. *The Dynamics of the Western New Guinea Problem*. Ithica (for Cornell University), New York, 1958.

Brongersma, L. D. and Venema, G. F. *To the Mountains of the Stars*. Hodder and Stoughton, London, 1962.

Harrar, H. *I Come from the Stone Age*. Rupert Hart-Davis, London, 1964.

Roscoe, G. T. *Our Neighbours in Netherlands New Guinea*. Jacaranda Press, Brisbane, 1959.

Smedts, M. W. *No Tobacco, No Hallelujah*. Kimber, London, 1955.

Important source material can be found in the following papers:

Handbook on Netherlands New Guinea. New Guinea Institute, Rotterdam, 1958.

Report on Netherlands New Guinea (to the U.N. Secretary General). Ministry of Overseas Affairs, The Hague, 1950.

Western New Guinea and the Netherlands (a statement of the Dutch case). State Printing Office, The Hague, 1954.

West Irian an Essential Part of Indonesia (a statement of the Indonesian case). The Indonesian Embassy, Canberra, 1963.

Statement by Sir Garfield Barwick to the House of Representatives. Canberra (*Hansard*, 21 August, 1962).

Statement by Sir Percy Spender to the First Committee, U.N. General Assembly, 9 November, 1964.

Statement by M. Subandrio before the U.N. General Assembly, 9 November, 1961.

INDONESIA

Grant, Bruce. *Indonesia*. Melbourne University Press, 1964.
Wehl, D. *The Birth of Indonesia*. Allen and Unwin, London, 1948.
Westerling, R. *Challenge to Terror*. Kimber, London, 1952.

GENERAL ANTHROPOLOGY

Elkin, A. P. *Social Anthropology in Melanesia*. Oxford University Press, London, 1953.
Hogbin, H. I. *Transformation Scene*. Routledge and Kegan Paul, London, 1951.
———— *Social Change*. Watts, London, 1958.
Malinowski, B. *Argonauts of the Western Pacific*. Routledge, London, 1922.
Mead, Margaret. *Growing Up in New Guinea*. Pelican, Harmondsworth, 1942.
———— *New Lives for Old*. Morrow, New York, 1956.
Ratcliffe-Brown, A. R. *Structure and Function of Primitive Society*. Cohen and West, London, 1952.
Rivers, W. H. R. *Essays on the Depopulation of Melanesia*. Cambridge University Press, Cambridge, 1922.

CARGO CULTS

Kamma, F. C. *Messianic Movements in Western New Guinea*. International Review of Missions, Vol. 41, No. 162, 1952.
Lawrence, Peter. *Road Belong Cargo*. Melbourne University Press, Melbourne, 1964.
Stanner, W. E. H. *The South Seas in Transition*. Australasian Publishing Company, London, 1953.
Williams, F. E. *The Vailala Madness in Retrospect*. Kegan Paul, London, 1934.
Worsley, P. *The Trumpet Shall Sound: A Study of Cargo Cults in Melanesia*. Macgibbon and Kee, London, 1957.

INDEX

Index

247